CHILDREN'S SOCIAL AND EMOTIONAL WELLBEING IN SCHOOLS

A critical perspective

Debbie Watson, Carl Emery and Phil Bayliss, with Margaret Boushel and Karen McInnes

First published in Great Britain in 2012 by

The Policy Press
University of Bristol
Fourth Floor
Beacon House
Queen's Road
Bristol BS8 1QU
UK

Tel +44 (0)117 331 4054
Fax +44 (0)117 331 4093
e-mail tpp-info@bristol.ac.uk
www.policypress.co.uk

North American office:
The Policy Press
c/o The University of Chicago Press
1427 East 60th Street
Chicago, IL 60637, USA
t: +1 773 702 7700
f: +1 773-702-9756
e:sales@press.uchicago.edu
www.press.uchicago.edu

© The Policy Press 2012

British Library Cataloguing in Publication Data
A catalogue record for this book is available from the British Library.

Library of Congress Cataloging-in-Publication Data
A catalog record for this book has been requested.

ISBN 978 1 84742 513 3   paperback
ISBN 978 1 84742 523 2   hardcover

The right of Debbie Watson, Carl Emery and Phil Bayliss, with Karen McInnes and Margaret Boushel, to be identified as authors of this work has been asserted by them in accordance with the 1988 Copyright, Designs and Patents Act.

Cover design by The Policy Press
Front cover: image kindly supplied by www.istock.com
Printed and bound in Great Britain by TJ International, Padstow
The Policy Press uses environmentally responsible print partners

Dedications

We would like to thank all our family members for their constant support, encouragement, love and patience: Neil, Charlie and Will; Jean, Josie, Lois and Mark; Linda, Tom and Will; Colin, Sophie and Millie; and Garvan and Corra.

Contents

List of figures and tables

Figures

Table

Acknowledgements

This book owes a debt to all the children, young people, practitioners, policymakers and families who have participated in the various studies jointly presented, or who have been willing to add accounts of policy and practice. Several of the studies were externally funded and our thanks go to the Welsh Assembly Government (and Arad Consulting), Esmeé Fairbairn Foundation, United Nations Children's Fund (UNICEF), School of Education and Social Work, University of Sussex, and Scope, UK.

In particular, we would like to thank Carl Emery's researcher, Hil Bichovsky, for her tireless support in researching evidence and sourcing references. Special thanks also to Yvonne Page, Steph Wilcock, Karen Newton and Rachel Muter.

Lastly, we would like to extend our gratitude to the support of Alison Shaw and the team at The Policy Press for giving us the opportunity to embark on this writing and in making this book possible.

List of abbreviations

AASP	Activity Apperception Story Procedure
ALC	Active Learning Capacity
C4EO	Centre for Excellence and Outcomes in Children and Young People's Services
CASEL	Collaborative for Academic Social and Emotional Learning
CFE	*Curriculum for Excellence*
CR	Conflict Resolution
DCSF	Department for Children, Schools and Families
DfE	Department for Education
DfEE	Department for Education and Employment
DfES	Department for Education and Skills
ECM	*Every Child Matters*
EHWB	Emotional Health and Wellbeing
EI	Emotional Intelligence
HLTA	Higher Level Teaching Assistant
LDD	Learning Difficulties and Disabilities
LEA	Local Education Authority
LLUK	Lifelong Learning UK
NCB	National Children's Bureau
NIAMH	Northern Ireland Association for Mental Health
NICE	National Institute for Health and Clinical Excellence
OECD	Organisation for Economic Co-operation and Development
OFSTED	Office of Standards in Education
OLT	Objective List Theories
PATHS	Promoting Alternative Thinking Strategies
PEHAW	*Pupils' Emotional Health and Wellbeing*
QTS	Qualified Teaching Status
RA	Restorative Approaches
RRSA	Rights Respecting Schools Award
SEAL	Social and Emotional Aspects of Learning
SEDS	Social and Emotional Dispositions and Skills
SEELS	School Emotional Environment for Learning Survey
SEF	*School Effectiveness Framework*
SEL	Social and Emotional Learning
SEN	Special Educational Needs
SEWB	Social and Emotional Wellbeing
SMSC	Spiritual, Moral, Social and Cultural

TCP	*The Children's Plan*
TDA	Training and Development Agency for Schools
TLSA	Teaching and Learning Support Assistant
UKRP	United Kingdom Resilience Programme
UNCRC	United Nations Convention on the Rights of the Child
UNESCO	United Nations Educational, Scientific and Cultural Organization
UNICEF	United Nations Children's Fund
WAG	Welsh Assembly Government
WHO	World Health Organization

Biographical notes

Debbie Watson is a Senior Lecturer in Childhood Studies at the University of Bristol (School for Policy Studies) and an experienced secondary school teacher. She manages the BSc (Hons) programme in Childhood Studies and teaches across a range of child- and family-related topics. Her research interests are in social and emotional wellbeing for children and, specifically, the role of staff in schools in supporting children and young people, as well as theorising difference and diversity. She has managed research projects exploring the provision of learning support in schools and supporting families and children in children's centres, and consulted on a project for the Welsh Assembly Government (with Carl Emery) theorising and capturing non-academic achievements for young people in Wales. She is also part of an international team developing a postgraduate programme on child rights and public policy in Egypt and Jordan.

Carl Emery is a researcher and lecturer in Social and Emotional Development and Conflict Resolution. Over the past 10 years, he has worked closely with the former Department for Children, Schools and Families, the Qualifications and Curriculum Authority, the Welsh Assembly and a number of universities in developing and exploring social and emotional wellbeing in education with an emphasis on supporting disengaged young people. He lectures at Warwick University (conflict resolution/relationship building) and is undertaking a PhD at Manchester University examining the divergence and convergence in Welsh and English education policy regarding wellbeing in education.

Phil Bayliss retired from the University of Exeter in 2009. He is now working in Turkey on a European project 'Strengthening Special Education in Turkey', which seeks to align the Turkish education system with European systems of inclusive education. He has been a teacher, academic and researcher and has developed post-structuralist and postmodernist approaches to challenges in inclusive education, difference and disability.

Karen McInnes is a Senior Lecturer in Play and Human Development in the School of Psychology at the University of Glamorgan. Her recently completed PhD focused on utilising children's perceptions of their own play in order to take a playful approach and attitude to activities. Previously, Karen was a Senior Researcher with Barnardo's UK Policy and Research team. During this time, her research projects involved acting as a research consultant to a local Sure Start project and developing outcomes for local children's centres. She has extensive experience of working with young children as a teacher and speech therapist. She has published on various aspects of early years education, play and playfulness and is a strong advocate for practitioners taking a playful approach to their work with children in order that children may be playful.

Margaret Boushel is completing a PhD on professional understandings and approaches to children's rights. She is a qualified social worker and barrister with considerable experience as a manager, academic and social work practitioner. Over the past decade, she has been Assistant Director of Barnardo's with responsibility for a number of early years, social inclusion and Children's Fund projects; manager of a Sure Start trailblazer programme; and director of a BSc (Hons) programme in Early Childhood Studies. Her research interests include children's rights, child welfare within an ecological perspective and inter-professional practice. She was a member of the National Evaluation of Sure Start Steering Group, has reviewed aspects of professional education for the Social Care Institute of Excellence and the Care Council for Wales, and contributed to the evaluation of UNICEF's Rights Respecting Schools initiative.

CHAPTER 1

Introduction

Wellbeing[1] as a concept has crept into policy agendas and practice in a range of settings, notably in health care and in regards to work and employment. Increasingly, attention is focused on child wellbeing with reports of increased mental and emotional health needs in children, bullying in schools, and major reports such as the United Nations Children's Fund report on child wellbeing in rich countries (UNICEF, 2007), which suggested children and young people were less satisfied with their lives, less happy, have a poor quality of life and report a lower subjective wellbeing. Such reports have resulted in the almost uncritical acceptance of the need to *improve wellbeing* among school-aged children in the UK through the *Every Child Matters* agenda (DfES, 2004a), *National Healthy Schools Standard Promoting Emotional Health and Wellbeing* (DFEE, 2005), and the *Happy, Safe and Achieving their Potential* guidance in Scotland (SE, 2004), with parallel debates occurring elsewhere in the world and led by organisations such as the World Health Organization (WHO, 1999).

Why social and emotional wellbeing?

Although this book explores a range of wellbeing perspectives, the emphasis is on what we have termed 'social and emotional wellbeing' (SEWB) in education. SEWB is an umbrella term that encompasses the wide range of concepts, skills, dispositions and attitudes infused within UK education policy and promoted through programmes such as Social and Emotional Aspects of Learning (SEAL), Promoting Alternative Thinking Strategies (PATHS), Second Step, Creating Confident Kids, the UK Resilience Programme, and Getting Connected. The term SEWB includes both programmes focused on positive models emphasising and promoting social and emotional wellbeing, and deficit or negative models that seek to repair or develop responses to socially problematic issues such as depression, anxiety and anti-social behaviour. The National Institute for Clinical Excellence (NICE) stated that SEWB encompasses:

- happiness, confidence and not feeling depressed (emotional wellbeing);

- a feeling of autonomy and control over one's life, problem-solving skills, resilience, attentiveness and a sense of involvement with others (psychological wellbeing); and
- the ability to have good relationships with others and to avoid disruptive behaviour, delinquency, violence or bullying (social wellbeing).[2]

As SEWB has developed across the UK, practice and policy terminology has morphed. Many early programmes were launched under the banner of 'Emotional Intelligence' or 'Emotional Literacy'. By the mid-2000s, this had become Social and Emotional Learning and, in particular, SEAL (the Department for Children, Schools and Families' schools-based programme). By 2008, the dominant term had become Emotional Health and Wellbeing, and later Emotional Resilience. Alongside this, the phrase 'teaching happiness' moved into the public consciousness and still sits there, albeit somewhat stalled.

In an interview with one of the authors in 2011, an expert commentator on SEWB, Neil Humphrey, reflected that SEWB was:

> "An umbrella term that's used to describe a whole range of things that may well be qualitatively different. It's used in reference to mental health, as a kind of synonym for mental health, but it's also used to refer to children's competence, social skills – something that is slightly separate from mental health. It's also used interchangeably with social and emotional learning, social and emotional literacy, and social and emotional intelligence. It is a fuzzy and intangible concept."[3]

It is indeed a fuzzy and intangible concept. Current policy and academic literature uses such terms as 'soft skills', 'emotional intelligence' and 'emotional resilience' interchangeably. A fluidity of terminology for educational wellbeing is symptomatic of the challenges and questions we wish to explore in this book. The ever-widening range of terms (emotional intelligence, emotional literacy, emotional health and wellbeing, skills for work and life, emotional resilience, employability skills, social and emotional learning, soft skills, non-academic achievements, social and emotional competency, mental well-being etc) points to the need within education to 'talk' a version of SEWB irrespective of the name being applied to it.

The issue of childhood wellbeing in education crosses a wide range of academic disciplines, from psychology and measurement to educational research, health education and promotion, and welfare and counselling literatures. Speaking of the linking of emotional intelligence with knowledge and behavioural constructs, but characteristic of the whole field, Bar-On and Parker's (2000) *Handbook of Emotional Intelligence* noted that 'research progress is perhaps impeded by a lack of consistency in how these constructs are conceptualised and operationalised' (p 157; for a more detailed critique of 'Emotional Intelligence' and the way it has been operationalised, see Watson and Emery, 2010).

In this book we have settled on the term 'social and emotional wellbeing' to capture the wide-ranging discourse taking place as well as allowing space to acknowledge the cross-disciplinary and somewhat slippery range of concepts, practices and programmes included in it. The focus of the book is on *all* children and young people's SEWB in school contexts. In illuminating this, we sometimes draw on research and experiences with particular groups of children who are deemed to be the most disadvantaged or vulnerable in schools (very young children, those with special educational needs [SEN] or disabilities, or children from minority ethnic groups). However, these examples are offered as exemplars from which the reader can apply the issues, as appropriate, to all children.

'Social and emotional wellbeing' in schools

If there is little consensus of what constitutes wellbeing (we use this in a general way here as most literature does not specify SEWB) for children in schools (see eg Coleman, 2009), then there is even less agreement on the place of wellbeing in schools or how wellbeing can be fostered among children (Weare and Gray, 2003, DCSF, 2008b). Given the rise in programmes and measures that aim to address wellbeing in the UK and throughout the world, it is appropriate to question the base premises as, with very few exceptions (Craig, 2007, 2009; Ecclestone and Hayes, 2008, 2009), it remains relatively unchallenged in educational contexts. The challenges that have been posed focused on the question of whether improving the emotional wellbeing of children should be an educational goal in itself, and the implications of allowing the emotional imperative to lead the academic. Ecclestone and Hayes (2009, p 385) illustrated this emotional turn to:

> An unchallenged orthodoxy that children and young people want a personally relevant, 'engaging' education where adults and peers listen and affirm them. This view presents subject disciplines as reactionary, irrelevant and oppressive.

It encourages assumptions that topics and processes can
only be engaging if they relate directly to the self and its
feelings about life and the world.

Ecclestone and Hayes (2009, p 385) challenged the validity of 'creating
a hollowed-out curriculum as an instrument for "delivering" a plethora
of attributes, skills, values and dispositions' and saw this influence in
education as an example of a 'therapeutic culture', building on the work
of Frank Furedi (2003), which has crept into mainstream schooling,
where a discourse 'of emotional well-being and engagement reveal
a pessimistic tone that privileges damage, vulnerability and fragility'
(Ecclestone, 2007, p 464). The work of Ecclestone has been challenged
as suggesting that the emotional dimensions of learning and learners
are unimportant in school contexts; but she counters this by arguing
that it is not wellbeing *per se* that is out of control in educational policy
and practice, but the 'normalising of therapeutic interventions around
self-esteem, emotional intelligence, emotional literacy and emotional
well-being' and the need for 'resistance to their underlying diminished
images of human potential and resilience' (Ecclestone, 2007, p 467).

Carol Craig has also been an outspoken commentator on the
place of wellbeing in schools. She claimed that we have permitted
a psychological and mental health perspective to predominate what
we understand as wellbeing; and that in doing so we have protected
children from experiencing the range of emotions necessary for
healthy emotional development. She cited the positive psychologist
Martin Seligman as stating that children need to experience negative
emotions and low self-esteem in order to be challenged and motivated
to succeed and to develop persistence and resilience in the face of failure.
She also suggested that there is a good body of evidence to support
the fact that an excessive focus on self-esteem in children results in
'unhealthy materialism and individualism and so undermines, rather
than contributes to, wellbeing' (Crocker and Park, 2004, cited in Craig,
2009, p 6). In agreement with Ecclestone and Hayes, she argued for
teachers to return to being good teachers 'not as surrogate psychologists
or mental health workers' (Craig, 2009, p 16).

While these arguments and challenges are persuasive, what neither
Ecclestone's, Hayes' nor Craig's works have addressed are the ways in
which wellbeing has and can be conceptualised. It is to this problem
of wellbeing as a concept that we turn in order to introduce some key
ideas and theories upon which the book will be based.

Wellbeing as a concept – some theoretical tools

While the book is designed to appeal to all audiences concerned with children's wellbeing in schools, there are a number of theoretical approaches that we have taken that demand some engagement with a critical understanding of wellbeing in epistemological terms. Wellbeing is a **concept** and it is our intention in this book to **deconstruct** this concept in order to explore and understand its use. It is for this reason that we now take the reader through a consideration of concepts more generally, as this approach is applied to wellbeing in later chapters. **Deconstruction** involves following the **genealogy** of a concept and enabling oneself to (re)think, (re-)prioritise, (re)analyse and to see the components and the roots of the concept anew. Foucault defined genealogy as: 'the union of erudite knowledge and local memories which allows us to establish a historical knowledge of struggles and to make use of this knowledge tactically today' (Foucault, 1980a, p 83).

The purpose of philosophy is to create concepts, whereby they 'are created as a function of problems which are thought to be badly understood or badly posed (pedagogy of the concept)' (Deleuze and Guattari, 1994, p 17). Concepts have functions, and the way in which a concept is utilised effects how it is determined and experienced. Deleuze wrote that: 'philosophical theory is itself a practice as much as its objects … it is a practice of concepts, and it must be judged in the light of other practise with which it interferes' (Deleuze, 1989, p 280). Thus, a concept is defined by its intersections with other concepts, both in its field and in surrounding fields. The intersections of concepts form a 'plane of immanence' (May, 1997), which aligns a **Deleuzian plane** with a Foucauldian **discursive practice** (Foucault, 1972), where the meaning of the concept (as an effect of its operation) emerges through the unity it articulates among its constituent parts. The **consistence** of the concept emerges through the bringing together of heterogeneous elements into a whole, where the components are inseparable.

A concept also has a **force**, which creates **effects** across a conceptual field as it passes through and by the elements and concepts of that field. A concept, then, is not a representation in any classical sense. Rather, it is a point in a field – or, to use Deleuze's term, on a 'plane' – that is at once logical, political and aesthetic. It is evaluated not by the degree of its truth or the accuracy of its reference, but by the effects it creates within and outside of the plane on which it finds itself. The concept, wrote Deleuze and Guattari, 'does not have reference, it is autoreferential, it poses itself and its effect at the same time that it is created' (Deleuze and Guattari, 1994, p 22). This gives rise to the following questions that we will address regarding wellbeing:

• What is our concept? What are the intersections between our concept and surrounding fields/concepts?
• What are its constituent parts and how are they consistent?
• What are these heterogeneous parts and how are they brought together into a whole that is at once distinct and inseparable from those composing elements?
• How do we understand our concept as a productive force that reverberates across a conceptual field, creating effects as it passes through and by the elements and concepts of that field?
• What is its practice? What are the effects? How does our concept function as an operation?
• Are we either rearranging the plane, articulating a new plane or forcing an intersection of that plane with others?

Our concept is that of 'social and emotional wellbeing' (herein referred to as SEWB or just 'wellbeing'). The literature surrounding wellbeing is contested as to its nature, because the intersections of the concept of wellbeing and surrounding fields and concepts are dense and unarticulated (see Figure 1.1).

The constituent parts of our analysis are derived from surrounding fields and in many ways the meaning of 'wellbeing' can only be understood through reference to other fields of enquiry (psychology, sociology, health studies, disability studies, childhood studies, law, ethics, education etc) (see Figure 1.2). These act as context to our concept of wellbeing and will be drawn in as referential contexts through our discussions of wellbeing.

What is the 'force' of the concept of wellbeing? The effect of the concepts at the level of the 'body politic' (Scheper-Hughes and Lock, 1987) has potentially driven UK educational policy towards fundamental change in schools, which have been acknowledged in the various international ratings of wellbeing and happiness (WHO, 1999; UNICEF, 2007), which rank the UK in low positions. This, we argue, is the 'force' of the concept when reduced to quantitative measurement, rather than ethical or educational practice, which may see wellbeing in different ways. Indeed, we argue that the effects of the concept of wellbeing are, in Deleuze and Guattari's terms, 'inconsistent'.

What is the practice of wellbeing? In several chapters we address the professional issues arising from the concept of wellbeing as its effects are understood in educational practice. We argue that because the concept is understood in inconsistent ways, to reduce the complexity of wellbeing to a set of indicators that derive from professional practice is to subject the concept to the law of unintended consequences, where, following Ecclestone and Hayes' (2009) critique cited earlier, the result is **pathology** and **therapy**, rather than wellbeing.

In our presentation are we rearranging our concept (plane) or creating a new one? Or are we forcing an intersection with other planes in ways that lead to consistency, rather than inconsistency? Our aim is the latter. We are not attempting to create a *grand theory of wellbeing*, since 'truth', to emphasise Deleuze and Guattari, lies in the **operation of concepts**, not in some (external) transcendental truth that reifies and legitimises one model (theory) over another. Our aim is pragmatic: how can we develop consistent intersections in the theory and practice of SEWB that have applications to and improve the experiences of children. There is no panacea that provides a recipe; rather, that policy and professional practice must be derived from consistent concepts.

We can ask further questions about the purpose of the concept, its place (site) of action and the effects derived from the concept as a productive force, and this has given rise to three key propositions that will be explored in this book. First, that wellbeing is embodied; the concept does not exist outside of human agency and social institutions. But **body** is not univocal; instead it should be seen as a multiplicity. The body(ies) is (are) simultaneously:

1. viewed as a phenomenally experienced, lived individual body(ies)/ self(ves);
2. may be seen as a social body(ies), what anthropologists term a natural symbol for thinking about relationships among nature, society and culture; and
3. seen as a body(ies) politic, artefacts, inscriptions of social and political control (Scheper-Hughes and Lock, 1987, p 6).

The levels of bodily experience just outlined conform to what Deleuze and Guattari called a 'juncture' (or a 'conjuncture' in discourse analysis) (Deleuze and Guattari, 2009; Bayliss and Dillon, 2010); that is, the lived body cannot be understood in isolation from the social and political bodies that compose it. This is the first proposition: SEWB is **subjectively experienced**.

Who are the subjects, and what are the objects, of wellbeing? Are we concerned to understand wellbeing in terms of the phenomenological body (lived experience) of individuals? Are we concerned with the locus of the 'social body'; that is, how is wellbeing used in schools? Or are we concerned with the 'body politic' – the macrosystemic use of the concept, which allocates resources and determines policy directions (Scheper-Hughes and Lock, 1987)? The response we make to these questions is 'all and none of these, what we are concerned with are the circumstances' (Deleuze and Guattari, 1980, p xiii). This leads us to the second proposition: SEWB is **contextual and embedded**.

If an elucidation of the concept can help us to think differently, then we can follow Foucault's project:

> There are times in life when the question of knowing if one can think differently than one thinks, and perceive differently than one sees, is absolutely necessary if one is to go on looking and reflecting at all ... what is philosophy today ... if it is not the critical work that thought brings to bear on itself: in what does it consist, if not in the endeavour to know how and to what extent it might be possible to think differently, instead of legitimising what is already known. (Mayo, 2000, p 104)

Who are the subjects of Foucault's project? If individual practitioners (professionals, para-professionals) are concerned with enacting an embodied concept (SEWB), then individuals do not act in isolation from each other or from 'regimes of truth' (Foucault, 1980b), which legitimise action on the *objects* of truth regimes (in the case of educational practices, children/learners). In this book, we derive understandings taken from Deleuze and Guattari, Foucault and other post-structuralist thought in understanding wellbeing as a singularity – as a set of circumstances and encounters. Thus, in a school, family or any other context, we would also like to offer the third proposition: SEWB is **relational**. These propositions are expanded in Figure 1.3 as a visual heuristic to frame our position and ideas related to children's SEWB in schools.

A road map

The book is divided into three parts, with the first part describing the conceptual, policy, practice and operationalised dimensions of SEWB. In Chapter 2, we deconstruct wellbeing in general as a concept and trace the genealogy of this through philosophy and other disciplines of thought. This leads into an examination of the policy frameworks in the four countries of the UK and elsewhere in the world within which SEWB in schools has emerged as a priority (Chapter 3). In

Chapter 4, we consider the programmes and initiatives in schools that aim to improve children's SEWB and challenge the evidence base for their effectiveness on several counts; not least being the inconsistency of the way in which wellbeing is understood and operationalised. In Chapter 5, we present a critique of the measurement movement as it has been applied to considerations of children's wellbeing.

In Part 2, we build on the themes that have been raised and explore thematic examples of policy, practice and research that address the new opportunities raised in Chapter 2 and that arise from critiques in the chapters in Part 1 concerning, namely: the purposes of education, and the links between achievement and wellbeing and how these contribute to inclusive discourses in schools (Chapter 6); methods for foregrounding minority voices on SEWB in meaningful dialogue (Chapter 7); and the importance of positive relationships and a consideration of school-based approaches aimed at tackling conflict in schools (Chapter 8). Karen McInnes discusses opportunities for playful expressions of wellbeing in schools (Chapter 9); and Margaret Boushel considers a reconceptualised status for children through a rights-based discourse and the role of children's rights in their wellbeing experiences (Chapter 10) and new understandings of professionalism and professionals in supporting children's wellbeing (Chapter 11). Each of these chapters will explore the three propositions offered regarding SEWB within a particular context.

Part 3 addresses the substantive issues concerning wellbeing in earlier parts and we address these from the perspective of professionals supporting wellbeing, with an invitation that there is a space for all professionals in schools to *do* wellbeing differently (Chapter 12). In Chapter 13, we return to the policy and practice dimensions of SEWB and question future directions for wellbeing under the new Coalition government. To date, there has been no formal statement from the incoming government on children's SEWB.

The conclusion sees us teasing out emergent themes and revisiting this excursus of concepts. We ask what wellbeing has to do with education and how our deconstructive approach to wellbeing as a concept has revealed new understandings about SEWB for children in UK schools.

A note about voice

This book is co-authored by Debbie Watson, Carl Emery and Phil Bayliss, with individual authored chapters supplied by Margaret Boushel and Karen McInnes. Given the number of voices involved, we were minded to consider using the third person pronoun in order to 'smooth' out the dissonances that might be present. However, we believe that the third person in presenting our positions on wellbeing creates a distance between the authors (us) and the audience, and the topic/concept. As we explain later in the book, Martin Buber (Buber, 1996) distinguished between an 'I–thou' relationship and an 'I–it' relationship. 'I–thou' creates a relational intersubjectivity, which is reflexive, while an 'I–it' distances subject and object. Given that a key aspect of our writing is to advocate for the former, it seemed inappropriate to write in a way that contradicted our base propositions.

Furthermore, traditional approaches to theoretical or conceptual writing that adopt the third person are open to manipulation through a use of language that shifts the focus to 'timeless' and 'objective' constructions (not least through the use of the passive voice, which elides the subject:'the agentless passive').We wish to avoid 'agentless'/'timeless' constructions, as the point we are trying to make is that SEWB is an encounter: between subjects and objects and concepts, which do not exist apart from each other. By using 'I/we' in our encounter with the concept of SEWB, we emphasise our connections with 'others' (learners, children, children with SEN, disabled children, minority children etc) in that wellbeing emerges through such encounters, rather than being imposed by a 'superior subject' (subjection, subjectification, abjection).

Notes
[1] Please note our spelling of 'wellbeing', which is explained in Chapter 2. Where we quote others, we use their spellings.

[2] See www.nice.org.uk/nicemedia/pdf/
MentalWellbeingChildrenReviewWhole.pdf

[3] From interview transcript.

Figure 1.1: Surrounding fields and concepts of wellbeing

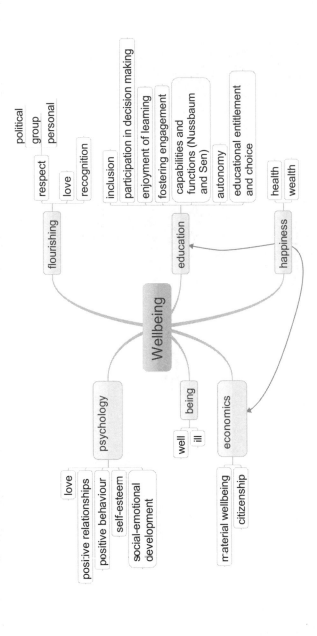

Note: These 'fields and concepts' also form a plane of immanence and should be read in conjunction with Figure 1.2. They are taken from the literature discussed in this chapter.

Figure 1.2: A 'plane of immanence' for the concept of wellbeing

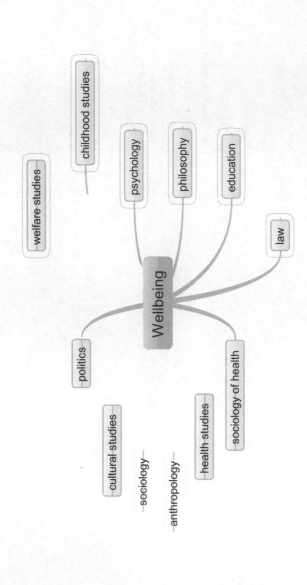

Note: The figure only shows first order relationships. Within each discipline area, it is possible to complete further links to create a conceptual map of increasing complexity. The figure is intended to be indicative, not exhaustive.

Figure 1.3: Visual heuristic

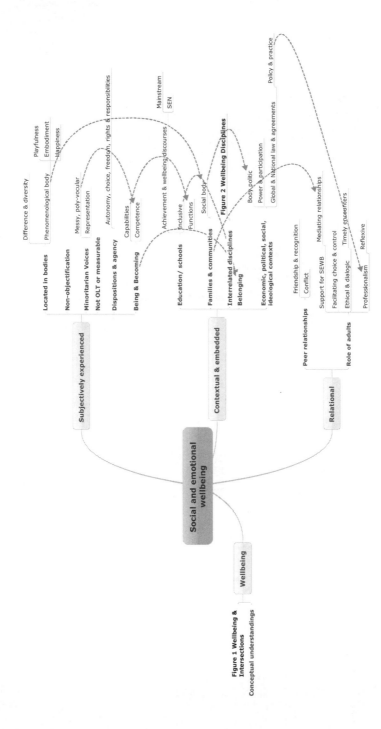

Part I
Context

In this Part we introduce the context for our critical debate of childhood SEWB. This begins with a theoretical and conceptual analysis of wellbeing and how this relates to children and childhood. we then consider contemporary wellbeing policy in the four countries of the UK. How these policies have emerged as educational practices and specific wellbeing programmes are then considered. Finally, we conclude this section explaining the measurement of wellbeing and the problematic issues inherent in measuring what we deem to be a fuzzy and complex concept.

CHAPTER 2

Conceptual dimensions of wellbeing

Introduction

In this chapter, we introduce key debates in philosophy, and beyond, in respect of wellbeing (in general, as this is how it has emerged in the literature) and attempt to unpack and deconstruct the concept of wellbeing in order to problematise and challenge the normalisation that has occurred. To this end, this chapter is theoretically focused, and at times conceptually challenging. We address the policy and practical application of these ideas in later chapters. There is also not a specific focus on schools or education in this chapter as the definitions of wellbeing as a concept are explored in the contexts in which theorists have described wellbeing (usually philosophical, medical and economic). Therefore, this chapter lays the foundations to engage in a critical examination of the roots of wellbeing, which will be developed and applied in later chapters.

A deconstructive approach has been used in order to foreground children's social and emotional wellbeing experiences as it allows a more ethical stance to be taken: 'from a feminist poststructural perspective, resistant practices such as deconstructive talks make possible another form of power production – not only more emancipatory, but also more ethical and responsible' (Dahlberg and Moss, 2005, p 111).

We do not seek any **truth** of wellbeing, nor do we intend to break down existing models in order to engage in a (re)making; but instead attempt to trace the history and development of the concept to address the questions in the Introduction about wellbeing as a concept. The ambition is to raise new questions; and describe the conditions for epistemological 'smooth space', as opposed to 'striated space' (Deleuze and Guattari, 2004), for new ways of thinking to emerge, where:

> The striated is that which intertwines fixed and variable elements, produces an order and succession of distinct forms, and organizes horizontal melodic lines and vertical harmonic planes. The smooth is the continuous variation,

> continuous development of form; it is the fusion of harmony
> and melody in favour of the production of properly
> rhythmic values, the pure act of the drawing of a diagonal
> across the vertical and the horizontal. (Deleuze and Guattari,
> 2004, p 478)

The 'smooth space' allows for greater 'de-territorialisation' (Deleuze
and Guattari, 2009) of the concept, and for its components to be
brought into focus in order that we may (re)consider them. Deleuze
and Guattari (2009) proposed that concepts had four key propositions:

• 'every concept relates back to other concepts, not only in its history
  but in its becoming or its present connections';
• 'what is distinctive about the concept is that it renders components
  inseparable *within itself*;
• 'each concept will therefore be considered as the point of coincidence,
  condensation, or accumulation of its own components'; and
• 'The concept is not discursive, and philosophy is not a discursive
  formation, as it does not link propositions together' (Deleuze and
  Guattari, 2009, pp 19–20, italics in original).

Drawing these ideas together:

> The concept is therefore both absolute and relative: it
> is relative to its own components, to other concepts, to
> the plane on which it is defined, and to the problems
> it is supposed to resolve; but it is absolute through the
> condensation it carries out, the site it occupies on the plane,
> and the conditions it assigns to the problem. As whole it
> is absolute, but insofar as it is fragmentary it is relative.
> (Deleuze and Guattari, 2009, p 21)

As outlined in the Introduction (Chapter 1) we are focused on an
aspect of the concept of wellbeing for children and young people as
situated and located within education and schooling systems specifically
(as illustrated in Figures 1.1 and 1.2). As Deleuze and Guattari (2009)
suggested, wellbeing is relative to other concepts such as health,
education, happiness, poverty, to name a few, and this is the 'plane of
immanence' explored in the Introduction. Wellbeing is also contextually
located in family, school and societal circumstances. As all these other
concepts and contexts change and evolve, so does wellbeing. This
fluidity and relationality has tasked philosophers for centuries.

Limited models of wellbeing that underpin everything

Constructions of wellbeing have long been debated and problematised with philosophers, psychologists, medics and economists occupying different positions and perspectives on what it means to be a *well being*. Such debates began in classical times with considerations by many, including Aristotle, of what constituted happiness and notions of well-living, and it is here that we see the changing nature of concepts as philosophers engage in 'recasting and even changing their concepts' (Deleuze and Guattari, 2009, p 21). In *The Nicomachean Ethics*, Aristotle described three lines of life – sensual enjoyment, the public life and a life of contemplation – and he viewed the 'Chief Good' as being happiness, whereby: 'happiness is shown to possess two characteristics of the Chief Good, inclusiveness of all other ends, and being in itself sufficient' (Aristotle, 1847, p 13).

Such terms as 'happiness', the 'good life', 'well-living' and 'positive psychology' have a long history and have been debated by many (Seligman and Csikszentmihalyi, 2000; Gasper, 2004; Crisp, 2008; Deci and Ryan, 2008; Ryan et al, 2008). In modern philosophy, the categorisations of wellbeing first developed by Parfit (1984) have been widely applied to philosophical ethics (Gasper, 2004). This classification includes the following three approaches to wellbeing.

Hedonistic accounts of subjective wellbeing, which centre on pleasure/pain and feelings of happiness and have since been subsumed under an umbrella of 'subjective wellbeing' (Diener and Biswas-Diener, 2000; Eid and Larsen, 2008). The simplest form of hedonism was described by Bentham 'according to which the more pleasantness one can pack into one's life, the better it will be, and the more painfulness one encounters, the worse it will be' (Crisp, 2008). But clearly not all experiences that bring momentary pleasure are necessarily good-making, or will enhance one's wellbeing, and therefore hedonistic theories have been challenged as a comprehensive theory of sustained wellbeing.

Desire theories (Scanlon, 1993) are where the focus is on achieving desire preference and fulfilment and in revealing levels of satisfaction with one's life achievements as opposed to the pure pursuit of pleasure indicative of the hedonistic theories. Desire theories are based on 'the assumption that preference fulfilment always or nearly always brings satisfaction' (Gasper, 2004, p 7). Other philosophers have increasingly described a form of 'desire theory' as *Eudaimonia* (Deci and Ryan, 2008) (drawing upon Aristotelian notions of living well and with virtue).

Eudaimonia derives from the Greek for happiness, and 'calls upon people to live in accordance with their daimon, or true self' (Ryan and Deci, 2001, p 146). Such approaches are evident in contemporary attempts to capture the essence of well-living from a subjective perspective, and are seen to be less egotistical and introspective than pure hedonistic approaches to positive psychology or subjective wellbeing.

Objective List Theories (OLTs) 'list items constituting wellbeing that consist neither merely in pleasurable experience nor in desire satisfaction [such as] knowledge or friendship' (Crisp, 2008). Examples of OLT approaches include Neo-Aristotelian capabilities approaches, such as those of the economist Amartya Sen (Sen, 1985, 1993), who identified the core values of *agency*, *freedom* and *dignity*, and the philosopher Martha Nussbaum, (Nussbaum and Sen, 1993; Nussbaum, 2000) who sought to establish a set of ethical principles for wellbeing for international governments and agencies to accept and implement – what she called her 'thick, vague conception of the good' (Nussbaum, 1992, p 214). Nussbaum identified some 10 capabilities as categories in formal lists and they ranged from *living a long life* and *having bodily health* to *living in a fruitful relationship with animals and the environment*. Her work has been criticised as being too universal (and therefore lacking in any specificity), and for her commitment to the sometimes incompatible essentialism of Aristotle (as defining a naturalistic theory of the good) and political liberalism of John Rawls (emphasising the collective right over the good) (Otto and Ziegler, 2010), which is a general criticism of many attempts to define wellbeing.

Other Neo-Aristotelian OLT approaches have included the work of Axel Honneth in defining human recognition (Honneth, 1995). His theory built on Aristotelian ethical criteria of a good life and combined this with Hegelian struggles to unite morality and ethical living in a struggle for recognition. Humans are seen to have an imperative need for recognition, and for the recognition of others, and this has resonance with the intersubjectivity theories of George Herbert Mead. Honneth identified three patterns of intersubjective recognition – *Love*, *Rights* and *Solidarity* – and three operational subcategories of *self-confidence*, *self-esteem* and *self-respect*. Such a perspective is important to consider when applying wellbeing to children and schools as this acknowledges the highly relational nature of humans and the importance of others in an individual's strive for happiness or wellbeing as 'efforts to achieve happiness and the good life perforce involve movements towards universalisation, and vice versa, movements towards universal justice are inevitably located in local communities of culturally shared identities and interests' (Alexander and Pia Lara, 1996, p 130).

Other OLTs appear to have derived from a Neo-Kantian perspective, where moral reasoning is applied to derive universal basic needs. Examples include the works of Len Doyal and Ian Gough (Doyal and Gough, 1991) who described the requirements for human flourishing and emphasised these as consensus-based, where emotional capacities were also included. Their approach was a hierarchical process that started with philosophical reasoning. This provided the potential to prioritise basic needs and add additional ones according to material and other circumstances. They utilised a two-step process:

1. universal basic needs are identified for health and autonomy; and
2. codified and experiential knowledge is drawn upon to understand satisfiers and intermediate needs and to challenge cultural relativity.

There are also accounts of wellbeing drawn from a tradition of OLT that do not seem to derive strongly from any philosophical foundation, but that have emerged from a more utilitarian approach of defining what particular groups in society need in order to survive, or to have a good standard of living. These are evidenced in the Quality of Life (QoL) movement. Such approaches are found in writings on disability, which consider QoL in respect of dimensions of experience and human potential, as well as outcomes (Schalock, 1997; Cummins, 2005). For example, Veenhoven suggested a systemic fourfold model of QoL which integrated *life chances* and *life results* with the *outer and inner qualities* of the life in question. The combination of these two 'dichotomies' gave rise to four dimensions of *Liveability of the Environment, Life-ability of the Person, Utility of Life* and *Appreciation of Life* (Veenhoven, 2000).

There is the opportunity for numerous subjective formulations of QoL in the approaches available without resorting to objective lists and this resonates for those people with profound disadvantages or disabilities. But, in operationalising these, QoL theorists have tended to describe the integration of the objective and subjective components of the person living the life, and do generate lists (Cummins, 2005) and measures of the dimensions, which arguably negates the subjective potential of QoL approaches.

In all of the OLT approaches, the question of course arises as to what should go on the list. There are also criticisms that list theories are elitist as they rest on other people's judgements of what is good for you, even if you do not agree. The conceptual foundation of OLTs is also heavily debated – at what level of concept should the list operate? Needs, wants, pleasures, capabilities, satisfactions, virtues and desires all operate at different conceptual levels and are differentially positioned and understood in respect of whether their effect is experienced by the individual, collective or entire society. Even within a conceptual framework such as Nussbaum's capabilities, there are different orders of capability referred to (ie they are not all survival-based, and some may be more important to individuals/societies than others). In ethical terms, Aristotle also introduced the problems of morality and virtue, which involved a value judgement about the kind of life one should live for greater human fulfilment as opposed to just a focus on selfish egoism (Crisp, 2008). Such moral- and, often, welfare-based judgements colour the decisions underpinning what goes on the list, and what does not.

Subjective/objective theories

The categorisations of wellbeing theories by Parfit (1984), while having theoretical utility, do not have direct utility in describing children's social and emotional wellbeing and a more nuanced approach drawing from across philosophical boundaries may be more appropriate. A useful way of separating out wellbeing theories may be according to their subjective or objective stance. Subjective theories of human good are sometimes taken to be those that 'make welfare depend *at least in part* on some mental state' (Sumner, 1996, p 82; emphasis in original). The intended contrast is with objective theories of wellbeing, which 'make the well-being of an agent depend entirely on states of the world apart from the state of mind of the agent whose well-being is under review' (Arneson, 1999, p 121). For children, the 'state of mind of the agent' is something that is not taken into account. Recent formulations of wellbeing indices (eg Bradshaw and Richardson, 2009) ask for a satisfaction rating for the indices: the voice of the child does not challenge the nature of content of the indices themselves (this is a discussion we return to in Chapters 5 and 7).

Where subjective aspects of family or peer relationships are seen as lying outside of policy (as policy cannot change these aspects of wellbeing), the objective list approach does not need the individual (in this case, child) to subscribe either to a hedonistic or desire fulfilment view of wellbeing. This was illustrated strongly in the findings of a report commissioned by the Department of Children, Schools and Families (DCSF) to gauge children's and families' understandings of wellbeing (DCSF, 2008b), which found widespread lack of use of the term and understanding of the concept by children and families, yet these were the recipients of the wellbeing policies (for further elaboration, see Chapter 3).

Thomas Scanlon (1993, p 188) asserted that what 'is essential is that these are theories according to which an assessment of a person's well-being involves a substantive judgement about what things make life better, a judgement which may conflict with that of the person whose well-being is in question'. Scanlon suggested the label 'substantive good theories' for this class of views on the ground that they 'are based on substantive claims about what goods, conditions, and opportunities make life better' (Scanlon, 1993, p 188).

The OLT approach to wellbeing ('substantive good theories') does not require judgement on the part of the child; rather, judgement lies in the domain of the parent, school or school system, where these are acting *in loco parentis* (and making substantive claims). As Gough (2002, p 16) stated in discussion of a capabilities approach to wellbeing: 'children may require enforced protection of and stimulation of their capabilities, for example through compulsory education'. If we accord person status to the child, their educational wellbeing could depend on hedonistic or desire theories, which are subjective and assume that the individual is in a position to determine their own sense of wellbeing (their mental state contributes to their own understanding). However, where the status of the child does not accord autonomy (although the achievement of autonomy is a goal of education generally), then OLTs posit external (objective) *good*, which may be resisted by the autonomous individual in any given case.

Functions and capabilities

Another fruitful line of theorising can be identified in the extent to which wellbeing is viewed as contingent on a person's *capabilities*, or the extent to which a *functionings* approach is sufficient in capturing what people need to flourish, be happy and well. If we use a functionings approach to children's wellbeing, then we arguably delimit their potential to an analysis based on (in certain circumstances) basic survival, and this rests on lists of human needs as illustrated by such humanist writers as Maslow (1943). In many affluent parts of the world, this list may not be so survival-oriented, as we see with the emergence and dominance of *Every Child Matters* in England and Wales (DfES, 2004a). Has this become the objective list by which society judges children's wellbeing?

If we adopt the approach of Nussbaum and Sen (1993) to understand wellbeing based on the 'capabilities approach', predicated on concepts of agency and empowerment (Alkire, 2005), then wellbeing ceases to be an ordered list and goods should not be seen as ends in themselves, but as opportunities (for activity):

> Sen (1985), and many writings subsequently, defines capabilities as what people are able to do or able to be – the opportunity they have to achieve various lifestyles and as a result, the ability to live a good life. He differentiates this from what he calls functionings – the things a person actually does and experiences. Functionings may vary from the elementary, such as being adequately nourished and being free from avoidable disease, to complex activities or personal states, such as taking part in the life of the community and having self-respect. (Anand et al, 2005, p 11)

Nussbaum (2001) argued for 'multidimensionality' as a rational set of capabilities (life, bodily health, bodily integrity, thought, emotions, reason, affiliation, other species, play and control over one's environment). This set is derived from Nussbaum's political philosophy and claims that they would underpin agreement of how wellbeing should be understood. She recognised that capabilities were interdependent with functionings, but that capabilities should be the focus for political activity, in the sense that a definition (or realisation) of capabilities should not be enforced, but should form the focus of political (democratic, rational) debate to establish the ground of the capabilities. Instead the realisation of capabilities should be up to the individual:

> I shall [examine] compassion in connection with a form of political liberalism, a political conception that attempts to win an overlapping consensus among citizens of many different kinds, respecting the spaces within which they elaborate and pursue the different reasonable conceptions of the good. (Nussbaum, 2001, p 401)

If we are to pursue a liberal political agenda, then concepts of wellbeing should be seen as a process of deliberation, which casts education as a deliberative process of inducting children into wider society. It should also be based on compassion as, following Nussbaum, the central ethic of an educational process (Nussbaum, 2001, p 426). This is also in accord with the general philosophy of Nel Noddings (1984), whose ideas, along with other feminist ethics of care writers, are explored further in Chapter 12.

Within the wider discourse of welfare, education can be seen as a good, something that has utility within a wider context of wellbeing (ie it is a component of wellbeing) and acts as a functioning. Or we suggest that within an educational discourse, it can be seen as a good in itself. The international surveys position education as an opportunity to promote wellbeing (a functioning), while the search for indicators of wellbeing argue that education should be seen in terms of itself (ie educational wellbeing = a capability). So we question: is education a functioning or a capability?

Interrelated terminology renders wellbeing meaningless

Wellbeing is a social construct that is fluid in nature and has an ever-evolving and contextual set of definitions. This socially constructed nature presents a high degree of ambiguity, and while many theorists dating back to ancient philosophy have attempted to *fix* the concept theoretically, it is important to acknowledge the usage of words and the potential discourses that are communicated.

A recent report for the DCSF by a discourse analysis consultancy (Ereaut and Whiting, 2008) raised important questions about our modern usage of the term 'wellbeing' and how it has crept into policy documentation in the UK. They provided a linguistic analysis and raised the interesting observation that there is no obvious **binary opposite** (Derrida, 1976) as the obvious word would be 'unwell', but this has clear links to bodily health and wellbeing appears to have a wider remit than this. The only other possibility would be 'ill-being', but this does not function as a proper word in the English language; and to be 'ill' also limits the perspective of wellbeing (Ereaut and Whiting, 2008, p 6). While this may seem like little more than a curious linguistic puzzle, and while there is evidence that 'ill-being' is used in development studies to capture the experiences of people living in poverty(Camfield and Tafere, 2009), there is substance to the claims. What is it that the term wellbeing attempts to capture? That which 'represents an ideal, a generically desirable state. It is *just good* – but not set against any specific *bad*' (Ereaut and Whiting, 2008, p 6; emphasis added).

Derridean deconstruction (Derrida, 1976) explained that all words have a socially and culturally constructed binary opposite and one is always more powerful than the other, such as man–woman, good–bad, hard–soft, with the latter being subordinated in these pairings. The absence of an accepted word as the opposite to wellbeing is interesting –

as if to be not a *well being* in any absolute way is not a concept that we want to have a language for, other than to resort to bodily definitions of ill-health. This raises questions for people with profound disabilities or chronic illnesses as their bodily health (in a biological and physiological sense) may be very *poor* or *ill*; but does that mean that taken as a whole they are not a well being? What about emotional wellness, positive relationships or a spiritual or religious sense of being well?

To extend the linguistic analysis further it is important to appreciate that *well* and *being* are two words, or **signifiers** (Saussure, 1959) that over time have become conflagrated with one another. This may account for why we find it hard to fix a meaning (that which is **signified**) for wellbeing, as there is more than one signifier involved. Why this specific combination of words? For instance, how is *welfare* different to *wellbeing*? Is welfare more about social measures of people's wellness? Is welfare more concerned with what can be done to support those in need? Welfare, it seems, is more associated with economic support and services (Kamerman et al, 2010). The terms are often used interchangeably, but it appears that wellbeing has replaced welfare in modern usage. Jordan (2008) argued that an economic model of welfare that rests on individualistic accounts of what is good for people have hampered our ability to consider wellbeing in anything more than an individual way, and that this has denied the progress of communal welfare and social value. This has echoes of Coalition Prime Minister David Cameron's interest in measuring wellbeing. He made reference to wellbeing in his speech to the Confederation of British Industry (Cameron, 2010), where he said that the government would set out in the coming weeks 'how we will bring in a new emphasis on wellbeing in our national life'.

Gasper (2004) argued that in modern history, wellbeing has been equated with 'well-feeling' and been the domain of utilitarian economics whereby the focus has been on pleasure seeking and achievement. But he believed that in more recent usage, wellbeing actually has a closer association to Aristotelian or Eudaimonic traditions of 'well-living' and that this should include conceptions of 'being well', but also of being, becoming and dying:

> Feeling and thinking, becoming and living and dying, and more, make up being. Wellbeing thus has diverse aspects. Rather than set up a precisely delimited, narrow single notion of well-being, and then try to police its 'correct' usage, we will do better to see wellbeing as an umbrella notion. (Gasper, 2004, p 7)

Arguably, most writers and uses of the term wellbeing focus on defining the *well* aspect of the term and there is an absence of the *person*, either in living or in dying. Gasper's account is one of the few to consider issues of quality of death and dying well, as well as those of life and living. This may account for the fact that while we could attribute a binary opposite to 'well' as being 'ill', when we combine the two signifiers to form 'ill-being' this becomes what is termed a 'nonce-word' by the *Oxford English Dictionary* (cited in Ereaut and Whiting, 2008, p 6) and the signified is poorly understood.

Ereaut and Whiting (2008) take this further into a minute discursive approach to the issue of how we should spell and write wellbeing and what difference this makes to its meaning. They claimed that wellbeing is used in a variety of formats:

1. As an adjective, with a presumption that we have a shared understanding, such as the policy use of 'the well-being agenda'. This is hugely presumptive and prevents the concept being problematised, and is arguably the way in which it has entered policy and practice discourses.
2. Without inverted commas, which suggests that it is taken for granted and unremarkable.
3. With the removal of the hyphen from 'well-being' to form 'wellbeing', which has the effect of normalising.
4. By dropping the first capitalisation of 'Wellbeing', which has the effect of preventing it standing out as something too overt and open to challenge.
5. Finally, by placing it alongside other words as if it has equivalence with established terms and concepts such as health, or even by creating a link between terms to objectify its use, for example, 'health and wellbeing' – which is a term regularly seen in policy literature.

In this book, we have chosen to use *wellbeing* in a deliberate manner – we do not use it as an adjective, except in our reporting of policy usage in Chapter 3. We have not used inverted commas or a capital first letter as this becomes repetitive, and while wellbeing is the phenomena being discussed, we felt it would be excessive to reiterate this all the time. We have chosen not to hyphenate for the simple reason that we believe that wellbeing is normalised in contemporary society – just not well articulated, particularly in the context of children. While the specific focus is children's social and emotional wellbeing (SEWB) we use wellbeing and SEWB fairly interchangeably as a mirror of the specificity of the literature available.

Ereaut and Whiting (2008) also considered the discourses underpinning the use of wellbeing in UK government departments. These were mapped out by them as a series of overlapping circles, much like a Venn diagram, and include five different discourses as follows:

- Medical heritage – this is based on the association of 'health and wellbeing' and seems to rest on an extension of the term health to include emotional and mental health and possibly the importance of relationships. The author's claim this to be the most dominant wellbeing discourse in UK policy and is prevalent in schools through the *Healthy Schools* agenda in England and Wales (DfEE, 1999) and through initiatives to tackle childhood obesity through the *National Child Measurement Programme* (DH, 2010).
- Operationalised discourse – whereby wellbeing is only known and understood in respect of a set of indicators and measures such as the five *Every Child Matters* outcomes. Wellbeing is understood *as* ECM, and does not need to be theorised, conceptualised or challenged as the outcomes provide indicators and arenas for measurement that are all shared and understood. Examples include wellbeing programmes based upon ECM such as Social and Emotional Aspects of Learning (SEAL) (DfES, 2005c) and PATHS (Channing-Bete, 2010).
- Sustainability discourse – wellbeing appears to be linked with environmental sustainability and is forward-projecting in respect of the wellbeing of society. Issues of climate change and environmental sustainability are focused on a great deal in schools and by children, but arguably not seen as essential to their wellbeing under OLT approaches such as ECM.
- Discourse of holism – this moves beyond bodily health to incorporate ideas of spirituality, relationships, the environment and the need to consider the whole person.
- Philosophical discourse – with roots in Aristotelian philosophy and the ideal of a good and ethical life, there are writers whose works in happiness, subjective wellbeing or positive psychology have filtered into policy discourses (Seligman and Csikszentmihalyi, 2000; Eid and Larsen, 2008).

These account for ways in which wellbeing can be identified in policy and raise the possibility that the majority usage of wellbeing for children rests in the *medicalised* and *operationalised* discourses, and these are explored later. The populist usage of wellbeing has, we argue, been denigrated to a debate of *wellness* (in a medical way) where the issue is more of the site of wellness (mental, bodily, emotional health) as opposed to debate and discussion about the *person* (or, in this case, the child) and their role in being well. This discourse of wellbeing reduces individual or community engagement and responsibility for being well and potentially disenfranchises individuals from their bodies and control over living well.

The space to do something different

Rather than get lost in circular and long-standing debates about wellbeing, well-living, flourishing and so on – debates that far more informed philosophers have not yet managed to resolve – we believe that this book offers, through the deconstruction of wellbeing as a concept, a space to do something different. We should not be wrapped up in terminology and conceptual confusions, rather the challenge is to distil the *essence* of the debate regarding children's wellbeing and creating new understandings from which better policy and practice in wellbeing research can emerge. This is a debate that we will identify in educational policy and practice in subsequent chapters, but one that is also prevalent in contemporary politics, the media and in the consciousness of parents and carers. This demands that we introduce a number of strands of thought that will underpin the later chapters. It is to these that we now turn.

Revisiting the status of the child

The last 30 years have been marked in childhood studies by debates concerning the extent to which childhood is a natural, biological state and transition on the way to adulthood (becoming theories) or whether it is a state of being in its own right (being theories) (Qvortrup, 1991; James et al, 1998; Jenks, 2001; Mayall, 2002). The work of sociologists of childhood has been to challenge taken-for-granted assumptions about childhood. As Rousseau strikingly wrote in the preface to his fiction *Émile*:

> We know nothing of childhood: and with our mistaken notions the further we advance the further we go astray. The wisest writers devote themselves to what a man ought to know, without asking what a child is capable of learning. They are always looking for the man in the child, without considering what he is before he becomes a man. (Rousseau, 1979, p 7)

Debates remain as to the extent to which children are in a state of *being*, and social actors in their own right, or *becomings*, as adults in the making, who are judged as incompetent against adult standards. Some authors suggest that to foreground one state as having predominance over the other creates a tautology; as children are actually locked into both states at once and to try and proclaim the importance of one over the other ignores the biological manifestations of growth and development that inevitably occur through what we know as the period of childhood (however this is framed and described). Nick Lee acknowledged that we are all (children and adults) denoted as both simultaneously *being* and *becoming*, as such analyses rest on judgments of relative competence and we cannot achieve complete competence at everything, just because we claim the state of adult (Lee, 2001). We are also all ageing biologically whether we are a child or an adult.

Emma Uprichard addressed this dichotomy by drawing on a conception of time from the Nobel prize-winning chemist Ilya Prigogine, conceived of as an arrow that has an epistemological component (the marker of time) and an ontological component (the intrinsic internal feature of the thing itself): 'in other words, for all things in the social and physical world, time is reversible and irreversible, external and internal to the thing itself, and always and necessarily "being and becoming"' (Uprichard, 2008, p 307). Applied to children, the being discourse is captured by the marker of time: the child living the experiences and being a child – the epistemological component that is external to the child. While the ontological component describes the ageing child – the becoming discourse – whereby the time component is concerned with the biological ageing process and is of the ontology of the body of the child.

Lee's work (2001, 2005) also challenged underlying assumptions about the relationship between children, adults and society and these were explored in ways that raised questions about children's rights, their autonomy and their ability to become and be a person. He proposed concepts of value, separability and possession to understand the 'apparent conflict of loving and caring for children and valuing them as individuals' (Lee, 2005, p 19). He used the concept of **de-territorialisation**, drawn from the writings of (Deleuze and Guattari, 1983, 2004), to challenge Kant's ideas that humanity emanates from our unique ability for rational thought as something to be discovered, and argued rather that human value is always built upon and is 'the diverse and changing consequence of processes of organization and re-organization' (Lee, 2005, p 140). De-territorialisation occurs as the human baby becomes more than just her nature or biology and her connection with her care-giver to a reacting and situated person in a social and physical world, and this development marks her 'separability' (as opposed to separateness) as an autonomous human being. His perspective acknowledges children's participation and their rights, and that includes deciding what is good for them, or what they need in order to be a well being. This poses a challenge to *who* determines wellbeing for children? As Lee (2005, p 152) commented: 'when children speak their minds and seek to differ with the adults who surround them, they are taking part in a de-territorialization from their family, but this need not make them strangers'.

Challenging Cartesian dualist ideas of wellbeing

So far in this chapter, we have explored the idea that wellbeing as it is used in modern parlance and policy documentation has transformed into the study of wellness, as opposed to a focus on well beings. The *beings* have been lost. Added to this observation is the ongoing debate about the nature of childhood that posits children in states of being and becoming, where the *becoming* aspect invites paternalism in respect of adult guidance and supervision of what is best for children (because they cannot possibly know). If we cannot understand whether children are beings in their own right, then arguably any concern for their wellbeing becomes an imposed judgement by adults that appears to have been diverted to questions of bodily and mental health, as opposed to debate concerning human (child) flourishing, value, needs or capabilities.

The *being* dimension of wellbeing for children is also not without problems and writers have attempted to understand the multiple and layered dimensions of bodies. One analysis that is useful to consider is that provided by Scheper-Hughes and Lock (1987) of the multiplicities of bodies comprised of the *individual body*, *social body* and *body politic*. Under these three conceptions, different formulations of wellbeing evolve. A perspective of the body as individually experienced and somatically understood raises age-old Cartesian mind–body dualisms as we lack a precise vocabulary to deal with experiences of the body that are truly integrated and combine mind–body and society. Instead, our language (particularly in medicine) attempts to dissociate feelings/ experiences into those of individual thoughts or experiences located in the physical substance of bodies that can be explained physiologically, for example, pain.

In most societies, the individual body is also understood as a social identity (one of responsibilities, awareness of others and a sense of communal life) as opposed to a purely individual identity, as we recognise the social nature of humanity. It is argued, however, that in modern Western society there is undue focus on the development of a strong sense of individual self at the cost of social selves. The social body is understood symbolically in relation to the social and cultural matrices and experiences of which the individual is party to. Cultural constructions of and about the body reveal views about society and social relations, and in respect of health and wellbeing, there is a direct correlation mapped between a healthy body and a healthy society. We see examples of this in contemporary propoganda about the state of childhood (Palmer, 2007) and how children's health and wellbeing are used as indicators for the wellbeing of society in general (DCSF, 2007b; UNICEF, 2007). Extending this symbolic association between individual bodies and societal wellbeing, Scheper-Hughes and Lock (1987, p 21) suggested that in ancient times and in non-Western traditional communities, there was a dominant discourse that connected individual mind–body with society and that:

> what is most significant about the symbolic and metaphorical extension of the body into the natural, social and supernatural realms is that it demonstrates a unique kind of human autonomy that seems to have all but disappeared in the 'modern', industrialized world.

The authors go on to explain that in societies where the social body predominates, 'the confident uses of the body in speaking about the external world conveyed a sense that humans are in control' (Scheper-Hughes and Lock, 1987, p 21) and this contrasts with the 'body alienation' they reported in Western countries where bodily dissatisfaction and separation have resulted in pathologising conditions of mental illnesses and body dysmorphias.

The relationship between individual and social bodies is also one of politics, and determined by power and control. Society determines at any given time, and for any given set of circumstances, the *correct* body that its citizenry should achieve. The politically and culturally correct body to achieve in the modern Western world is the lean, fit, androgynous type where health and fitness are earnt through living well and exercising hard. Some commentators have suggested that this reflects a nation's obsession with preparing for war (DeMause, cited in Scheper-Hughes and Lock, 1987). The body politic is experienced and exerted on individuals in many ways, and these are subject to other social forces such as gender. The epidemic in eating disorders among young girls and women may be testament to the dual expectations on them to be both hedonistic and fun-loving, while at the same time remaining slim, fit and composed. A response to such demands may be to eat and drink at will, but to manage one's body by excessive exercising, and bouts of vomiting and purging (Scheper-Hughes and Lock, 1987).

The body politic exerts power and control over individual bodies whereby 'the individual body becomes an element that may be placed, moved, articulated on others' (Foucault, 1991a, p 164). Foucault (1991a, 1995) developed the concept of 'docile bodies' to describe the manipulation and subjugation of individuals that occurs through bodily domination, particularly in institutionalised settings such as the army, prisons, churches or schools. Discipline is the tool of docility and it helps to divert power away from autonomous beings to docile subjects:

> Discipline increases the forces of the body (in economic terms of utility) and diminishes these same forces (in political terms of obedience). In short, it dissociates power from the body; on the one hand, it turns into an 'aptitude', a 'capacity', which it seeks to increase, on the other hand, it reverses the course of the energy, the power that might result from it, and turns it into a relation of strict subjection. (Foucault, 1991a, p 138)

More integrated and holistic understandings of wellbeing for children require engagement with complex and nuanced understandings of children as comprising all three bodies and to understand how these bodies express and experience their being well. As Scheper- Hughes and Lock (1989, p 31) concluded: 'the individual body should be seen as the most immediate, the proximate terrain where social truths and social contradictions are played out, as well as a locus of personal and social resistance, creativity and struggle'.

Voice

An OLT perspective on wellbeing presupposes that others in positions of authority have decided what goes on the list for children and young people. The ECM agenda (DfES, 2004a), along with international agreements on child rights such as the *United Nations Convention on the Rights of the Child* (UNCRC) (UN, 1990), reinforce the notion of 'universal goods' that are to be achieved for all children and young people and this negates the problematic and highly complex and situated nature of wellbeing for children living in very different economic, social and familial circumstances. Such a view of wellbeing as imposed upon children also denigrates their right to speak about their wellbeing, or to vocalise on matters that concern them and children collectively. This runs counter to the sociology of childhood movement that affords primacy to children's rights and their voices as enshrined in Article 12 of the UNCRC (UN, 1990), and sees them as competent actors who can narrate their own lives. While there are pockets of research and practice in the UK attempting to access children's accounts on wellbeing or what they determine to be a *good* childhood experience (UNICEF, 2007; DCSF, 2008b; Layard and Dunn, 2009), these are limited, wrought with methodological difficulties and often include a particular section of society, as will be expanded upon later in Chapter 7. The exclusion of children, young people, families and practitioners from deciding what is right and good for the flourishing of each individual is evidence of the dominance of what Deleuze and Guattari (2004) termed 'majoritarian' discourses, where:

> one is given a perspective, together with a set of categories and presuppositions, by the historical, social, cultural and economic site one occupies, a site expressing pre-conscious interests … dominant social presuppositions take on the mask of necessity through reflection: everyone knows them and can understand them. (Goodchild, 1996, p 54)

Under this conception, wellbeing is formulated into *medicalised* or *operationalised* lists of things to achieve and becomes objective and unproblematic. How wellbeing is defined is fluid and interchangeable, but arguably not determined by children and young people themselves; rather, it is constituted as hegemonic knowledge in a 'majoritarian' discourse. This reflects a model of childhood as being locked into a 'being' state only and that denies the room for growth and development as earlier discussions have elaborated: 'that is why we must distinguish between: the majoritarian as a construct and homogeneous system; minorities as subsystems; and the minoritarian as a potential, created and creative becoming.… There is no becoming-majoritarian; majority is never becoming. All becoming is minoritarian' (Deleuze and Guattari, 1987, pp 105–6).

This is important to appreciate as working with 'minoritarian' discourses provides room for change and growth as it is a becoming state, rather than the 'majoritarian', which is effectively a hegemonic constant against which 'minoritarian' can be understood. So, if the 'minoritarian' knowledge of wellbeing can be revealed and the experiences of children, young people, families and professionals are foregrounded, then this could provide a vehicle for the voices of all of the participants involved to emerge, be heard and valued, rather than relying on imported concepts and constructs from an uncritical and poorly conceptualised notion of wellbeing.

This aspiration could permit new ways of regarding the 'minoritarian' fictions of children and young people, as 'only fiction [*real accounts of experience*] can invent a people' (Goodchild, 1996, p 55):

> Fiction is a privileged medium of social and political thought … since it is not bound up with any theoretical illusions: it is no longer a question of 'telling the truth' in order to bring people to a reflective consciousness of their real situation, for when the minorities are colonised by majorities, the people (as a set of modes of existence) are still missing (insofar as the only consciousness available to the oppressed is that of the majority) and only fiction can invent a people. (Deleuze, 1989, p 216, cited in Goodchild, 1996, p 55)

The concept of fiction challenges any suggestion that there are 'truths' to be revealed; rather, there is a need to access lived realities and find a language for sharing and communicating these realities. This brings new challenges, as it is reliant on the ability to bring to visibility (Foucault, 1972) concepts and constructs that have had a complex history, and about which there is little agreement. These ambitions – to reveal the 'minoritarian' fictions (voices) and to find more valid and embedded methods to understand wellbeing for children and young people – form the basis of Chapter 7, where we explore attempts to access children's and professionals' voices on wellbeing.

Not pathologising difference/Othering

The concept of wellbeing in education is an expression – it has form and content and is created through, and in itself creates, a **discursive practice**, which positions children in varying ways as becoming – child. Such 'becomings' for children designated as 'having special educational needs', 'disabled' or 'different' are '**Othered**' in that the expression creates the boundary between normal and abnormal. As Foucault noted: 'an Other is always pushed aside, marginalized, forcibly homogenized and devalued as [Western] cognitive machinery does its work' (Foucault, 1983b, p 19).

In interrogating 'majoritarian' positions, there are questions as to who has the power to make expressions. Who is the subject of enunciation? Who are the priests of the 'majoritarian' theory? Who, then, forms the subject of the statement (to whom is the expression directed)? How do subjects of the statement become subjectified? For the project of resisting objectification, are there possibilities of breaking out – of deterritorialisation – which break the connections between expression and content to allow for a radical disruption?

Such understandings challenge the liberal views of education based on compassion (Nussbaum, 2001) or care (Noddings, 2002) in that minoritarian engagement is based on encounter and responsiveness: 'responsiveness suggests a different way to understand the needs of others rather than to put ourselves into their position.... One is engaged from the standpoint of the other, but not by presuming the other is exactly like the self' (Tronto, 1993, p 135). And responsiveness underpins respect, where 'respect for others is also openness to and welcoming of difference' (Dahlberg and Moss, 2005, p 83).

The concept of wellbeing that begins to emerge here is one of dynamic exchange between people (adults and adults, adults and children, children and children), which is not predicated on objective lists that constrain moral behaviour. Instead, we have a politics of becoming, as emergence, where wellbeing is not predicated by OLTs or is resolutely hedonistic or desiring, but is an ethics of encounter (Bayliss, 2009). These ideas are particularly revisited in Chapters 11 and 12.

New understandings of professionals and professionalism

Which professionals are vested with the wellbeing of children in schools and what models of wellbeing practice are engaged in by adults who support children's wellbeing? Such questions rest on analyses of what it is to be a 'professional', and sociologists and economists have long debated the concept of 'professional' or indeed 'professionalism'. Most attempts have been based upon professionalism as a normative value system. Durkheim, for example, assessed professionalism as being a 'form of moral community based on occupational membership' (Evetts, 2008, p 399). Evetts (2008, p 399) argued that there were two dominant discourses in respect of how professionalism and its effects in society are understood: as a 'value system [that] is guardedly optimistic about the positive contributions of the concept to a normative social order'; and as an 'ideology [that] focuses more negatively on professionalism as a hegemonic belief system and mechanism of social control for "professional" workers'. Not surprisingly, she argued that professionals themselves adopt the 'value system' with the 'normative discourse' in describing their work with clients.

We suggest that professionals in schools also ascribe to the normative discourse of professionalism in respect of their wellbeing 'work' with children and young people. But accountability and audit of performance for professionals (in this case, teachers, and based on academic achievement) places demands on how they evidence their professionalism, where achievement targets (because they are easily evidenced in exam marks) arguably take priority over 'softer' mental health or wellbeing outcomes. The appeal of professionalism is:

> exclusive ownership of an area of expertise and knowledge, and the power to define the nature of problems in that area as well as the control of access to potential solutions. It also includes an image of collegial work relations of mutual assistance and support rather than hierarchical, competitive or managerialist control. (Evetts, 2008, p 407)

Yet, schools *are* hierarchical in nature, with some employees 'qualified' (and paid) at higher levels than others. Even pupils are hierarchically arranged according to age. Given the pressures on teachers to meet achievement outcomes, it is clear that support for wellbeing becomes a minority concern. Increasingly, non-educational and non-qualified educational staff are being encouraged to work together with teachers in joined-up ways to support the 'whole child', and there is some evidence of teachers resisting the engagement of other professional groups appropriating 'part of the pastoral role that traditionally lay with the classroom teacher' (Spratt et al, 2006, p 367), creating professional jealousies across boundaries, with teachers viewing schools as their professional domain.

The literature outlines a number of models and tensions for how wellbeing can become part of the remit of schools and there are challenges in all of these. Traditionally, wellbeing has been part of wider agendas of 'health promotion' or 'mental health' work in schools and relied heavily on the specialist inputs of health personnel. The effect of such limited interventionist approaches 'is that the school environment does not shift towards the prevention of ill health or the promotion of wellbeing' (Wyn et al, 2000, p 599). Specialists are concerned with individuals, not with the wider promotion of wellbeing across the whole school (Spratt et al, 2006).

Alternative approaches to wellbeing in schools include the direct teaching of wellbeing by teachers who embed 'Positive Education'

(Seligman et al, 2009) across curriculum subjects, and this rests on specific training for teachers understanding aspects of 'positive psychology: resilience, gratitude, strengths, meaning, flow, positive relationships and positive emotions' (Seligman et al, 2009, p 304). These approaches arguably reinstate teachers' professional knowledge over other professional groups, and place wellbeing firmly within their domain of responsibility. But this is a very specialist and psychologically framed approach that requires specialist training.

Increasingly, schools are being encouraged to take a 'whole school ethos' approach to wellbeing (as opposed to whole child?) based on a World Health Organization report, whereby it was claimed 'the advantages of a positive school environment can be greater well-being and happiness, an improved sense of belonging and better quality of life for those engaged with the organization' (WHO, 1999, p 5). These approaches are based on the large benefits for whole populations (universal) as opposed to targeted work with those deemed particularly in need. While the World Health Organization and many others support the importance of whole school, holistic approaches, based on ecological models of wellbeing (Roffey, 2008), fostering 'connectedness' (Rowe et al, 2007) and building on ideas of 'social capital' (Spratt et al, 2006; Rowe et al, 2007), there is little account of *who* is responsible for the wellbeing agendas in schools.

These models parallel the targeted–universal arguments that we will explore in later chapters. In one model, we have professionals protecting their specific body of knowledge and skills (targeted) and a small number of children benefitting. The alternative model rests on universal approaches that draw on everyone's (and no one's) knowledge and sense of responsibility. We suggest, however, that there are other *informal* models of support for wellbeing that exist in schools, where we see (particularly para-professional) groups who resist the 'ideological discourses' (Evetts, 2008) underpinning their professionalism and engage in value-based practice with children and young people that resists the diminished construction of their professional identities.

Conclusion

We have raised a number of questions about how wellbeing is understood, and have attempted to trace the origins of a number of theories and models of wellbeing throughout history and across a number of disciplines. Our ambition has been to problematise 'wellbeing', 'being well' and children as 'beings' and 'becomings'. This is not about generating a new or true model of children's wellbeing in schools; but rather about grappling with the complexities and uncertainties of using the concept at all, and to understand the *inconsistencies* inherent in the concept. The deconstruction and examination of existing theories and models is of value in itself in trying to understand how, why and in what circumstances wellbeing has taken such a strong hold in our language, policy and practice with children and young people.

CHAPTER 3

Policy on the promotion of wellbeing in schools

Introduction

This chapter critically reviews some key UK educational policies focused on the promotion of social and emotional wellbeing (SEWB) in schools over the last decade. We also offer some wider context to this policy formation and the drivers behind it. Each of the four countries of the UK is considered separately as there are different policy frameworks in each region. Table 3.1 shows estimated relative youth (under 18) populations across the UK as context for this discussion.

The rise and rise of wellbeing in education policy

Within education policy, wellbeing, and its offshoot SEWB, is a relatively new discourse, reflective of much of the New Labour agenda post–1997. What policymakers understand by wellbeing is far from clear (Ereaut and Whiting, 2008), as we outlined in Chapter 2.

Dartington Social Research Unit (Axford et al, 2009) identified five 'lenses' (needs, poverty, quality of life, social exclusion and children's rights) through which policymakers observed and acted on children's wellbeing and suggested that policymakers' understanding of these lenses is inconsistent. The route policy has taken, however, does show consistency. Both in the UK and internationally it has favoured operationalised or Objective List Theory (OLT) definitions. UK examples of lists of wellbeing indicators integral to policy include *Every Child Matters*' five outcomes, and the Scottish *Curriculum for Excellence*'s four capacities.

Table 3.1: Estimated youth populations in the UK regions

England	12,400,000
Scotland	1,000,000
Northern Ireland	50,000
Wales	651,800

Source: Based on figures from the UK Children's Commissioners' report to the UN Committee on the Rights of the Child (UKCC, 2008).

The United Nations World Health Organization (WHO), the Organisation for Economic Co-operation and Development (OECD) and the United Nations Educational, Scientific and Cultural Organization (UNESCO) have all influenced UK policy on SEWB in schools. Several comparative international reports (UNICEF, 2007; Bradshaw and Richardson, 2009; OECD, 2009) suggested that UK children fare worse than their counterparts in many other countries. The UNICEF report ranked the UK 21st out of 21 rich countries surveyed.

The UNICEF report was based on a concept of wellbeing grounded in the United Nations Convention on the Rights of the Child (UNCRC), and this resulted in some difficult findings for the UK. Just over 40% of the UK's 11, 13 and 15 year olds found their peers kind and helpful, the worst score of all the developed countries. The UK had the highest proportion of young people who smoke, abuse drink and drugs, engage in risky sex, and become pregnant at too early an age. Also, 30% of the 15 to 19 year olds were not in education or training or were not looking beyond low-skilled work. In direct regard to education, the UK came 17th out of 21 countries. Sensational headlines stated 'Bottom of a league table for child well-being across 21 industrialised countries' (BBC, 2007), and comment followed that 'there is a crisis at the heart of our society and we must not continue to ignore the impact of our attitudes towards young people and the effect that this has on their wellbeing'.

Further adverse comparisons were to come. In 2009, Bradshaw and Richardson's (2009, p 5) 'Index of Child Wellbeing in Europe' ranked the UK:

• 24th out of 29 countries for child health (although doing quite well on health behaviours such as exercise, eating fruit and brushing teeth, the UK scored badly on immunisation rates);
• 21st out of 28 countries for subjective wellbeing;
• 24th out of 26 countries for material resources (because of the high number of children living in families where neither parent is employed); and
• 22nd out of 27 countries for education (although the UK was slightly above average in the sub-domain of educational attainment).

This low ranking was also reflected in *Doing Better for Children* (OECD, 2009), which looked at 30 countries and, using six comparative domains and data mostly from 2005 or 2006, ranked the UK as follows: fourth for quality of school life; 12th for material wellbeing; 15th for housing and environment; 22nd for educational wellbeing; 20th for health and safety; and 28th for risky behaviours.

Matching these damning pressures to act on wellbeing were internal forces such as child poverty, anti-social behaviour and the need for 'employability'. New Labour declared 'Our historic aim will be for ours to be the first generation to end child poverty' (Blair, 1999). This was intended to draw a clear dividing policy line between New Labour and what had gone before, but direct wealth redistribution was not on the cards. It was perhaps for this reason that New Labour's notion of child poverty broadened to include child wellbeing: 'concepts of child well-being are particularly helpful in broadening the discussion on poverty among children from a mainly income-focused perspective to a more comprehensive understanding of the multiple factors influencing children's life situations' (Huby and Bradshaw, 2006, p 4). 'Although child poverty is a different concept to wellbeing, poverty influences each aspect of wellbeing and is a major impediment to delivering better wellbeing' (Child Poverty Action Group, 2009, p 2).

In 2002, then Prime Minister Tony Blair set out a new vision for UK civil society in which the lives of all individuals would be regulated and modified by state legislation 'to tackle antisocial behaviour that damages communities' (Blair, 2002). No clear definition was given, but the behaviour in mind seemed to range from dropping chewing gum to assaults by collectives of 'feral children'. The new 'respect agenda' assumed untrustworthiness and supplied more and more state guidance on how to relate and behave. In schools, this approach formed a platform for Social and Emotional Aspects of Learning (SEAL), the approach to emotions that would come to be modelled, taught and managed through the school curriculum (see Chapter 4).

The issue of employability and the 'skills deficit' also raised the profile of wellbeing-related issues in education. In 2003, a Learning and Skills Council report identified one fifth of reported job vacancies as unfilled due to a lack of applicants with generic, transferable skills, including many elements of what we now know as social and emotional learning. According to Bunt et al (2005, p 29), employability meant motivation and flexibility; willingness to work and learn; appearance, behaviour, confidence; and positive gestures and mannerisms. The Qualifications and Curriculum Authority joined the debate to assert that any future curriculum should 'give substantial weight to personal, social and emotional education' (QCA, 2005, p 6; see also WHO, 1999).

Pressures also came from outside the UK. Since 2003, the WHO has called for 'health promoting' schools, and provided templates to work to. Together with UNESCO, the World Bank and others, it produced

Creating an Environment for Emotional and Social Well-Being, a guide to 'psycho social environment profiling' in schools (WHO, 1999), which defined wellbeing as involving the whole school community 'including administrators, cleaners, secretarial staff, volunteers, and, where applicable: playground monitors, cafeteria staff, the school nurse, and traffic safety patrol' (WHO, 1999, p 68). This guidance has been translated into Chinese, an example of the growing global reach of the 'wellbeing brand'. The report was influential in the creation of the UK 'Healthy Schools' programme, set up in 1999, which was a joint initiative between the Department for Education and Department of Health designed to promote a whole school/whole child approach to health, including emotional health and wellbeing. The involvement of all school personnel in wellbeing measures is enshrined in SEAL (see Chapter 4), a social and emotional learning programme that is used in most UK schools in England. An OECD report concluded that 'Governments should continuously experiment with policies and programmes for children, rigorously evaluate them to see whether they enhance child well-being, and reallocate money from programmes that don't work to those that do' (OECD, 2009, p 163).

Other influences played a large but mostly unspoken part in the rise of child wellbeing as a policy objective. In at least three of the four UK regions, abuse, murder and suicide directly impacted policy. In England, *Every Child Matters* was a response to Laming's report on Victoria Climbié's murder by her carers (DH, 2003). In Wales, certain children's homes were found to have 'allowed some of society's most vulnerable youngsters to be sexually, physically and emotionally abused by the very people supposed to protect them' (*The Independent*, 2000). In Northern Ireland, national debate has been highly concerned with suicide (Leavey et al, 2009, p 19 and *passim*).

The regions and wellbeing policy

England

In England and parts of Wales, *Every Child Matters* (ECM) was the name given to the policy framework (DfES, 2004a) that would implement the 2004 Children Act. ECM advocated whole system change through inter-agency cooperation, which explains why 16 different government departments put their name to it.

Every Child Matters: Change for Children (DfES, 2004a, p 6) asked those involved in the policy to 'clarify what we all want to achieve locally and nationally', apparently encountering the definitional ambiguity

Ereaut and Whiting (2008) had commented on. Within ECM, wellbeing (spelled 'well-being') occurs with three variants; in the phrase 'economic well-being', a term that presumably describes not being poor; as an umbrella term within which the five outcomes are held (see later in this chapter); and as an adjunct of achievement, for example, 'the outcomes are inter-dependent. They show the important relationship between educational achievement and well-being' (DFES, 2004a, p 8). ECM does not explicitly link wellbeing with physical or social and emotional health, though it is linked to 'enjoying' as this passage shows:

> Children and young people have told us that five outcomes are key to well-being in childhood and later life – being healthy; staying safe; enjoying and achieving; making a positive contribution; and achieving economic well-being. Our ambition is to improve those outcomes for all children and to narrow the gap in outcomes between those who do well and those who do not. (DFES, 2004a, p 4)

Here 'children and young people have told us' suggests consultation, and may be intended to sugar the pill of government-prescribed life values, but no source is given. Adult language projects onto children the aim of 'wellbeing in later life' and wellbeing blurs into 'welldoing'. There is a claustrophobia to the world as modelled by ECM. We reproduce here a diagram from *Every Child Matters: Change for Children*. Recipients of policy sit targeted at the centre of a policy vortex with no visible means of escape.

It is an irony that children and young people became a central focus for New Labour at a time when both the aging population and single and childless households rose in number (Office for National Statistics, 2007). Alexandra Dobrowolsky (2002, p 44) commented:

> The figure of the child had no specific gender, race or class and it appealed to the mainstream. For those who remained committed to social justice, the child could be used to legitimize redistributive measures. Even on the right, who else but a curmudgeon would admit to being opposed to improving children's conditions?

Following on from ECM, *The Children's Plan* (TCP) (DCSF, 2007b, p 7) stated: 'If we can establish good habits in childhood, this will provide the basis for lifelong health and wellbeing'. TCP was conflicted about parenting, saying 'governments do not bring up children, parents do'

Figure 3.1: 'A national framework for change'

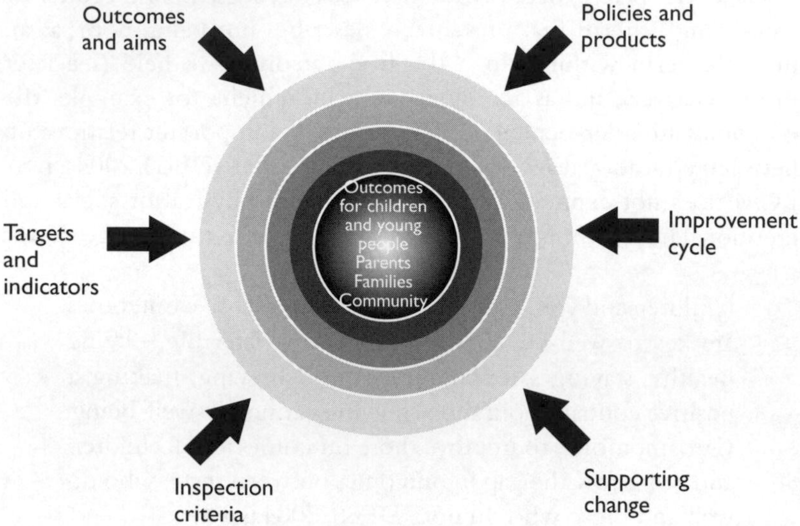

Source: Reproduced under the Open Government Licence from *Every Child Matters: Change for Children* (DfES, 2004a, p 6).

(DCSF, 2007b, p 5), while allocating £34 million 'to place expert parenting advisers in every local authority' (DCSF, 2007b, p 6). TCP also aimed to consult widely over whether the nation wanted to 'enhance children and young people's wellbeing, particularly at key transition points in their lives' or for 'all young people participating in positive activities to develop personal and social skills, promote wellbeing and reduce behaviour that puts them at risk' (DCSF, 2007b, p 14), but such self-evident 'goods' are a poor focus for public consultation. By 2010, a report from the Centre for Policy Studies titled *Cutting the Children's Plan: A £5 Billion Experiment Gone Astray* (Burkard and Clelford, 2010) demolished TCP's record on living up to its own rhetoric of 'a vision for change to make England the best place in the world for children and young people to grow up' (Burkard and Clelford, 2010, p 2):

> Underlying these programmes is a remarkable confidence in the ability of the state to regulate the lives of its citizens and to control their destinies. This confidence appears to be misplaced for it is hard to find much benefit from many of the programmes (the weakness of many of the programme evaluations is also to be condemned). The centralised approach, where a Whitehall department creates and funds

> an endless stream of new programmes, is a model which
> must now be questioned. (Burkard and Clelford, 2010, p 44)

ECM and TCP have contradictions typical of childhood wellbeing
policy discourse. Both policies place consultation with children at
their core, but the *voice* of children is absent or hard to find in both.
Furthermore, both policies advocate state intervention to control the
actions of children, a role exacerbated by the introduction in TCP of
parenting advisors. This centralised model of intervention (Burkard and
Clelford, 2010) challenges the rhetoric of aiming to 'put the needs of
families, children and young people at the heart of everything we do'
(DCSF, 2007b, p 3).

The deficit model of wellbeing (Ecclestone and Hayes, 2009)
underpinning ECM and TCP sees children as lacking, in ways
categorised by the policies: our children are unwell and need fixing!
Humphrey (Humphrey, 2011, p 17) describes how 'a 'moral panic'
(Cohen, 1972) of sorts is generated when a rationalist education system
and society are painted as sources of emotional distress, and children
and young people are cast as disempowered victims'. In contrast, both
ECM and TCP offer a flow of feel-good rhetoric that invites those
involved to 'enhance children and young people's wellbeing' or see
children 'enjoy and achieve': aims difficult to contest or open any form
of debate with (White and Pettit, 2004). The utopian language belies
the rather controlling and authoritative nature of both schemes.

In 2008, the DCSF commissioned *Childhood Wellbeing* (DCSF, 2008b),
a large piece of research that interviewed children, young people
and parents throughout the UK on what contributed to childhood
wellbeing. A number of concerns were raised, including: the ubiquity of
pornographic images in cyberspace; the selling of school sports grounds
to private buyers; the lack of free safe public spaces for children to
spend time in; and the unintended consequences of non-competitive
'politically correct' ('PC') policies in schools, which parents believed
discriminated against children who excelled in non-academic areas.
None of these concerns were directly addressed, either by this piece
of research or in subsequent policy. Their specific gritty nature is ill
met by the vagueness of language such as 'staying safe'. The authors of
Childhood Wellbeing (Counterpoint Research) were briefed to observe
use of the word 'wellbeing'. They write: 'This was not a term anyone
in the sample spontaneously used, and being asked to react to it …
made parents and carers feel uncomfortable' (DCSF, 2008b, p 23). A
few participants are described as recognising the word from childcare
or social research courses. One of these commented: 'I should have

brought my books with me!' (DCSF, 2008b, p 23). Participants were initially nonplussed by the term wellbeing, but once attention was drawn to it, they 'felt this topic was of fundamental importance, and it was frightening that it was so rarely discussed' (DCSF, 2008b, p 14). Thus, the research appears to have created, rather than simply observed, debate about 'childhood wellbeing'.

Scotland

In 2009, the Scottish framework for educational policy became *Curriculum for Excellence* (CFE) (Curriculum Review Group, 2004; CFE, 2010), which, like much educational wellbeing policy, tends to transfer responsibility for weathering an increasingly difficult wider environment to the individual. Scotland's new curriculum arose in response to various challenges, not least of which was 'the need to increase the economic performance of the nation; reflect its growing diversity; improve health; and reduce poverty' (Curriculum Review Group, 2004, p 10). CFE charts SEWB in schoolchildren with detailed wellbeing descriptors, or model answers, intended to be assigned by teachers to each child. In theory, the children involved could be as young as three. An example of which is: 'I value the opportunities I am given to make friends and be part of a group in a range of situations' (CFE, 2010, p 3).

Behaviour control is implied, but not explicitly stated, in CFE's aims, which include proactively promoting 'positive behaviour in the classroom, playground and the wider school community' (CFE, 2010, p 1). Positive is not defined. CFE would like to deliver 'robust policies and practice which ensure the safety and wellbeing of children' because 'good health and wellbeing is central to effective learning and preparation for successful independent living' (SE, 2006). CFE uses an operationalised wellbeing model, with four components called *capacities*: 'The four capacities will make students successful learners, confident individuals, effective contributors and responsible citizens' (Curriculum Review Group, 2004, p 12). Wellbeing is located in the confident individual's capacity. Such individuals can:

> relate to others and manage themselves; pursue a healthy and active lifestyle; be self-aware; develop and communicate their own beliefs and view of the world; live as independently as they can; assess risk and take informed decisions; achieve success in different areas of activity. (Curriculum Review Group, 2004, p 12)

Would 'developing and communicating their own beliefs and view of the world' include proselytising for a Jihad or the legalisation of cannabis? Would 'living as independently as you can' stretch to missing school to attend paid work? If a child furthers their own wellbeing by reading a book during a lesson, is this 'positive behaviour'? Is it wellbeing-promoting behaviour? In Scotland, as throughout educational SEWB discourse, behind bland language stands a covert rubric of values, un-debated and on which consensus is assumed.

Wales

Welsh developments take place within a comprehensive schooling system, and policy definitions of wellbeing show a more social bias. *The Learning Country* (WAG, 2001), a key policy document, described a mix of factors shaping individuals' lives, including 'social, economic, environmental and cultural factors', all of which have a part in determining health, and the Welsh Assembly Government (WAG) sought to improve wellbeing by addressing these factors (WAG, 2002, p 5). The Welsh government supports school councils and uses a language of empowering its youth. School councils, although varying in effectiveness, do institutionalise student influence to some degree. The term wellbeing is defined in Wales through the seven core aims from the UNCRC – that all children and young people:

- have a flying start in life;
- have a comprehensive range of education and learning opportunities;
- enjoy the best possible health and are free from abuse, victimisation and exploitation;
- have access to play, leisure, sporting and cultural activities;
- are listened to, treated with respect and have their race and cultural identity recognised;
- have a safe home and a community that supports physical and emotional wellbeing; and
- are not disadvantaged by poverty.

In Wales, wellbeing is positioned as realising the rights of the child: 'The Welsh Assembly Government believes that following a rights-based policy approach will support all children and young people across Wales to achieve improved emotional health and well-being' (WAG, 2010b, p 4).

In 2008, Wales introduced the *Children and Young People's Well-being Monitor* (WAG, 2008a), which used a variety of child wellbeing indicators and other statistical and research sources to analyse and identify progress against the seven core aims. The *Monitor*'s aims were broad and its moral compass aimed at the reduction of child poverty within a holistic model, because 'there is very little information available on children and young people's own priorities and experiences, and how these vary by geography, age, gender, socio-economic circumstances and other factors' (WAG, 2008a, p 27). Wales was the first region to appoint a Children's Commissioner, and Wales has created *Funky Dragon* (Funky Dragon, 2008), an assembly for the young people of Wales. *Funky Dragon* surveyed 10,000 young people on what they thought the usefulness was of Personal and Social Education (PSE) lessons. Around 45% were positive and 55% thought it was not useful or were not sure (Funky Dragon, 2008). This is the only poll we know of in which young people have collected views on wellbeing education. It is the only evaluation in the field that has been carried out by young people themselves (with guidance and support).

The messages in *The Learning Country* on the role of wellbeing in education were developed further through the publication of the *School Effectiveness Framework* (SEF) (WAG, 2008b), a Welsh school improvement plan with wellbeing at its heart. The SEF 'describes the key characteristics required to build on existing good practice and improve children's and young people's learning and wellbeing throughout Wales' (WAG, 2008b). The SEF definition of wellbeing was directly linked to the seven core aims mentioned earlier. Building on the messages and purpose set out in the SEF, *Thinking Positively, Emotional Health and Well-Being in Schools and Early Years Settings* (WAG, 2010b) guides Welsh schools to focus on emotional health and wellbeing, a term not used in the SEF. *Thinking Positively* states the hoped-for benefits of emotional health and wellbeing as being 'improvements in classroom and whole school atmosphere' (WAG, 2010b, p 3).

Thinking Positively defined school improvement as improvement in behaviour, attendance, teaching, learning, staff recruitment and retention. It supports the children's rights agenda, and links to the child poverty strategy. Emphasis was placed on school councils, pupil counselling services and pupils being involved in decision-making processes: 'Pupils can and should take an active role in developing the policies that will impact positively on the emotional health and well-being of pupils and staff' (WAG, 2010b, p 5). A whole school approach of the kind advocated by the WHO, and discussed earlier, was encouraged. The emotionally healthy school is diagnosed by questioning whether pupils and staff feel nurtured, supported and valued by the school, and whether good relationships are valued and 'given priority in the organisation both explicitly and through its structures' (WAG, 2010b, p 22). Practice in this area was encouraged to be a 'taught and caught' process – taught through explicit teaching of social, emotional and behavioural skills and caught through the promotion of these across all aspects of school life. The concept of an emotionally healthy school is further supported by the Welsh Network of Healthy School Schemes (WAG, 2010a).

Northern Ireland

In 2006, the Northern Irish government published *Our Children and Young People, Our Pledge, A 10 Year Strategy for Children and Young People in Northern Ireland 2006–2016* (Northern Ireland Assembly, 2006), which set out six broad outcomes and a supporting framework designed to let children 'thrive and look forward with confidence to the future' (Northern Ireland Assembly, 2006, p 5). Outcome four stated: 'We have achieved our shared vision if ... our children are experiencing economic and environmental well-being' (2006, p 7). Wellbeing features as one of the six key themes in the report, but, in common with the other regional policies discussed earlier, there is no definition of it as a term. The political context is cited, with an acknowledgement that 36% of those killed in the Troubles in Northern Ireland were children and young people and that although there has been progress since the Good Friday Agreement, 'sectarianism and division within Northern Ireland is still affecting the well-being of our children and young people' (2006, p 30). This report also stated: 'our commitment to tackling social exclusion and social need is reflected in the "economic and environmental wellbeing outcome"' (2006, p 82). There was reference to a new policy framework 'to assist schools to make effective arrangements for supporting the health and well-being of pupils and staff' (2006, p 34) and the assertion that 'a child experiencing economic and environmental well-being is also more likely to be healthy' (2006, p 9).

Another key influence on Northern Ireland policy was the *Flourishing Society* report, published by the Northern Ireland Association for Mental Health (NIAMH) (Leavey et al, 2009), which examined the cost of mental illness, health inequalities and social exclusion in the region. *Flourishing Society*'s remit was to measure progress against three key strategies: the *Bamford Review of Mental Health and Learning Disability* (2007); the *Promoting Mental Health: Strategy and Action Plan 2003–2008* (DHSSPS, 2003); and *Protect Life: A Shared Vision – The Northern Ireland Suicide Prevention Strategy & Action Plan 2006–2011* (DHSSPS, 2006).

This report attributed the up to 30% higher levels of psychiatric morbidity than the rest of the UK in part to fallout from 30 years of sectarian violence, and there was particular concern for rises in suicide rates among young men. *Flourishing Society* called for a more coherent and unified Northern Irish strategy to promote wellbeing, including within schools.

More recently, the term 'emotional health and wellbeing' has appeared in the *Pupils' Emotional Health and Wellbeing Programme* (PEHAW) (Northern Ireland Department of Education, 2005), the new policy vehicle for delivering wellbeing in education in the region, formulated by the Department for Education, the Department of Health, Social Services and Public Safety and a range of key statutory, voluntary and community-sector organisations. Where PEHAW fits into the 10-year strategy outlined earlier is unclear, since it uses a construction of wellbeing grounded in mental health, rather than economic or environmental issues. According to the Department for Education's website, PEHAW is intended to 'contribute to the building of resilient emotional health and well being of pupils'. It is also described as a 'glue' to integrate a range of policies and services from non-academic and curriculum activities, like counselling, pastoral care systems, and suicide prevention, with the *Healthy Schools* initiative (Northern Ireland Department of Education, 2005).

In February 2010, the Northern Irish Education Minister said: 'It is expected that … PEHAW, once established, will make a significant contribution to the wider strategies around improving mental health in our community' (Northern Ireland Assembly, 2010). Although developments in the other UK regions shared some similar concerns, the term 'mental health' is rarer in the wellbeing literature that we have studied outside of Ireland. This mental health focus was a delaying factor in the development of PEHAW because of the cross-departmental blurring involved in merging mental health and educational issues. In the words of one committee:

> The Department's view is that the inclusion of any additional duty relating to mental health ought to be carefully thought through in order to avoid an overlap with the duties and functions of the Department of Health, Social Services and Public Safety. (Northern Ireland Assembly, 2009)

Structural elements have slowed Northern Irish developments too. The role of the five Education and Library Boards in Northern Ireland is to deliver local education, youth and library services, in PEHAW's case paying, for teacher training support. Meanwhile, funding needed by schools and pupils to introduce PEHAW is held by the Department for Education. A number of other obstacles impede policy change, including school selection processes, sectarian issues and a historical lack of public consultation. There is a consequent lack of consistency in how policy in relation to wellbeing is applied across the region.

The unheard debate

Although governments across the UK have developed policies regarding childhood wellbeing in education, there is public debate yet to be had. As Evans (2011, p 347) put it: 'certain values, feelings and behaviours' are promoted in a way that 'raises a key ethical and political challenge: should the state dictate such values and feelings?'. We appear to have skidded from governmental guidance on social and emotional health promotion to full-blown governmental management of these areas; a model with all the usual trappings of targets, outcomes, measures and success criteria.

A comparison with physical health policy may be enlightening here. The UK government recommends us to eat five portions of fruit and vegetables per day, but what would public reaction be if instead of guidance, the state mandated daily menus that provided the five portions, and then weighed, measured and assessed our fruit and vegetable intake and directed us to remedial classes if we ate, say, four or three portions of fruit and vegetables daily?

Similarly, can, or should, the state decide on the legitimacy of feelings? If an individual's personal wellbeing at some stage is connected to being pessimistic and somewhat misanthropic, does that make them deviant in terms of government policy? If so, and I am 14 years old, will I be managed by state policy in order to meet the criteria? As Evans commented: 'Within happiness and well-being there are many "truths" that could be challenged. For example, Cigman (2008) asks how we know what feelings are unconditionally good, pointing out that it can be appropriate to feel fear and shame' (Evans, 2011, p 347).

On a biological level, we have learnt more about the plasticity of adolescent brains. According to Strauch (2004), physical aspects of the brain strongly influence teenage behaviour and, as such, teenagers are not entirely responsible for their sullen, rebellious and moody ways. One wonders how this model meets the normalising and prescriptive nature of SEWB programmes in schools. A similar question arises regarding social development during adolescence and its relationship to rebellion, testing, deviation and subversion.

Finally, SEWB policy, particularly in England, has a focus on the individual behind it. Yet this contradicts much of what we know about SEWB: that it is best nurtured through our families, friends, communities and networks. Many commentators have remarked on the uncomfortableness of the individual model, noting that it places too much focus on the importance of the self, fuels the individualistic society (Michalos, 2007) and fails to recognise that we value things that do not make us especially happy (see eg Layard and Dunn, 2009).

Conclusion

Wellbeing policy burgeoned under New Labour. But in a period dominated by the term 'evidence-based policy' (Wells, 2004), both the term 'wellbeing' and the evidence supporting policy were contested (Hird, 2003; Coleman, 2009). Despite this, wellbeing has dominated the minds of many policymakers, ushering in sweeping changes in how we work with and support children in schools.

Child poverty has been pivotal. If increased income was not sufficient to improve wellbeing (Layard, 2005), something else would need to be supplied – that something became SEWB. Other more hidden drivers have also influenced policy in this area. Reluctance to overtly acknowledge the universal issue of children's mental health has meant the disguising of a response to this real phenomenon in the 'sugared' language of wellbeing. In Scotland, Northern Ireland and Wales, this factor has been even more influential on policy than in England.

Evidence for interventions such as SEAL and other regional SEWB policy vehicles in schools remains inconclusive. Schumer (cited in Waterhouse, 2006) gave three reasons why human beings may believe in ideas lacking sound evidence:

1. *credo consolans*, an unproven idea may be comforting if it predicts a good outcome, makes us feel powerful, or makes us feel in control;
2. *immediate gratification*, an unproven idea may be attractive if it offers instant solutions for difficult problems; and
3. *easy explanations*, an unproven idea may be accepted if it offers a simple story about something that is difficult. (Waterhouse, 2006, p 219, italics and numbering added)

If we apply these three reasons to SEWB policy in schools, an interesting picture emerges. First, *credo consolans*: did the wellbeing agenda give New Labour a feeling of control regarding the management of anti-social behaviour and personal responsibility? Perhaps it assuaged some of the guilt regarding the childhood poverty gap? The language of wellbeing opened a policy door that allowed the government to attempt to intervene with unprecedented detail in how children should be socially and emotionally reared and taught. The hand of government reached into the family unit, both at home and in school, and directed the behaviour of children, and often implicitly adults too (Burkard and Clelford, 2010).

Second, *immediate gratification* was offered by SEWB taught in schools. Although elusive, the idea of SEWB programmes for young people made adults, including politicians feel good – as though they possessed a tangible solution to a rather amorphous problem. Third, *easy explanations* – the very term 'childhood wellbeing' implies a simple description for what is in fact a complex reality facing society and the role of children, smoothing over territory that is difficult to understand and intervene in.

With the introduction of the Coalition government, it is already clear that many of the key New Labour policies will be left to wither on the vine or be quietly closed down. The National Strategies, a forum through which much wellbeing policy was developed and enacted, has been closed down, and much of its online resources and information deleted. The two main policy documents ECM and TCP, although Acts of Parliament, look likely to be significantly modified as the Coalition strives towards devolved models of practice and a reduced role for the state. While wellbeing in general has been placed central to Coalition policy, the role of education in it is yet to be clearly defined.

CHAPTER 4

Practice of social and emotional wellbeing in schools

Introduction

The decade 2000 to 2010 saw a vast increase in UK school-based programmes that focused on various interpretations of social and emotional wellbeing. These approaches either emphasised building the positive skills and capabilities of young people (resilience, confidence, social skills, self-esteem) or attempted to reduce mental illness, bullying, depression and anxiety (Smart and Vassallo, 2008). A range of labels were applied to these approaches, from 'emotional intelligence' (EI) (Goleman, 1995), 'emotional literacy' and 'emotional health and wellbeing' (EHWB) to 'social and emotional wellbeing' (SEWB) (DCSF, 2005), and 'social and emotional dispositions and skills' (SEDS) (Watson and Emery, 2010). Shared objectives were employability, lifelong learning, relationship building, improved behaviour and academic achievement.

The creators of these school wellbeing programmes ranged from independent private organisations through to local authorities, individual schools, not-for-profit social agencies, charities and universities. A 2007 report produced by Futurelab and the Qualifications and Curriculum Authority (Facer and Pykett, 2007) highlighted 19 programmes running across the UK, noting that many others existed. The combined impact of all of these, however, is negligible compared to the main subject of this chapter: 'Social and Emotional Aspects of Learning' (SEAL) (DFES, 2005c, 2007b, 2007c).

What are Social and Emotional Aspects of Learning?

SEAL first emerged as 'Social, Emotional and Behavioural Skills' (SEBS), part of the National Behaviour and Attendance Pilot in 2003 (Hallam et al, 2006). By 2007, it was delivered in more than 80% of primary schools and, by 2010, in 90% of primary and 70% of secondary schools across England, a high rate of coverage for a non-compulsory programme (Mills, 2009). Guidance documents, learning materials and background papers were placed on the now defunct National Strategies website (DfE, nd).

Taking *Every Child Matters* as its policy template, *Promoting Emotional Health and Wellbeing through the National Healthy School Standard* (DH and DfES, 2004) set out the framework for SEAL. This report explicitly linked improvements in child wellbeing with the development of their social, emotional and behavioural skills. It defined EHWB as 'a holistic, subjective state which is present when a range of feelings, among them energy, confidence, openness, enjoyment, happiness, calm, and caring, are combined and balanced' (Stewart-Brown, quoted in Weare and Gray, 2003, p 19).

By 2007, Healthy Schools produced a comprehensive practice guide for schools that asked for evidence of a whole school approach to EHWB, which it linked to behaviour management, and school leadership, which can 'create and manage a positive environment which enhances emotional health and wellbeing in school – including the management of the behaviour and rewards policies' (DCSF, 2007a, p 20). The link with behaviour remained a rationale throughout the implementation of SEAL.

From 2006 onwards, SEAL occupied a central role in education policy and practice, assessing students' social and emotional learning against 42 (primary) or 50 (secondary) key outcomes, for instance, at secondary level: 'I have a range of strategies for managing impulses and strong emotions so they do not lead me to behave in ways that would have negative consequences for me or for other people' (DFES, 2007d, p 53). It should be noted that in discussions with one of the key SEAL creators, it became apparent that, certainly for this player, the learning outcomes were meant to be non-prescriptive examples of how you might apply the programme. However, this was not how the programme was interpreted in schools.

According to the now-disbanded Department for Children, Schools and Families (DCSF), SEAL was 'a comprehensive, whole-school approach to promoting the social and emotional skills that *are thought to* underpin effective learning, positive behaviour, regular attendance, and emotional well-being' (DCSF, 2007f, p 4, italics added). It is interesting that a department concerned with evidence-based practice launched a national programme based on the teaching of skills merely *thought* to support wellbeing. We explore the issue of evidence later in this chapter.

The primary SEAL programme set out to provide schools 'with an explicit, structured whole-curriculum framework for developing all children's social, emotional and behavioural skills' (DfES, 2005a, p 5). The five social and emotional skills within SEAL are the domains in

Goleman's EI framework (Goleman, 1995); social skills, motivation, self-awareness, managing feelings and empathy. SEAL requires these to be explored, reflected on and taught both in and out of the classroom and progress to be made in them. SEAL secondary guidance requires schools to promote these skills through:

- discrete lessons that focus on the social and emotional skills;
- the encouragement of a review of the social and emotional climate and conditions for learning, to ensure pupils can learn, practise and consolidate the skills across the school;
- the encouragement of teachers to review their approaches to learning and teaching to ensure that the approaches implicitly promote social and emotional skills. (DfES, 2007b, p 7)

In 2007, SEAL received funding of £13.7 million to support its expansion across the secondary sector. According to a DCSF press release, SEAL promoted the 'hard-edged social and emotional skills all children and young people need to thrive' (DCSF, 2007g). Ed Balls, the Children's Minister at the time, cited a wide range of benefits, including that the programme would 'make sure that all children understand the importance of being confident and interacting with other children in a respectful and positive manner'. SEAL was described as a set of powerful tools for teachers 'to make sure good behaviour and an atmosphere of respect are the norm in all schools'.[1] Around the same time, fines were announced for parents deemed not to be managing the behaviour of their excluded children.

An interesting point to note here, particularly in regard to the claims being made for SEAL by the DCSF, is that for all the talk of evidence, primary SEAL was nationally launched in May 2005, 10 months *before* the pilot evaluation was reported on. Likewise, secondary SEAL was launched nationally three months *before* its pilot evaluation was reported on. This approach seems somewhat confusing with pupils and practitioners being asked to reflect on their own experiences, while policymakers do not undertake the same process. In fairness, perhaps this process just reflected the *realpolitick* of funding realities at the time.

Origins of Social and Emotional Aspects of Learning

Three factors drove the creation and implementation of SEAL: the work of Daniel Goleman; American social and emotional learning programmes, chiefly the Collaborative for Academic Social and Emotional Learning (CASEL, 2009); and Weare and Gray's (2003)

UK report *What Works in Developing Children's Emotional and Social Competence and Well-Being?*. In 2006, *The Origins of the Primary SEAL Programme* (DCSF, 2006, p 1) stated:

> The stimulus for the development of the SEAL resource was the growing evidence base from the US on the impact of social and emotional learning (SEL) on a range of areas including school achievement, and government's wish to draw together preventative work on mental health and work to tackle behaviour issues in schools.

The 'growing evidence base' referred to here is worth exploring further. SEL first came to academic consciousness in 1990 when psychologists published a series of papers examining people's ability to deal with emotions (Mayer et al, 1990). They found that some people were better than others at identifying their feelings and managing their emotions, and that these people were better at adapting to the environment. Salovey and Mayer are credited by many as the first proponents of 'emotional literacy', but their work remained obscure until Daniel Goleman (1995) chose the title *Emotional Intelligence* for his book. With Salovey's permission to use the term, *Emotional Intelligence* was published in 1995 and a bandwagon was born. On 2 October 1995, *Time* magazine's cover epitomised the *Zeitgeist* by asking 'What's your EQ [emotional intelligence quotient]?' adding in smaller type 'It's not your IQ [intelligence quotient]. It's not even a number. But emotional intelligence may be the best predictor of success in life, redefining what it means to be smart'.

Goleman's book sold millions, perhaps because the idea of emotional intelligence challenged the highly successful *Bell Curve* (Herrnstein and Murray, 1994), which had argued that conventional IQ was the main barometer of future success and was unequally spread among the population. Emotional intelligence by contrast was non-intellectual, emotion-based and could be developed by anyone – a philosophy that offered hope for ever-increasing equality of opportunity. SEAL documentation, as well as the work of supporting academics like Weare and Gray, saw the cultivation of emotional intelligence not just as the inspiration, but as the intellectual and empirical rationale for social and emotional education. Popular support for the notion of EI remains strong, but Goleman's claims for the concept have been discredited in academia. The following quotes (and there are many more) are typical of the criticism:

> [Goleman] exemplifies more clearly than most the fundamental absurdity of the tendency to class almost any type of behaviour as intelligence ... if we cannot measure them how do we know they are related?... The whole theory is built on quicksand; there is no scientific basis. (Eysenck, 2000, p 109)

Indeed, as other writers have noted, there are major conceptual, psychometric and applied problems and issues to be overcome before EI can be considered a genuine, scientifically validated construct with real-life practical significance (Matthews et al, 2004, p 192).

Goleman acknowledged that in the early years, criticism was justified, in particular that statements made then about the benefits of EI were not founded on research specifically testing the effects of EI. In his view, that situation arose because of the newness of EI as a concept and the fact that researchers and others in the field had not yet had time to design, produce and analyse EI-specific research (Goleman, 2006). Yet it is on the work of these early years that SEAL is built. For example, one SEAL guidance document, citing Goleman, repeated the popularised belief that 'emotional and social competences have been shown to be more influential than cognitive abilities for personal, career and scholastic success' (DfES, 2005a, p 48). If EI had been shown to be this reliably predictive of life outcomes, it would be irresponsible of educators to ignore it. In our opinion, the actual evidence is harder to interpret and more ambivalent than that.

The Collaborative for Academic Social and Emotional Learning

The second US-based factor that drove the adoption of SEAL in UK schools was the formation in Chicago of CASEL. While it would be disingenuous to say that only one voice has existed in the US regarding the introduction and teaching of social and emotional learning programmes, CASEL is the dominant player in what is close to a monolithic discourse.

Founded in 1995, CASEL is a not-for-profit research organisation whose mission is to 'establish social and emotional learning (SEL) as an essential part of education' (CASEL, 2010). CASEL has conducted a number of studies examining the benefits of SEL across the US, concluding that it aids: cognitive development, student focus and motivation; relationships between students and teachers; school–family partnerships (which help students achieve); and student confidence and success. CASEL is a platform not only for its own research findings but for academic comment. It spearheads SEL through research papers, the most recent as we go to press being 'The Impact of Enhancing Students' Social and Emotional Learning: a Meta-Analysis of School-Based Universal Interventions' (Durlak et al, 2011) assessing effects on behaviour and academic outcomes. While it found benefits to SEL programming: 'Nevertheless, current findings are not definitive' (Durlak et al, 2011, p 419). Effects followed up (by only 15% of projects studied) are described as 'statistically significant for a minimum of 6 months after the intervention' (Durlak et al, 2011, p 405). According to Michael Wigelsworth at Manchester University:

> Headline findings show 0.6 effect, which is massive, but digging down, it's because everything has been thrown in together. More specific measures show much more tentative findings. I think the best summary of the study is the headline news that the programmes work and in the same report, the statement that 50% of the tools are unpublished, no reliable psychometrics, etc.[2]

Whatever else it is, CASEL is *not* a non-aligned, independent, open forum for critical debate about SEL. Neither is it a publicly funded university department. CASEL is in effect a publishing house and lobbying organisation with a mission to make SEL a dominant discourse and practice in education. CASEL's stronghold on educational thinking positions SEL as a 'majoritarian discourse' (Deleuze and Guattari, 2004), whereby 'dominant social presuppositions take on the mask of necessity' (Goodchild, 1996, p 54). The dominant presupposition here is that SEL requires educational interventions. CASEL desires to increase its influence, believing that:

> the SEL field needs an organization that can reach across disciplines such as research, education practice, policy, and communications to take advantage of the opportunities before us. With investments from donors large and small and the commitment of both long-time collaborators and the field's growing numbers of supporters, CASEL can be that organization. (CASEL, 2009, p 2)

A field dominated by one player will always minimalise challenge. Hoye (2010) suggested that CASEL personnel could become driven by groupthink, and he questioned CASEL's evidence base:

It would be best if these [CASEL's] studies were not limited to the schools themselves, but to the community at large within a school district. This current review of the literature did not find any evidence that this is being undertaken. Indicators of economic progress, reduction in violence, and better living conditions within communities must be taken into consideration in longitudinal studies. Only in this way will we know if SEL is a panacea for poverty, and not merely a placebo to assuage the guilt of the dominant groups of American society. (Hoye, 2010)

The UK influence: Weare and Gray

In 2002, Katherine Weare and Gay Gray were commissioned by the then Department for Education and Skills (DfES) to study 'how children's emotional and social competence and wellbeing could most effectively be developed at national and local level' (Weare and Gray, 2003, p 5), with a brief to identify the broad approaches that showed most promise. Their subsequent report became the evidential foundation for SEAL.

Their study took a threefold approach: a literature review, case studies of practice and interviews with professionals. In their literature review, and by their own admission, 'texts were not subjected to rigorous criteria for inclusion' (Weare and Gray, 2003, p 5). The case studies, although informative of practice developments in different Local Education Authorities (LEAs), offered no consensus on SEL practice precisely because of their variety. Finally, all interviewees were active practitioners with a clear interest in the CASEL-style SEL model being adopted. No voices of dissent or alternative practice appeared in their study, which became the bridge that allowed US SEL rhetoric to translate itself into UK national practice.

Weare and Gray drew from another meta-study that looked at studies of universal mental health promotion or disease prevention in schools (Wells et al, 2003). Wells et al began their review with 8,000 publications, chose 423 for further review and finally chose 17 (12 of them in North America) for analysis. Weare and Gray reported Wells et al as finding that 'work in this area can achieve the following outcomes: 1. greater educational and work success; 2. improvements in behaviour; 3. increased inclusion; 4. improved learning; 5. greater social cohesion; 6. improvements to mental health' (Weare and Gray, 2003, p 33).

However, the 17 programmes surveyed by Wells et al were so disparate (ranging from suicide prevention to self-esteem, conflict resolution and transition programmes) that meaningful cross-comparison is difficult. Most were in US elementary schools in socially disadvantaged areas and, of these, 10 were categorised 'analysis not adjusted for school/ classroom effects' (Wells et al, 2003, p 203). In other words, because of the mix of influences, it was impossible to trace effects definitively back to SEL interventions. Furthermore, only four of the programmes looked at positive mental health, perhaps as close as it is possible to get to the SEAL model. Although only two of the 17 cases studied by Wells et al were whole school interventions, the whole school approach is affirmed in the Wells report. Towards the close of their report, Wells et al state that what they had studied did not show that such programmes would work in a UK school setting (Wells et al, 2003, p 218).

In 2008, a report from Manchester University for the DCSF found comparatively little research provided evidence for SEAL. The authors reported that the existing body of evidence threw up the following methodological problems:

> Lack of control groups ... ; Lack of longitudinal assessment for whole-school approaches ...; Assessment of targeted interventions used to make claims for whole school results ...; Success criteria based on teacher satisfaction .... (DCSF, 2008d, p 12)

Weare and Gray called for further sifting of the evidence in order to distinguish hopes from sound, demonstrated effect (Weare and Gray, 2003, p 29). Matthews et al (2004) found serious methodological problems with cross-comparing school-based projects, including 'non-equivalence of experimental and control groups, poor documentation of methods, over reliance on self report criteria of success, poor generalizability of methods, and failure to assess longer-term outcomes' (Matthews et al, 2004, p 542). Craig made the point that SEAL is not a suitable comparison for its American forerunners in that it was designed to be implemented year on year, throughout schooling from age 3 to 18 (Craig, 2007).

As we explore what SEWB looks like in UK education, it is necessary to turn attention, if only for a short time, to 'teaching happiness'. Built around the positive psychology model developed by Seligman at the University of Pennsylvania, teaching happiness programmes generally combine Cognitive Behavioural Therapy, elements of philosophy, spirituality, mindfulness and a range of self-esteem activities. A good summary of the positive psychology movement is presented by Alistair Miller: 'It is the central contention of positive psychology that people can be recrafted into goal achievers, able to control their emotions and harness all their positive energies in the service of their goals' (Miller, 2008, p 595). He also reflected on the inherent paradox and stated 'that unless you know already exactly what you want and are therefore by definition motivated to achieve it, these are impossible tasks' (Miller, 2008, p 595).

According to Seligman, 'We took some ideas from ancient philosophy and married them to the new scientific study of happiness. Aristotle never had the benefit of the seven-point scale'.[3] In the UK, the teaching happiness movement was given both credence and impetus through the work of Lord Layard, a Labour government advisor and eminent economist. His work has directly endorsed teaching happiness, and created an economic driver to fuel the movement in the UK (Layard, 2007). In 2008, Seligman reflected 'nowhere in the world have [my ideas] been so taken up by public policy as in the UK. There is a real buzz here about the politics of wellbeing' (cited in Suissa, 2008, p 576).

Happiness programmes contain many features seen in SEWB programmes across Europe and America, particularly in regard to the learning and teaching of new ways of thinking, but they differ in comparison with SEAL in that they aim to increase pupils' 'happiness' rather than develop their interpersonal skills or attitudes. Both the state and private sector in England have picked up on the teaching happiness model. The best known private proponent is Wellington College, a fee-paying school in Berkshire, where head teacher Anthony Seldon believes that 'Wellbeing classes are an important part of moving British education beyond its "toxic obsession" with exams and tests, towards a more holistic idea of education that gives young people the cognitive skills they need to cope with the ups and downs that they will inevitably face in life' (Evans, 2008).

From the state school perspective, a pilot scheme in 2008, which involved South Tyneside, Hertfordshire and Manchester LEAs, funded teachers and council officers to visit the University of Pennsylvania to be trained by Seligman. The trip alone cost Manchester City Council £25,000. This programme has since developed into the United Kingdom Resilience Programme (UKRP), a scheme that we explore in more detail in Chapter 13. In 2007, Jenny Andrews, Manchester City Council's Assistant Chief Education Officer at the time, said that 'research shows that resilience to setbacks can actually be learned and it can be a huge benefit for children in later life' (Qureshi, 2007).

One does wonder where the theory and practice of teaching happiness fits in regarding the multitude of structural inequalities faced by many of the Year 7 children who took part in the UK programme. Where are issues such as racism, sexism, family breakdown and economic inequality placed in the context of learning to be happy? Is there not a danger inherent to all these programmes that we are in fact teaching young people to accept their lot rather than challenge, question, subvert and change the structures of society? Is it ever permissible in the nature of these schemes to be unhappy? To better understand what is happening on the ground, under the banner of SEL and SEWB approaches, we interviewed some practitioners across the UK. No critique is offered here, but rather a description of what is delivered.

Manchester

Through its Healthy Schools programme, Manchester LEA intended that by April 2010, 40% of Manchester high schools would have implemented a combined approach to SEWB to ensure that 'children and young people are emotionally resilient and have a strong sense of emotional well-being' (Jayne, 2010, p 14). The top two key statistics driving these aims were '55% of primary pupils and 74% of secondary pupils worry about at least one problem "quite a lot" or "a lot"' (Student Health Education Unit, 2010).

In the summer of 2010, we spoke to the lead Healthy Schools officer in Manchester, who viewed SEWB as fundamental to schooling and underpinning all learning. To define wellbeing, he looked to the Healthy Schools documentation, seeing it in terms of protecting vulnerable children, having a whole school ethos and building character. He was broadly supportive of SEAL, although critical of local variations in resources to carry it through. He reported that teachers' responses to SEAL were often positive and that it built good team spirit and made explicit skills that were already present. He was concerned that teachers should be clear about where their responsibility ended. He gave three examples of specific local schemes that had arisen in response to the SEWB agenda.

The first was a housekeeping club where pupils were supported and given access to free washing and laundry facilities in order that they had a clean school sports kit. This was developed with the aim of reducing the bullying and stigma of children who did not have clean clothes. Obviously useful in some ways, it nevertheless raises questions regarding parental responsibility, and the boundaries between school and home. The second project was the Exceeding Expectations programme, a theatre project aimed at reducing homophobic bullying in schools.[4] The third Manchester SEWB initiative was training for 471 school staff, which was intended to create understanding of SEWB and focused on modelling, self-reflection, context, and building awareness of the key skills needed to support children.

According to this officer, a key driver behind SEWB, which he called 'Emotional Health and Wellbeing' (EHWB), was behaviour, which got funding and priority. He understood 'mental health' and 'EHWB' as interchangeable, but used EHWB 'as it's softer for people'. It involved 'training staff to recognise, model and manage EHWB in schools'. He described a model of EHWB as built on how good mental health can help young people achieve their dreams. He specifically thought SEAL could be viewed as a social programme designed to effect change in families and communities in order to 'repair broken society'. Measurement was an issue raised with the impact of interventions being inconsistently assessed via academia, OFSTED and other methods.

Scotland

SEAL is less prevalent in Scotland because, in general, Scottish schools take a devolved approach, choosing projects that meet localised needs. This has involved a range of SEWB schemes, including: the American Promoting Alternative Thinking Strategies (PATHS) (Channing-Bete, 2010); Being Cool in School (Report of the Discipline Task Group, 2001); and Creating Confident Kids (Creating Confident Kids, 2010). Unlike the English Department for Education, the Scottish government has not developed specific school wellbeing programmes, but has provided leadership and coordination in this area. However, *Curriculum for Excellence* (CFE), launched in 2010, was the first move towards a more prescriptive framework for delivering programmes to address wellbeing in schools. The role of wellbeing is explicit in CFE: 'learning through health and wellbeing promotes confidence, independent thinking and positive attitudes and dispositions' (SE, 2006, p 10).

CFE categorises wellbeing as having four elements (mental, emotional, social and physical). Emphasis is on lifestyle and health, rather than behaviour. There are only four references to behaviour in the CFE guidance documentation, in contrast to the 135 in the *SEAL Primary School Guidance* document (DfES, 2005a). CFE makes every teacher responsible for contributing to outcomes, an expectation that raises questions regarding staff training and accountability. Anne Ballinger, General Secretary of The Scottish Secondary Teachers Association, recognised this challenge:

> We would absolutely agree that health and wellbeing is the responsibility of every teacher and would only ask that

adequate training is provided for those teachers who feel uncomfortable with that role. Being able to teach physics or maths or English does not mean you are adept at discussing health and wellbeing with pupils.[5]

CFE contains outcomes reminiscent of SEAL, but, surprisingly, intended to span from the early years (5–6) through to stage four (15–16). For example:

> I understand the importance of mental wellbeing and that this can be fostered and strengthened through personal coping skills and positive relationships. I know that it is not always possible to enjoy good mental health and that if this happens there is support available. (CFE, 2010, p 2)

Dorothy Gair, a development officer for Healthcare in Schools, is trialling the new Scottish Health and Wellbeing in Schools programme in one of four pilot areas. The prescriptiveness of descriptors like the one above concerned her, as does measurement and assessment. However, as often with a new practice, the determination and desire to deliver, rather than the question of ethics, dominates. Dorothy questioned the academic rigor of the programme and how that may affect its effectiveness:

> We are not doing any academic research. There is no external evaluation. We don't have the funding for this. This does concern me and I wish it was different. If we create change it concerns me that due to the lack of academic evidence we cannot prove this. We also cannot say with conviction that any change seen is true. It's very frustrating and I hope it doesn't mean things get lost.[6]

Another Scottish initiative, the Pupil Wellbeing Questionnaire, has been developed by the Edinburgh Council's Growing Confidence project, in conjunction with a web development business called ReSURV (sic) (Edinburgh Council, no date). The questionnaire was designed for primary school children and aims to track and measure social and emotional development. It was intended to be a self-evaluation tool for schools and not an individual measurement tool. Measurement is done through a series of 30 statements rated anonymously online by individual children, covering themes such as self-respect, empathy, confidence and resilience. Examples include 'I enjoy being in school' and 'I think I have good ideas'. Each statement is rated by the child filling in the questionnaire circling one of four scaled responses: 'Yes, definitely'; 'Yes, most of the time'; 'No, only some of the time'; 'No, not really'. Results are gathered and findings are used to inform school decision-making.

In conversation with Patricia Santelices, one of the project team, we explored the background to the questionnaire. There were three key drivers to its development: first, criticisms regarding the lack of measurement tools offered by SEAL and the vacuum this created; second, current research in the field of resilience; and, third, the importance of relationships for children. Santelices believed that the findings of the questionnaire demonstrate the need for, and importance of, work in these areas. Administering an online questionnaire to children immediately raises methodological queries: children's responses may vary by the hour, they may confer with others while responding, the questionnaire does not recognise social and cultural variations, the scale appears skewed and so on. Once the questionnaire is in the public domain, moreover, pressure may be put on schools to use it as an outcomes measure. Santelices shared this particular concern.

This scheme shows in microcosm some of the tensions played out in the wider wellbeing-in-schools debate. Well-meaning adults seek to investigate and support wellbeing, only to find that passing children's emotions through any sort of objectifying data-gathering process is distorting. The model of wellbeing underpinning the Pupil Wellbeing Questionnaire is holistic, based on community and relationships, by definition a difficult area to record for a questionnaire filled in individually.

Working across 28 schools in Edinburgh, Growing Confidence prioritises staff training in SEL through a programme called Confident Staff, Confident Children, designed to ensure staff understand and model SEL skills expected of children and better understand factors affecting emotional wellbeing. It also aims to increase 'capacity and skills to better promote positive mental health and well-being in ourselves and the children and young people we work with' (Edinburgh Council, 2008). This programme has recently been rolled out to over 350 parents and carers as part of the organisation's commitment to promoting EHWB.

Wales

The Welsh version of EHWB in schools is built on the seven core aims of the Welsh Assembly Government's (WAG's) vision for children and young people, in turn based on the UN Convention on the Rights of the Child. In common with the Scottish government, the Welsh Assembly, until recently, offered policy leadership, rather than a direct practice model. This has resulted in many Welsh schools pursuing SEAL. However, with no one prescribed programme in place, a wide range of initiatives are used in Wales, including: PATHS (Channing-Bete, 2010); Antidote's School Emotional Environment for Learning Survey (SEELS) (Teaching Expertise, 2009); and Getting Connected (Young Adults Learning Partnership [YALP]) (The National Institute of Adult Continuing Education, 2001).

The last few years have seen the development of Demonstrating Success, in which two of the authors of this book have been involved, intended as a whole Wales framework for recording and observing young people's progress in a range of social and emotional dispositions and skills (SEDS). Demonstrating Success offers no teaching or learning materials, and attempts to present a more subjective model of wellbeing, with emphasis on dialogue, relationships and observation between the young person and practitioner. With Demonstrating Success, WAG has invested in a Welsh framework for guiding SEL practice. This framework will not prescribe outcomes, but act as a guide for practitioners to develop and capture SEDS through locally contextualised programmes.

A member of our team spoke with Lowri Gravell and Anna Riley, two Educational Psychologists based at Conwy LEA, which through its emotional health multi-agency forum has been proactive in developing and providing school-based SEL activities and support programmes. They both saw SEWB as fundamental:

> It's a key aspect to our service. It's something that drives many of the different kinds of services that we offer, and it's foremost in our minds really when we look at interventions, evaluating and deciding on which programmes we're going to be introducing in to schools.[7]

Also 'it's underpinning everything really, isn't it? That's something we've always felt. It's something that's coming out now in all of the OFSTED and ESTYN [Her Majesty's Inspectorate for Education and Training in Wales]'.[8] As to what their model of SEWB looked like:

> I think wellbeing for young people is the concept of feeling safe, secure, successful, wanted – attached, in positive ways with their main carers, with key personnel who work with them in different stages of their lives. And that they have a positive sense of self-worth really and sense of self.[9]

Key theories behind their favoured model of SEWB were Rutter's work on risk and resilience (Rutter, 2008), Bowlby's attachment theory (Bowlby, 1988) and Seligman's positive psychology teachings (Seligman, 1990). In relation to risk and resilience, there is some consistency with the model discussed by their colleague in the Manchester Healthy Schools programme. Gravell commented on the journey SEWB has taken, reflecting on the developing interest and language used to describe the concept: 'It's gone from dyslexia to autism to emotional health and I think what it's taken them a long time to realise is that this does underpin it all'.[10]

A range of programmes currently operate across Conwy from Seasons for Growth, addressing social and emotional competence, bereavement and loss (described in more detail in Chapter 7), to the Friends programme, a 10-week, small group work scheme dealing with issues of anxiety and depression and utilising cognitive behavioural therapy. Conwy has also provided the US PATHS programme to 54 of the 73 primary schools in the district (incurring the considerable expense of translating it into Welsh). This is currently delivered twice a week as part of PSHE [Personal, Social and Health Education].

The Welsh perspective seems to be to develop diffuse responsibility for wellbeing of the type promoted by the WHO (WHO, 2010) where, 'It's everybody's responsibility, isn't it? School is the first place, and personnel within school, but then all the outside agencies as well who are supporting schools'.[11]

Northern Ireland

In Northern Ireland, schools SEWB developments have generally been viewed from a perspective focused on health and social inequalities. Three key factors of suicide prevention, mental health and community cohesion have driven much of the debate. One initiative, Pupils Emotional Health and Wellbeing (PEHAW) has been much discussed across the region's governmental departments and is expected to lead practice in schools. According to the Minister of Education: 'It [PEHAW] will bring together the range of activities already occurring at school level and provide a consistency of delivery and availability across the education sector, focusing initially on the post primary sector' (Northern Ireland Assembly, 2009). It is intended that PEHAW will 'contribute to the building of resilient emotional health and wellbeing of pupils' (Northern Ireland Department of Education, 2005).

At the time of writing, Northern Irish pupils' EHWB is being progressed in post-primary schools through PEHAW's personal development curriculum and a series of support materials to be used in homework diaries. These colourful and cartoon-style materials are built around 10 themes (self-confidence, keeping yourself safe, bullying, family problems, sex and relationships, being different, peer pressure, bereavement, feelings and drugs, and alcohol and smoking). For each theme, a series of simple tips and advice is offered followed by the contact details for organisations offering support in this area. Four definitions of mental health and emotional wellbeing are offered, which, according to the booklet, young people helped to develop (Northern Ireland Department of Education, 2005).

The meaning of wellbeing at the practice level has been debated, and responsibility is divided between education and health service departments. PEHAW will not be launched before 2011 and even then may not serve as a national practice model, but as an umbrella covering initiatives and programmes that range from school counselling schemes to universal guidance on critical incident responses. Activities expected to be incorporated include pupil counselling, pastoral care systems, suicide prevention, anti-bullying, discipline processes and the Healthy Schools initiative.

At the local level, Northern Ireland schools have generally adopted individual approaches including SEAL and a locally contextualised version of the US PATHS programme. This is delivered by a charity called Together 4 All, which was launched in 2008 and is still running in the Craigavon district. According to previous Chief Executive Nuala Magee, Together 4 All has:

> Adapted a proven international model of intervention (PATHS) on social and emotional regulation and married this with units of Mutual Respect and Understanding to create a unique programme for Northern Ireland that meets the requirements set by the Department of Education. Teachers will receive ongoing support from Specialist Coaches to enable effective classroom delivery, while parents will receive support from a Home School Liaison Coordinator to help them engage with the programme. (Together 4 All, no date)

Paul Edwards, Acting Chief Executive of Together 4 All, states that the schools programme is designed to promote and develop social skills and emotional literacy, as well as reduce aggression and general behavioural problems. Among other things, it sets out to increase self-control, enhance self-esteem and self-confidence, improve communication about emotions and feelings, and improve understanding of how one's behaviour affects others. Teachers deliver approximately two lessons of the programme each week, with each lesson taking between 15 and 25 minutes once a teacher is confident in implementing the programme (Together 4 All, no date). A mixed-method evaluation of Together 4 All is currently being carried out by the Institute for Effective Education at the University of York and Johns Hopkins University.

Conclusion

The process of devolution has meant regions can flavour their own approaches to SEL. England has invested heavily in a universal, prescribed programme focused on behaviour, individual responsibility and the 'teachability' of emotional wellbeing. In Scotland and Wales, the story is of a somewhat different model of practice, with less interest in emotional intelligence, and a focus on delivering wellbeing through children's rights and the community. In Northern Ireland, progress on developing wellbeing programmes has been slow, perhaps showing caution towards the complexities involved.

While different areas of the UK have developed individual responses, the most established and widespread wellbeing-related educational programme in the UK is still SEAL and, as we have argued, evidence of its impact is problematic. SEAL operationalises children's emotional lives according to adult concepts. Given its status as a widely prescribed programme for three to 16 year olds, SEAL is an unprecedented large-scale experiment on children's emotions. Its expansion has met little resistance – after all, who would not want to see young people more confident, happier, building long-lasting balanced relationships and engaged in school life?

Benign hopes have smoothed the path for thousands of children across England, and to a lesser degree the UK, to be taught how to be emotionally intelligent. To paraphrase *Newsweek* in October 2009 (Bronson, 2009), how did biased science lead to an emotional intelligence curriculum in all UK schools? A full answer to that question is beyond the scope of this chapter, but one possible account that may shed light on the popularity of SEAL was given by Shermer (1997) – *credo consolans*, immediate gratification and easy explanations. We have set out these categories in Chapter 3 and feel they may have some relevance for understanding the spread of SEAL.

From a practitioner's perspective, it would be anxiety-provoking not to do what everyone else is doing. Faced with the buzz and chatter, not to mention the 'evidence' given for SEAL, fears of not being seen to support children's wellbeing, or to strive for academic standards, may have been high. Daily teaching demands leave little time to explore questions of the validity of curriculum materials and many, perhaps most, practitioners would not see it as their place to raise the evidence against curriculum content for fear of professional exclusion and reprisals. In fact, to challenge a programme presented as definitively as SEAL would be hard for a teacher. Deep questioning is much easier for researchers, reviewers of policy and authors. One such body of research produced for the DCSF in 2008 found that:

> In terms of impact, our analysis of pupil-level outcome data indicated that SEAL (as implemented by schools in our sample) failed to impact significantly upon pupils' social and emotional skills, general mental health difficulties, pro-social behaviour or behaviour problems.... A greater emphasis needs to be given to the rigorous collection and use of evidence to inform developments in policy and practice in this area; in particular, there should be proper trialling of initiatives like SEAL before they are rolled out on a national level. (DCSF, 2008d, pp 2–3)

A further critical perspective has been developed by Humphrey (2011) who challenged assumed truths propagated by SEAL, for instance, that 'social and emotional learning is conceptually coherent'. Humphrey questions this, suggesting that the field is protean, vague and ultimately intangible. What SEL means appears to differ depending on which text one consults. A second assumed truth that 'whole-school social and emotional learning is more effective than other forms of intervention' leads Humphrey (2011) to cite Blank as saying that studies of truly whole school approaches to SEL are thin on the ground, 'the literature to support whole school approaches is not well developed' (Humphrey, 2011, p 12). Two recent major reviews have not found any advantage of multi-component approaches over single-component approaches (Durlak et al, 2011).

In March 2011, BBC Radio 4 broadcast 'Testing the Emotions', an analysis of the SEAL story with contributions from policymakers and practitioners. The Department for Education stated the current governmental position regarding SEAL as 'the lack of any overall positive impact from SEAL reinforces the need to prevent further time and resource expenditure on this project' (BBC, 2011).

Notes

[1] BBC News home page 7 July 2007.

[2] Email correspondence with authors, June 2011.

[3] This quote is attributed to Seligman in a blog at: http://www.politicsofwellbeing.com/2011/01/teaching-emotional-resilience.html

[4] See http://www.exceedingexpectations.org.uk/

[5] Anne Ballinger in conversation with the author in 2010.

[6] Dorothy Gair, Chief Nursing Officer Directorate, Scottish government, in conversation with the author, March 2010.

[7] Lowri Gravell, Deputy Principal Educational Psychologist, Conwy Additional Learning Needs, interview with the author, September 2010.

[6] Anna Riley, Educational Psychologist, Conwy County Council, interview with the author, September 2010.

[9] Lowri Gravell, Deputy Principal Educational Psychologist, Conwy Additional Learning Needs, interview with the author, September 2010.

[10] Lowri Gravell, Deputy Principal Educational Psychologist, Conwy Additional Learning Needs, interview with the author, September 2010.

[11] Lowri Gravell, Deputy Principal Educational Psychologist, Conwy Additional Learning Needs, interview with the author, September 2010.

CHAPTER 5

The measurement of wellbeing

Introduction

In Chapter 3, we explored issues of policy and wellbeing and, in Chapter 4, we examined the practice in schools to promote wellbeing, with a particular emphasis on the Social and Emotional Aspects of Learning (SEAL) programme. Policy (and its resulting practice) is dependent on measurement. The purpose of policy is to enable change, and change can only impact on those aspects of social life that can be measured. Measurement is necessary as part of processes of the *examination* (Foucault, 1991a) of the public body underpinning the ability of the state to regulate the lives of its citizens and to control their destinies.

Such measurement is focused on the 'social body', through the action of the 'body politic' (Scheper-Hughes and Lock, 1987). Policy also impacts on the phenomenological body of the person. Through the discursive practices of examination and the modern concept of intervention, the measurement of wellbeing is increasingly used to identify problems in the population (especially children) as part of an accepted policy strategy of early intervention: spot problems early and they can be eradicated. The shift towards emphasis on the phenomenological body, as opposed to action focused on the social body, reflected a shift in the neo–liberal agenda pursued by New Labour during their term of office. In 1997, on taking power, Tony Blair emphasised activity focused on the failings of the phenomenological body:

> Social exclusion is about income but it is about more. It is about prospects and networks and life-chances. It's a very modern problem, and one that is more harmful to the individual, more damaging to self-esteem, more corrosive for society as a whole, more likely to be passed down from generation to generation, than material poverty. Getting government to act more coherently is the key. Everyone knows that the problems of social exclusion – of failure at school, joblessness, crime – are woven together when you get down to the level of the individual's daily life, or the life

> of a housing estate.... Our actions on exclusion reflect our
> values and those of the British people. It offends against our
> values to see children with no prospect of work, families
> trapped in poverty, neighbourhoods blighted by crime. But
> this isn't just about compassion. It's also about self-interest. If
> we can shift resources from picking up the costs of problems
> to preventing them, there will be a dividend for everyone.[1]

This statement ignored the welfare agenda, which evolved through the post-Second World War consensus. The concern of the welfare agenda was to eradicate poverty through the creation of work and social opportunities. Blair's shift was away from a 'pure' welfare agenda of 'opportunity creation', and towards a stance that involves personal responsibility. This shift requires a shift from 'government' to 'governmentality' (Foucault, 1980a; Rose, 1996; Lemke, 2000).

Assuming a theoretical position of governmentality allows for a more complex analysis of neo-liberal forms of government that not only feature direct intervention by means of empowered and specialised state apparatuses, but also develop indirect techniques for leading and controlling individuals. The strategy of rendering individual subjects 'responsible' (and also collectives, such as families, associations, etc) entails shifting the responsibility for social risks such as illness, unemployment, poverty and so on, and for life in society, into the domain for which the individual is responsible and transforming it into a problem of 'self-care' (Lemke, 2000).

This shift was reflected by Tony Blair in 2006: 'my thesis today is straightforward: some aspects of social exclusion are deeply intractable. The most socially excluded are very hard to reach. Their problems are multiple, entrenched and often passed down the generations'. (Blair, 2006). Intractable, entrenched problems are the problems of *individuals*, who do not avail themselves of the opportunities provided by state apparatuses.

The shift towards self-governance of the individual is what Cruickshank called the 'self-esteem' movement (Cruickshank, 1996). The 'self-esteem' movement, Cruickshank suggested, is not limited to the personal domain, as its goal is a new politics and a new social order. It promises to solve social problems by heralding a revolution – not against capitalism, racism, patriarchy and so on, but against the (wrong) way of governing ourselves. In this way, the angle of possible political and social intervention changes. It is not social-structural factors that decide whether unemployment, alcoholism, criminality, child abuse and so on can be solved, but individual-subjective categories. 'Self-esteem' thus has much more to do with self-*assessment* than with self-*respect*, as the self continuously has to be measured, judged and disciplined in order to gear personal 'empowerment' to collective yardsticks (Lemke, 2000).

Self-assessment, self-respect, bodily health, the whole concept of the 'active citizen', as individual-subjective categories are part of a process whereby individuals are to become 'experts of themselves', becoming educated and knowledgeable ('responsible') about self-care in respect of their bodies, minds, social relationships and the regulation of their own behaviour (Donzelot, 2009). These categories strongly resemble the categories contained in, among others, the *Every Child Matters* (ECM) policy (DfES, 2004a), where 'bodies', 'minds', 'social relationships' and 'behaviour' are amenable to normative descriptions, and deviance (as part of intractable and entrenched problems) can be examined, hierarchically determined and disciplined (Foucault, 1991a).

Here, we are talking about people. The entrenched problems that act as barriers to the Blairite modernist agenda are not located in social or cultural issues (of difference, discussed in Chapter 6), but are located in the phenomenological body of the individual, who is directed towards processes of 'responsibilisation' (see Scourfield, 2007) and the development of 'technologies of the self' (Foucault, 1991b). Thus, self-esteem is a technology of self for 'evaluating and acting upon ourselves so that the police, the guards and the doctors do not have to do so' (Cruickshank, 1996, p 234).

Measurement

Measurement (the process of examination) is crucial to this process. Measurement defines, categorises and lays out an ordinal progression from the normal to the pathological (Canguilhem, 1989) and allows the development of 'technologies' to normalise those deemed deviant or deficient (eg the SEAL programme). Thus, 'self-esteem' is amenable to constructions such as 'she suffers from low-self-esteem' (and this explains her failure); the direction for change is to 'increase self-esteem' (so that she will begin to achieve).

The 'ordinalisation' or ranking of a quality is programmatic, in the sense that the ranking of qualitative aspects, defined a priori, provides the definition of a technology that creates progress, and is designed to become a technology of the self, which becomes self-regulating by the individual. If we can embed one quality in a battery of qualities assumed under a general category of 'wellbeing', then we can tackle the intractable and entrenched problems experienced by socially excluded individuals. The various conceptual dimensions of 'wellbeing' have been explored in Chapter 2, but 'ordinalisation' can best be expressed (and measured) through the use of Objective List Theories (OLTs). The development of objective lists are subject to the criticisms raised in Chapter 2 and represents the manifestation of a 'majoritarian discourse' (Deleuze and Guattari, 2004).

'Majoritarian' discourses are enunciated by people who have the power to speak. In their speaking, they make statements and such statements create their objects (people, children), whose subjectivities are constrained by the power of the statement. But who is the subject of the enunciation? (Who has the power to speak or make statements?) Who are the *subjects* of those statements? How, through the power of the statement, is the subject created – who is the *object* of the statement? The statement we are considering is that of 'wellbeing' and, for the focus of this discussion, the 'objects' of the statements are children in schools; the 'subjects' of enunciation are the policy statements provided by the 'wellbeing agenda', created through governmentality.

If we assume the complex understanding of wellbeing as being located in a nexus of competing discourses, it is problematic to assume a singular form of measurement to allow perspectives of 'efficiency' in service delivery. Objective or subjective measures of wellbeing (and its associated concepts of 'human flourishing', 'life satisfaction' and 'quality of life') may distort the life experiences of children and lead to problematic policy formulations for the design and delivery of services. We develop a critique to support the development of new approaches to understanding the problem and meeting the needs derived from such a problem definition. In the recent past, there has been a growth of what Ecclestone (2007, p 467) described as the 'normalizing discourse of therapeutic intervention' in the area of the measurement of wellbeing, and we offer a critique of the measures that are available for use with children and young people.

What is the problem?

Chapter 3 provided a comprehensive review of policy with regard to wellbeing in the UK and internationally. The results of national and international surveys (UNICEF, 2007; Bradshaw and Richardson, 2009; OECD, 2009) have suggested that children in the UK are faring significantly less well than their counterparts in many other countries. The UNICEF report (2007, p 6) was based on the measurement of six categories:

- material wellbeing;
- health and safety;
- educational wellbeing – based on school achievement at age 15;
- relationships;
- behaviours and risks – based on health behaviours, risk behaviours (including getting drunk, smoking, under-age sex, drug abuse, using condoms and teenage fertility), and experiencing violence, including bullying; and
- subjective wellbeing – based on subjective feelings of healthiness, enjoying school life and personal wellbeing.

In this 'objective list' it is difficult to understand how different forms of 'wellbeing' (material, educational, subjective and personal) can be subsumed under the general heading of 'wellbeing'. The UNICEF report clearly stated the problem of aggregating survey data across different nation states, but used the six categories as proxies for 'wellbeing'. It noted, however:

> children's exposure to violence in the home both as victims and as witnesses, for example, could not be included because of problems of cross-national definition and measurement. Children's mental health and emotional well-being may also be under-represented, though attempts have been made to reflect these difficult-to-measure dimensions. (UNICEF, 2007, p 6)

The later OECD report stated that it omitted the:

> 'family and peer relationships' and 'subjective well-being' dimensions included in the UNICEF report….The reason is not because they are unimportant for child well-being, but because this report has a strong policy focus. It is unclear how governments concerned with family and peer relationships and subjective well-being would go about designing policies to improve outcomes in these dimensions. (OECD, 2009, p 29)

The Labour government's response was to commission the Office of Standards in Education (OFSTED) to consult on a range of 'Indicators of a school's contribution to well-being' (OFSTED, 2008). The indicators were based on the ECM proposals. The development of the indicators was designed to support schools in undertaking self-evaluation and in improving the quality of the education and care they provided for children and young people. The indicators were designed to measure and contribute an understanding of the relationship between the activities of the school and outcomes for pupils (OFSTED, 2008).

In addition to quantitative indicators, the consultation also required data for subjective wellbeing, obtained through parental and pupil perceptions of schools and schooling. These qualitative indictors relate to broad areas of health and a healthy lifestyle (exercise, smoking and sexual relationships), relationships, equality, access to the community and the exercise of choice in the areas of curriculum and post-school transitions. They also relate to the ECM outcomes.

As the 'subject of enunciation', the government's explicit or implicit responses to an observed failure 'to promote wellbeing in children' raise questions about the models of wellbeing ('the nature of the statement') used to determine the paucity of perceived flourishing and attempts to remediate this state of affairs. The nature of the statement for wellbeing, as it is enunciated, constrains the way schools can 'promote' the wellbeing of their pupils. If the statement is enunciated in the form of the UNICEF survey, the statement at the heart of this instrument (and findings) is what Warnick (2009) described as a convergence between 'wellbeing', 'happiness' and 'human flourishing'. The nature of the statement attempts to derive objective indicators of 'human flourishing' based on subjective reports of wellbeing and happiness. These three forms of the statement are on a conceptual plane that cannot differentiate between them: that is, you can describe wellbeing in terms of flourishing and happiness; conversely you can describe human flourishing in terms of happiness and wellbeing. These definitions do not escape the conceptual plane and any operationalisation of these terms is arbitrary. The subject of enunciation ('those who have the power to speak') can create an 'objective' statement that is open to criticism from the other dimensions of the conceptual plane (or other dimensions that lie outside of the main conceptual framework of happiness, flourishing or wellbeing).

For example, none of the earlier indicators explicitly used 'autonomy', 'freedom of choice' or 'critical thinking' (Warnick, 2009) as indicators of wellbeing – in a school context, the choice offered to children through the OFSTED indicators are restricted to curriculum choices and post-school transitions. The things we can measure 'converge' on those things we cannot measure and are taken as quantitative proxies or indices of qualitative understandings of broader concepts of happiness and flourishing. Policy cannot dictate happiness or flourishing directly, that is, the relationships between the conceptual dimensions are not causal.

An increase in wellbeing does not necessarily result in a correlative increase in happiness or flourishing (Warnick, 2009). Indirect factors that contribute to flourishing, within simple convergences, are not sufficient to establish common identity. Happiness and flourishing form two interrelated conceptual 'maps'. What are the overlaps in the two maps? What common aspects of happiness and flourishing provide a common identity (Warnick, 2009, p 93)?

Where measurement of wellbeing is contained within OLTs of human flourishing, the elements on the list are not (following Warnick) necessarily convergent. The conditions of the surveys cited earlier do not necessarily result in human flourishing or happiness or, actually, wellbeing. But where the neo-liberal agenda precludes a direct intervention in happiness (not least because we cannot measure it), we are constrained to use proxies and indices of wellbeing to make claims about happiness and flourishing.

The surveys discussed earlier and in Chapter 3 claim universal validity in that they can be used comparatively across nation states, but in the case of the UNICEF (2007) report: 'no single dimension stands as a reliable proxy for child well-being and several OECD countries have widely differing rankings to the dimensions. There is no obvious relationship between child well-being and gross domestic product (GDP) per capita' (Morrow and Mayall, 2009b, p 208). Is GDP per capita an indicator of human flourishing?

Flourishing and the individual's contribution to the general (social) happiness, within the liberal humanist philosophical tradition derives from the pragmatic and liberal philosophies of Bentham and Mill and are predicated on freedom (especially economic freedom), personal autonomy (choice) and material wellbeing (freedom from want). These concepts have a long history.

The developments over the recent past related to global and national policy initiatives are all based on the same concerns: how do we (the measurers) develop proxies or indices (relating to 'flourishing', 'standards of living', 'quality of life', wellbeing', 'happiness' etc) that can be counted, particularly through the collection of data relating to subjective wellbeing, in order to put in place social policy that is geared towards maximising human flourishing? Whatever the case, connecting flourishing with subjective wellbeing opens the door for social science research to enter into normative discussions of educational policy: 'Richard Layard's (2005) work on happiness has provided a conceptual map of what makes people happy: adequate financial situations, family relationships, work, community and friends, health, personal freedom and personal values'. (Warnick, 2009, p 93).

These convergent proxies for happiness can also be used as proxies for flourishing and wellbeing. For conceptual coherence, the circular arguments cannot be used to develop measurement instruments for the 'ordinalisation' of happiness (flourishing, wellbeing) – this ignores the cultural biases built into Layard's analysis (again, this is taken up in Chapter 6).

Measuring wellbeing

Layard's (2005) proxies are presented as 'objective' and 'subjective' indicators. Objective indicators can be obtained through population statistics. Subjective indicators are more problematic in that they relate to the 'personal' – the socio–cultural–historical constitution of personal identity. Subjectivity escapes the normalising examination of the individual. In order to pursue the wellbeing agenda, the subjective must be translated into the objective.

Subjective wellbeing (within a measurement focus) is dependent on self-report measures (rating scales). Such approaches should, following O'Hare et al, be based on the concept of 'continuous scales' derived from 'typical qualitative psychosocial and psychiatric assessments required in community programs' (O'Hare et al, 2003, p 117). This focus is on intervention programmes based on a concept of 'treatment'. Such scales are amenable to statistical procedures to demonstrate reliability and validity.

These approaches are based on psychometric principles and are subject to extensive testing for validity and reliability, but as rating scales, which require subjects to complete a survey, the process of eliciting such information is highly problematic given the issues we have discussed relating to the complexity of the construct (ie these instruments are open to criticism as to their construct validity). It is also highly questionable as to whether such approaches capture any sense of a voice of the child. This issue is complex and is beyond the scope of this chapter (it is interrogated further in Chapter 7).

Warnick's attempt to critique liberal positions on wellbeing corresponds to Nussbaum and Sen's model of 'capabilities' and 'functions' (Nussbaum and Sen, 1993). The state cannot intervene directly in capabilities (subjective states), but can provide opportunities (functions – objective states) to allow the development of capabilities, which lead to happiness and flourishing – again, there is an implicit understanding of a causal relationship between capabilities and functions. But, as Gasper (2004, p 1) argued:

> Well-being seems to have intuitive plausibility as a concept,
> but in practice we encounter a bewilderingly diverse family
> of concepts and approaches, partly reflecting different
> contexts, purposes, and foci of attention. Is there a unifying
> framework that yet respects the complexity and diversity of
> well-being? (Gasper, 2004, p 1)

An OLT provides such a framework requested by Gasper, but such lists are finite and, as we argued earlier, are based on a very specific historical conjuncture. Warnick (2009) also argued against such a unifying framework, in that establishing a 'core set of proxies' or 'indices' for human flourishing, and then measuring them through objective means of subjective self-report approaches, is subject to what is described as the problems of the 'central tendency'. Where the measurement of either subjective or objective indices of wellbeing is subject to statistical interpretation, non-homogeneous populations are collapsed into distribution curves and correlation indices. Such processes are subject to 'central tendencies' where decisions (in this case, educational policies) are made on averages, which hide difference. If a population index of happiness is formulated statistically, then individual happiness is subject to statistical relationships of variance and deviation from the norm. If policy is built around the central tendency, then individuals outside of this may be ill-served by a normalising process that does not take into account their (subjective) variance from the norm (Warnick, 2009).

This applies specifically to populations of children with special educational needs (SEN). The measurement of wellbeing is subject to the problem of central tendencies, it is also constrained by what the policymakers wish to count (the nature of the statement, ie what comprises the OLT), and it is subject to error in the processes of counting:

> In designing measures for satisfaction with life in general,
> or satisfaction with specific aspects of life, choices must be
> made with regard to the wording of questions, the response
> scale, the question context and the technique of data
> collection.... Each of these choices and each combination of
> choices can lead to different errors. (Saris et al, 1998, p 73)

Liberal philosophers place emphasis on freedom, personal autonomy and material wellbeing, but these are also not unitary concepts and raise issues about the nature of the questions, as noted by Saris et al. Peters (2009) noted that *freedom from* is different from *freedom to*, where *freedom from* (want, poverty, etc) in material terms does not necessarily imply the *freedom to* create a unique lifestyle. Similarly, autonomy, in the sense of rational choice, is only available to groups who exercise the 'right' choice. Implicit in these formulations is the invisible hand of hegemonic structures, which determine both the content of the concepts of freedom, autonomy and material wellbeing and also their limits. (*Freedom from* also implies revolution!)

Where government policy is concerned with the wellbeing of vulnerable groups, as the achievement of such groups impacts on standards of achievement, such policies appear to be based on a set of 'Victorian' values. Such values have a misplaced faith in convergence theories of the indicators of 'human flourishing' and the problem of error and central tendencies, which marginalise those who are the focus for normative policies in that difference is elided through the process of measurement.

Early intervention for children and adults at risk: clinical and educational measurement of wellbeing

The measurement of wellbeing is a central issue for governmentality and its implication in self-regulation (control) to address the issues of social exclusion raised by Blair in 1997, and its subsequent shift towards the emphasis on the phenomenological body of the individual. The shift towards the individual, who embodies the intractable and entrenched problems of social exclusion, implies that if early identification and intervention are undertaken, the state services can ameliorate the effects of personal pathology.

The English Department of Health has set national standards for the first time for children's health and social care, which promote high-quality, women- and child-centred services and personalised care that meets the needs of parents, children and their families (DH, 2004). The standards require services to provide information to families, promote health and wellbeing in children, and design early intervention programmes for children 'at risk'. For example, early intervention is aimed at providing (among other measures) an assessment of a child's physical, emotional and social development before the child's first birthday (DH, 2004). We find it difficult to understand how a process of surveillance can be effective to identify a child's psychosocial-emotional needs by the time of their first birthday.

In a comprehensive review of methods of intervention for social-emotional wellbeing, Storey and Smith (2008) argued that any intervention should be aimed at the reduction of the frequency and severity of physical symptoms of 'ill-being': psychosomatic effects of stress and anxiety. This is to be achieved through empowering individuals, by 'helping the child to understand and resolve their own problems, and to feel confident in becoming a competent problem-solver' (Storey and Smith, 2008, p 15). The report also indicated that 'preventative strategies may also need to consider the wider environment of interactions with family and peers, and with school' (Storey and Smith, 2008, p 15). But they also noted:

> Reviewers, however, tend to be guarded in their appraisals, because programmes have not been able to present evidence of sufficient rigor in terms of controlled trials or to demonstrate lasting effects. The real world settings in which school based trials are conducted sets a background environment of parents and family, school and community characteristics that impact on effectiveness of outcomes. (Storey and Smith, 2008, p 15)

These intervention approaches are subject to the common issues of normativity, construct validity and reliability, as well as raising questions about the nature of the population that was used to standardise them. Who are the 'normal' children who form the comparison group for 'disordered children'? These forms of measurement are also open to the criticisms that have been explored comprehensively in Stephen Jay Gould's book *The Mismeasure of Man* (Gould, 1971), which critiqued models of intelligence and intelligence testing. The concern here is not to criticise these instruments in terms of the technical validity of statistics. Instead, the 'majoritarian theory' (Deleuze and Guattari, 2004) of measurement acts as a discourse that creates its own objects: wellbeing exists as an object, which can be measured; there is a population of children who (for pathological reasons) do not possess it; and a range of professional experts who can diagnose it and offer intervention programmes to remediate the situation. Thus, to follow the typology offered in Chapter 2 (Ereaut and Whiting, 2008), such an understanding of wellbeing follows a 'medical heritage' and allows for the operationalisation of wellbeing as an un-theorised construct that can be 'delivered' through programmes. These approaches ignore the sustainability, holistic or philosophical discourses offered by Ereaut and Whiting and conform to Ecclestone's criticism of the need for 'resistance to [their] underlying diminished images of human potential and resilience' (Ecclestone, 2007, p 467).

Final comments

We do not wish to 'conclude' here. This chapter has interrogated the force and practice of the concept of wellbeing, its intersection with other concepts, and its representation through the forms of measurement of wellbeing and how this relates to policy and practice. The discussion so far has been located in a modernist discourse of the role of education and its relationship to the state ('governmentality'). The relationship of wellbeing to policy and practice (and the centrality of measurement as the basis of this relationship) is located within an understanding of the state (as a democratic institution) as providing the functional basis of developing capabilities in its citizenry.

A government (or its global equivalents, eg the Organisation for Economic Co-operation and Development [OECD], United Nations Educational, Scientific and Cultural Organization [UNESCO], World Bank etc) develops policy, which is directed at protecting, supporting and developing national wellbeing (or happiness, life satisfaction or quality of life) as it is realised through individuals. The concept of the 'body politic' (Scheper-Hughes and Lock, 1987) is seen as a homogeneous *socius* (Deleuze and Guattari, 1983; see also Patton, 2000). The *socius* represents the collective social investment that transforms the biological body into the social body. The *socius*, which developed out of 19th-century social-democratic changes, enabled modern education and social systems to develop. At a surface level of analysis, the democratic process has always been seen as a competition between political ideologies. At a deeper level of analysis (Deleuze and Guattari, 1983), the *socius* represents Western capitalist modes of production and social organisation, maintaining an underlying coherence and conforming to 19th-century liberal deontological ethics, that is, the policies so formulated all subscribed to a liberal-humanist conception of wellbeing, irrespective of their surface difference in political ideologies.

Blair's shift from a politics of social exclusion to one of personal intractable and entrenched problems in the population mirrors a shift from government to governance. Stephen Ball (2010) interrogated the relationships between social and education policy, social enterprise, hybridity, and new discourse communities, where he argued that we are experiencing a transformation of social and education policy, which has seen a shift from *government* to *governance*, stemming from a Cabinet Office briefing of 2006. The shift to governance is predicated on four key mechanisms of reform – choice, contestability, workforce reform and performance management – together with a shift from centralised and bureaucratic government to governance in and by networks (Ball,

2008). The shift has resulted in redistributed power and responsibility within the politics of education, away from local authorities and to both parts of the central state and other new and diverse actors and agencies. 'Diverse actors and agencies' include private enterprises, social enterprises, charities, individual philanthropists, quangos and non-governmental organisations (NGOs).

Governance is accomplished through the 'informal authority' of diverse and flexible networks, while *government* is carried out through hierarchies, specifically, bureaucracy. Governance, then, involves a 'catalyzing of all sectors – public, private and voluntary – into action to solve their community problems' (Ball, 2008, p 747). Ball also argued that the shift to governance involves a financialisation of policy: the production of new kinds of citizens and workers, with new sensibilities and values, who are responsible for their own wellbeing. The state's role is no longer that of providing the ground for human flourishing, but the 'responsibilisation' of the individual – seen, for example, in the shift between the labels of 'client', 'consumer' and 'service user' (Scourfield, 2007; McLaughlin, 2009). The shift also signals a change in the designation of coherent values and moral codes, which were assigned to civil authority, being replaced by corporations and philanthropic activity.

'Taken together this might be read as signaling the triumph of "the neo-liberal imaginary" within social policy' (Ball, 2010, p 3). The neo-liberal imaginary is constructing new forms of schools and schooling: City Technology Colleges, academies, special schools, faith schools and latterly 'free schools'. The schools are 'hybrids', run by the agents connected to networks discussed earlier. Ball (2008) provided several examples of the complex networks that have emerged since 2006. If 'biopower', discussed by Foucault in relation to the 18th and 19th centuries, was concerned with the normalisation of society based on state observation and measurement, the neo-liberal complexity of governance, in removing state biopower, replaces a centralised form with a localised, fragmented form of biopower (based on market, not social, ideologies). It is assumed that with the fragmentation of provision in the shift to governance, some form of overall state control (OFSTED) will be exercised, or at least delegated to consumers of education (the pupil, the parents, the community). The regulation of governance, it is assumed, would be based on 'indicators' of wellbeing. As we have argued, these indicators are un-theorised and flawed. As such, the form of social control exercised through the use of such instruments is 'bad for kids', but good for the commodification of education. The commodification of education implies that the discursive practices that emerge from this process will exacerbate inequalities.

Should wellbeing be an entitlement; a right; a fundamental attribute of being human; or a by-product of choice, contestability, workforce reform and performance management? However wellbeing is understood, if the basis for understanding is based on *measurement*, as it is presently constructed, then schools will divide, marginalise and exclude groups of children, as opposed to promoting human flourishing. It is to this concern that we turn in Chapter 6.

Notes

[1] Speech by Prime Minister Tony Blair on Monday 2 June 1997, at the Aylesbury estate, Southwark.

Part 2
Key issues

In this part, we consider the issues of concept, policy, practice and measurement in specific contexts. These contexts are derived from the authors' recent research experiences and are not designed to provide the 'elements' of wellbeing. Rather, they are lenses through which it is possible to consider the propositions made about wellbeing in Chapter 1: that wellbeing is subjectively experienced, contextual and embedded, and relational. They are also opportunities through which we explore the questions related to wellbeing as a concept in respect of the effects and practices of wellbeing. Each chapter is to be understood in the context of the visual heuristic introduced earlier (Figure 1.3).

CHAPTER 6

Inclusion in schools

Introduction

Chapter 2 established a conceptual framework for understanding wellbeing and its relationships to other concepts on a Deleuzian 'plane of consistency'. In Chapter 5, we explored the relationships between flourishing, happiness and wellbeing, and how these concepts are used interdependently to cross-refer to each to provide an understanding of wellbeing and, as far as measurement of the concept is concerned, its operationalisation as a concept.

In a similar way that flourishing, happiness and wellbeing are interrelated, so is wellbeing inextricably linked with concepts of inclusion. In the speeches of Tony Blair when he was Prime Minister, the theme of social exclusion was a central policy driver, and the focus for social policy was its corollary, social inclusion. Where such policy foundered on intractable and entrenched problems experienced by the individual, the shift towards education as a way of tackling entrenched problems shifted discussion of education within what is called the 'standards debate' and the role of schools in reducing social exclusion and promoting social inclusion.

'Inclusion' and 'exclusion' form the binary opposites underpinning social policy. Where 'social exclusion' is focused on the social body of children and young people who, through lack of achievement, do not gain access to the benefits of society, the social body represents difference as experienced through social, cultural or economic circumstances: the poor, ethnic minorities, youth subcultures, disabled children and so on.

A further set of binary opposites also exists: 'integration' and 'segregation'. This binary represents some form of human agency (government) that creates social groupings (sometimes through force). Thus, internationally, the apartheid regime in South Africa forcibly segregated black and white populations; Australian policies forcibly segregated white and Aboriginal populations; while in the US, civil rights legislation promoted integration (integrated schools in Alabama for black and white children); and, more recently, the

British government promoted the development of integrated schools in Northern Ireland to reduce the tensions between Catholic and Protestant communities.

There is a sense in which inclusion relates to Nussbuam and Sen's discussion of functions and capabilities, where inclusion is a function, which promotes capabilities (and social cohesion), while integration relates to government policies, not necessarily dependent on the promotion of human capability. We agree with White (2002, p 442) who stated that: 'a key aim of education is to help students to lead personally fulfilling lives. The aim has to do with the pupil's wellbeing, not – at least, not initially – with his or her moral responsibilities towards other people'.

If moral responsibilities are concerned not only with the generalised 'other' (people), but with also transcending dimensions of difference, then inclusion is not only about reducing social *exclusion* (seen in societal terms of economic or material access to society), but also about social *cohesion*. Moral responsibility (in White's terms) is reciprocal and is based on, as we argued in Chapter 2, Honneth's three patterns of intersubjective recognition – love, rights and solidarity – and the three operational subcategories of self-confidence, self-esteem and self-respect (Honneth, 1995). We argued that such a perspective is important to consider when thinking about wellbeing in respect of children and schools. Intersubjective recognition depends on the highly relational nature of humans, who are located in local communities of culturally shared identities and interests.

If we understand wellbeing, happiness and human flourishing as being linked with issues of material and economic wellbeing, and intersubjective recognition (described in terms of love, rights and solidarity, and self-confidence, self-esteem and self-respect [Could we add dignity here?]), and being located in communities of shared identities and interests, then the following questions emerge:

- To what extent is a school a community of shared identities and interests?
- To what extent does a school promote love, rights and solidarity, from which self-confidence, self-esteem and self-respect emerge through collective intersubjectivities?
- If a school provides the opportunities (*functions*) to develop the human *capabilities* that underpin such a view of wellbeing, can it be called 'inclusive'?

This discussion, stemming from White and Honneth, considers children as a generality, but the debate around 'inclusion' (or exclusion, integration and segregation) and 'social inclusion'/'exclusion' centres on the status of minorities. We rarely consider 'inclusion' to be an issue when considering schools that have a homogeneous population of children from the same social class, ethnicity, religion, economic status and so on. Each of the segregated schools in the US (black or white) or in Northern Ireland (Catholic or Protestant) could be consider 'inclusive' from the perspective of the schools themselves. This intra-cultural view only becomes a 'problem' when viewed supra-culturally, when it is recognised that schools organised on cultural homogeneities can be seen as 'segregated'.

The *Brown vs Board of Education* ruling in the US created the first concerns about integration/segregation when it ruled against the prevailing notion of 'separate but equal' as contravening the 14th Amendment of the US constitution by denying specific groups equal access to educational opportunities. The ruling referenced the work of Clark and Clark (1939), which argued that psychological damage was caused through segregation. *Brown vs Board of Education* was used as a springboard for the civil rights movement in the US, being the foundation of the Civil Liberties Act 1964 (NCPR, 2011). The psychological damage cited by *Brown vs Board of Education* relates to Honneth's view of wellbeing: segregation does not lead to love, rights and solidarity across cultural minorities.

In a recent review of inclusion 'across cultures', Alur and Timmons (2009, p ix) presented 'a vision of inclusion that is about societal reform. If we can successfully provide education to our most vulnerable children the education of all children will improve', and this statement reflects the shift in view that focuses on questions of disability as being the overriding dimension of cultural difference. We follow the intentions of this statement, but the statement itself reflects the fact that the inclusion debate focuses on issues of disability. While our following discussion follows the development of inclusion as it relates to disability and 'special educational needs', it should be kept in mind that our intention is to focus on 'all children'.

The findings of the *Brown vs Board of Education* case were transferred to children with disabilities in 1974 in the USA (US Rehabilitation Act), following *PARC vs Pennsylvania* in 1973 (PARC, 1971) and extended through the American Disabilities Act 1974 and the Individuals with Disabilities Act (IDEA, 1990). This legislation provided moral, civil, parental, ethical and legal rights for children with disabilities to be educated in ordinary schools, which rejected the ethic of 'separate but equal'. The legislation was anti-discriminatory, but did not enshrine the principles presented by the work of Clark and Clark (1939), where segregation as existed was seen as detrimental to the psychological wellbeing of children segregated from their peers. This discourse of rights was concerned with providing educational opportunities, but did not acknowledge the psychological consequences of segregation. The shift in the discourse to 'rights' has blurred this original distinction and it is generally accepted that inclusion is seen in terms of educational opportunity. This view has now shifted towards a global concern with 'inclusive education'.

Inclusion debates

In parallel with the ambiguity and confusion over what wellbeing might mean, there is also little agreement over what inclusion might mean for children identified as having disabilities that require additional or special needs, or for children in general (Goodley, 2007; Thomas and Loxley, 2007). Indeed, schools have become the site of normalisation ideologies where 'the standardization of inclusion and equity has re-territorialized difference as problematic' (Allan, 2004, p 420).

The concept of 'inclusion' is as slippery as 'wellbeing' – it lies in the eyes of the beholder. While the report *Removing Barriers to Achievement* (DfES, 2004b) acknowledged the importance of embedding inclusive practice in schools, there is no attempt to define inclusion. There is also little agreement over whether inclusion is a process – a road on which we travel towards an inclusive society – or whether it is a state – that is, in this school, under these circumstances, this child is achieving, within a safe and caring environment that ensures wellbeing and friendships: the child is included. These ways of seeing inclusion are complementary and there are schools that are inclusive and children or young people who are included. There are also a large number of children who experience educational failure, social stigma and rejection; there are children and young people who are emotionally, physically and socially abused, who are bullied, or who experience an increasing range of mental health problems.

The debates around inclusion have taken as tacit that inclusion is a 'substantive good' and therefore desirable in its own right. Debate about the general question of 'What are schools for?' has continued for millennia (Curtis and Boultwood, 1963), although educational philosophy no longer forms part of the training curricula for teachers. To amend the question slightly, we can ask: 'What is inclusion for?' (following Deleuze and Guattari's (1994) exhortation to evaluate concepts through their effects and functions). If White (2002, p 442) is correct that 'a key aim of education is to help students to lead personally fulfilling lives', then to what extent does inclusion result in children leading personally fulfilling lives? Where inclusion is part of a binary distinction (inclusion–exclusion), we can also ask: 'How does exclusion lead to a lack of fulfilling lives?'

Being well

Educational philosophy emanating from Aristotelian or humanist formulations locates education within a discourse of moral, personal and social development. In recent times (after the Education Reform Act 1988), early formulations of being well were focused on the school's role in promoting the Spiritual, Moral, Social and Cultural (SMSC) development of children. The statutory requirement that schools should encourage pupils' SMSC development was first included in the Education Reform Act 1988. This was followed by the Education (Schools) Act 1992, which required schools to report on the quality of SMSC development of pupils.

The purpose of supporting SMSC development was underpinned by a sense that in promoting healthy societal values, the ills of society could be diminished, and that schools were a central institution for the promotion of values. The central role of the school in promoting 'healthy values' was emphasised in a set of qualitative indicators of the ethos or hidden curriculum pursued by the school and staff ('climate and values' of the school) (OFSTED, 2004). 'Climate and values' included: relationships between staff, governors and pupils; forms of address; forms of conflict resolution; the quality of the physical environment; the nature of the formal curriculum; relationships with the wider community; and tone and content of the materials published by the school.

By 2008, this view had changed. The Office of Standards in Education (OFSTED) consultation document to develop indicators of a school's contribution to wellbeing foregrounded different aspects of the central aims of education and the statutory requirement to promote SMSC, as concerned with the development of the whole child and young person (OFSTED, 2008). The role of the school was seen as limited: the entrenched and intractable problems residing outside of the schools jurisdiction – 'Parents have the biggest influence on children's wellbeing' (OFSTED, 2008, p 4).

The shifts in focus between 1992 and 2008 show a shift towards what Roulstone and Prideaux (2008) described as a 'functionalist' understanding of education. As Tomlinson (2001, p 169) commented: 'the results of market competition did indeed work to the benefit of middle class and aspirant groups, and despite a rhetoric of inclusion, continued to perpetuate a divided and divisive system'.

Functionalism argues that social systems and institutions have evolved to have the best fit with a complex industrial society, characterising the process as 'a transformation of social solidarity due to the steadily growing development of the division of labour' (Durkheim, quoted in Roulstone and Prideaux, 2008, p 17). Applied to education, this approach suggests that education is essentially functional and appropriate (Roulstone and Prideaux, 2008), especially where divisions of labour depend on 'spurious notions of ability, which reflect the social class structure' (Tomlinson, 2001, p 168).

Functionalism requires concepts of 'efficiency' or 'effectiveness', which are measurable and can feed into policies to improve educational outcomes (seen primarily in terms of achievement). The shift towards functionalism has shifted the emphasis from the role of schools in promoting the holistic aspects of SMSC, towards the individual learner (in keeping with the neo-liberal stance on governmentality), who can develop knowledge and skills that contribute to their economic and social 'wellbeing'. Learners are required to demonstrate the ability to make informed choices about their own health and wellbeing, and to be able to contribute to community cohesion and sustainable development. Following the 2008 OFSTED indicators (OFSTED, 2008), where the learner can achieve their learning outcomes, the school can be seen to fulfil its central aim of promoting pupils' achievement; where the pupil fails to 'achieve', then this lies outside of the school's accountability. Failure in achievement within this shift of emphasis locates the failure of the child in external circumstances; either within the child themself, or with societal factors, beyond the control of school. The surveillance of children (Foucault, 1991a), in locating a failure to thrive as a barrier to learning, has created the recent educational concept of 'special educational need'.

The Warnock report of 1978 (Warnock, 1978) characterised the 'non-achiever' as having some form of 'special educational need'. This term shifted a view of *difference* based on concepts of disability (or as Warnock described it: 'handicap'), to that of 'a special educational need'. Up to 1978, children with ostensive disabilities ('handicaps') were educated in segregated environments, while low-attaining children were part of the minority of failure in ordinary schools. The process of educating children with disabilities has followed a path, based on Canadian experience, characterised by Andrews and Lupart (2000) as:

Exclusion → Institutionalisation → segregation → categorisation →
integration → mainstreaming → inclusion

'Mainstreaming' as a concept appeared first in the US in the early 1990s and was seen as a 'neutral' term for the educational placement of disabled children in the 'mainstream'. This term did not have the negative implications of 'integration' derived from the experience of desegregation of schools in the US. For non-disabled low achievers in schools (and the derivation of the concept of 'special educational need'), the main changes have been in the areas of categorisation, as a learning failure has come to be understood with respect to a range of psychological and socio-cultural factors.

Warnock developed the idea of a continuum of need, where a 'continuum of needs' require a 'continuum of provision' (Warnock, 1978, p 95). Matching environments (the social) to individual needs (the bio) supports learning (the psycho). The view of matching need to provision led to 'the Warnock Continuum', which advocated provision ranging from full exclusion (home tuition) to full inclusion (full-time education in an ordinary class with any necessary help and support). This latter term has become one of the definitions of full inclusion (Gallagher, 2007). But where Warnock sought to match need with provision, the ideological basis of inclusion has shifted, where inclusion, different from integration, requires a shift in the culture of schooling that allows all children in (Gallagher, 2007). This process is seen as a 'substantive good' in its own right, and should form the goal of a trajectory that starts with exclusion and ends in inclusion (characterised as a 'struggle') (Vlachou, 1997). Such a move has shifted the meaning of the concept away from an understanding of educational failure, and towards an understanding of (inclusive) education as relating to rights and differences.

Inclusion

Ellis et al (2008) report a policy review of inclusion for the National Association of Women Teachers and report that inclusion can be seen as:

- an ideology and/or aspiration: usually linked to a human rights agenda;
- a place: usually mainstream versus special school;
- a policy: normally from central or local government;
- professional practice: i.e. 'inclusive teaching'?

- personal experience: how an individual and their parent/
  carer experiences inclusion. (Ellis et al, 2008, p 8)

The factors noted by Ellis et al attempt to characterise inclusion in a multidimensional way, that is, the concept of inclusion is described through the intersection of subsidiary concepts or ideas. The way these different aspects of inclusion interrelate does not, in itself, provide a definition of inclusion, but the assumption emerges that if all of these dimensions are coherent, then inclusion happens; if they are discordant, inclusion fails. We start with inclusion as an ideology.

Ideology

The basis for understanding the development policies of inclusion and its links to concepts of opportunities is deeply rooted in political ideologies. Vitello and Mithaug (1998), in their comprehensive review of US policy determination through the 1980s and 1990s, argue that the thrust of the development of educational policy has been as shift from welfare arguments, through liberal, and towards conservative and libertarian (neo-conservative) models. The conditions of equality either require opportunities or protections (welfare/liberal) or are contingent on conduct/achievement (conservative/libertarian). The concern is that shifting ideologies have seen increases or reductions in the number of children placed in ordinary (mainstream) or special settings, depending on whether inclusion is seen as a right (and based on social values – welfare/liberal views) or based on learning outcomes (conservative/ libertarian) views (Mithaug, 1998).

Mithaug also discussed societal inclusion and equality as part of the 'something beyond integration'. It is unclear how 'societal inclusion' is derived from inclusion as a school process, particularly where, within a functionalist, post-welfare education system, social mobility is a major policy objective for government. The shift in policy frameworks towards a functionalist approach has resulted in the original policy of the 1980s and 1990s (post-Warnock and the Education Act 1981) of providing provision to meet needs, giving way to the recent changes in focus towards the contingent nature of pupil behaviour, in terms of achievement and conduct. This reflects the political shifts away from a welfare and liberal consensus and towards the conservative/ libertarian (neo-conservative) agenda since the early 1990s in Britain and in Europe.

This shift in focus has seen an enormous (epidemic?) rise in those pathologised oppositional behaviours associated with autistic spectrum disorders, or the construct of BESD/ADHD (behavioural, emotional and social difficulties/attention deficit hyperactivity disorder). Such individuals create problems for the education of other (non-disabled) children, which is the main contingent factor for their exclusion. If these oppositional children create barriers to inclusion, what is it about *inclusion* that oppositional behaviour creates barriers to it?

In moving towards conservative or libertarian models, inclusion has been predicated as a 'substantive good'. Thomas Scanlon asserted that what 'is essential is that these are theories according to which an assessment of a person's well-being involves a substantive judgement about what things make life better, a judgement which may conflict with that of the person whose well-being is in question' (Scanlon, 1993, p 188). He suggested the label 'substantive good theories' for this class of views on the ground that they 'are based on substantive claims about what goods, conditions, and opportunities make life better' (Arneson, 1999, p 5).

If inclusion is a 'substantive good', then this is an assertion, and its assertive nature is contained in the idea that it is 'beyond' integration, that is, beyond placement and provision and represents a quality in which its denial is an infringement of a basic right. The relationship between the right to inclusion and the provision of educational resources to enable achievement is a disjuncture, based on the judgement of the authority, 'which may be in conflict with that of the person whose wellbeing is in question' (Scanlon, 1993, p 188). The exercise of judgement underpins the entire inclusion industry of identification and classification, resource allocation, placement provisions, and tribunals[1]. The authorities who stand outside of the core of the judgement define the nature of the substantive good in their own way, and the problem of judgement reflects Warnock's original position that it is impossible to match need with provision, because of the complexities of such a position. Where the substantive good is ill defined, the child (as the person on whom such judgement is exercised) has no voice.

The 'inclusion as a substantive good' argument does not allow the autonomy of children (the child having no ontological status as an adult only allows the external 'good' to be defined for them), although, within the wellbeing discourse, subjective views are now generally sought to endorse the 'substantive good' and the child's reaction to it (again, the child has no agency to redefine the nature of that substantive good as it impacts on the child's life), and this is an argument we propose in Chapter 7. The policy framework is neutral towards the social determinants of wellbeing, but it does promote inclusion as a substantive good by operating within an equal opportunities framework to allow 'functioning', in Nussbaum and Sen's (1993) terms, which has the potential to promote 'capabilities', but does not guarantee them.

Inclusion is both a concept and an 'item' on an Objective List Theory (OLT) for quality of life or well-being (Schalock, 1997). Inclusion in this sense is humanistic and assumes an Enlightenment/post-Enlightenment assumption that 'solidarity' is a given 'good', together with the view that social relationships are a 'substantive good', on which well-being (especially psychological or emotional wellbeing) is predicated . However, social relationships (seen in the wider terms of community, teachers, adults generally, as well as peers) should *underpin* achievement rather than be in competition with it. Thus, the ethos of competition (achievement) in education (functionalism) creates difference, and pathologises the different. The OLT surrounding 'wellbeing' (determined by the unnamed 'general consensus') is open to critiques of cultural bias, where the 'deviant', who do not conform to the 'normal', are not accorded autonomy and may hate the 'certain things' that are good or bad for them.

Inclusion as policy

Policy, with an inclusion focus, is based on objective views of measurable phenomena: the answer lies in the maxim 'to improve something, first measure it'. Even the decision to measure helps set directions and priorities by demanding a degree of consensus on what is to be measured – that is, on what constitutes progress. Returning to the discussion of schooling, the UK government has never produced policy to influence human relationships in schools (and, following the Organisation for Economic Co-operation and Development's [OECD's] original caveat (OECD, 2009), it is difficult to see how such policy could be framed). However, since the 1990s, the government has adopted a policy of inclusion to address the concerns of minorities within society to provide equality of opportunity for children and young people, especially those deemed to have special educational needs, disabilities or who are at risk of social exclusion and experience cumulative disadvantage. In this sense, the policy framework has been 'anti-discriminatory', and the discourse has shifted to one of equal opportunities and rights.

The new anti-discriminatory climate has provided the basis for much change in policy and statute, nationally and internationally. Integration transformed itself into inclusion during the 1990s (Vislie, 2006) and inclusion has been enshrined at the same time that segregation and discrimination have been rejected. Articulations of the new developments in ways of thinking, in policy and in law include: the *UN Convention on the Rights of the Child* (UN, 1990); the *UNESCO Salamanca Statement* (UNESCO, 1994); and the *UN Convention on the Rights of Persons with Disabilities* (UN, 2006).

Since the period from 1981 to the present, successive UK governments have implemented various inclusive policies, which match the global frameworks adopted by the UN, especially the Salamanca Statement of 1994 (UNESCO, 1994). However, even with a plethora of inclusive policies, Roulstone and Prideaux (2008, p 16) argued that: 'on the two key measures of the number of disabled children educated in mainstream contexts and the number of school exclusions affecting disabled children, there is no significant evidence of improvement'. They also noted that within a functionalist view, education was a 'proving ground for ability ... a selective agency for placing people according to their capacities' (Roulstone and Prideaux, 2008, p 16). The major problem with functionalist evaluations of education is the assumption that the norms and values being inculcated are equitable, shared and advantageous to all. Parallel assumptions suggest that all children begin their educational journey at roughly the same starting point. Arguably, neither of these points are accurate reflections of the nature of education in a competitive industrial society (Roulstone and Prideaux, 2008). The outcomes of Warnock's (1978) report and subsequent legislation, even though it advocates integration for children with disabilities, has been continuing special education (whether this takes place in a special school, special class or unit) where children are educated separately.

Inclusion as a set of placement decisions

The House of Commons Select Committee on Education and Skills (HM Government, 2006, s 61) noted that: 'the debate over provision has for too long focused on an unhelpful interpretation of inclusion as a place (that is, special or mainstream) rather than on what the pupils achieve'. Ellis et al (2008) noted that an understanding of inclusion was predicated on place: usually mainstream versus special school. Placement decisions are subject to the Foucauldian system of producing 'docile bodies', which are predicated on processes of hierarchical observation, normalising judgement and examination (Foucault, 1991a). Such processes, as we have argued earlier, are based on judgement of capacity and contingent behaviour. The placement of a child is subject to quasi-legal processes (in England) of identification of need through procedures of assessment/diagnosis. Such processes are controlled by educational psychologists and local authorities. This was strongly criticised during the Select Committee Review of Education (HM Government, 2006), and, as we write, the present government is undertaking a review/reform of the system of placement. But given the policies of the last Labour government (and being continued by the present government) the shift towards the pluralism of schooling has led to the proliferation of independent special schools offering placement for children with significant learning difficulties (especially within the field of autistic spectrum disorders).

The continuum of provision advocated by Warnock is still in place and while inclusion is seen as the desired goal, placement founders on the ability of the individual school to provide an education for specific children that results in achievement and does not disrupt the education of other children. Placement is not predicated on the psychological effects of educational placement.

Inclusion as a professional practice

The 2001 guidance *Inclusive Schooling for Children with Special Educational Needs* offered the following statement: 'inclusion is about engendering a sense of community and belonging and encouraging mainstream and special schools and others to come together to support each other and pupils with special educational needs' (DfES, 2001, p 8). This statement reflects a Honneth-like concern for wellbeing.

Although the guidance spoke of community and belonging, it also provided a statement on inclusion as providing effective learning opportunities for all children, responding to individual needs and overcoming barriers to learning. The guidance also described the principles of an inclusive education service, where inclusion is seen as a process of developing school cultures. Such a process is dependent on the professional development of teachers and should focus on developing the potential of all learners.

If we consider inclusion to be a professional practice, then this begs the question of what is extra about *inclusive practice*, as opposed to ordinary professional practice. In the guidance, the distinguishing factors for inclusion are located in diverse learning needs and potential barriers to learning and participation. Participation is about integration, not inclusion in the way we are arguing.

Hegarty (2001) queried the relationship between a special educator and a general educator, and whether an inclusive school is synonymous with a 'good school': 'One may well accept that [there] are characteristics of *good* schools, but if inclusion and inclusive schools are to be useful terms they need a clear, specific domain of reference' (Hegarty, 2001, p 25; original emphasis).

Inclusive schools and 'good schools' still require a professional 'gaze' (Foucault, 1983a) based on examination and hierarchical judgement. How does the 'good school gaze' differ from the 'inclusive school gaze'? Special educational provision is predicated on an 'examining gaze' (especially a psychological gaze), which differentiates the 'normal' from the 'abnormal' (and the pathological). Given the plethora of professional engagement with 'special education' (through teachers, psychologists and para-professionals, including teaching assistants), the professonalisation of inclusion has moved the practice away from the 'general teacher' and towards the specialist, but the specific domains of reference (Hegarty, 2001) are not clear.

The discussion has so far followed the inclusion of children with special educational needs/disabilities, but has ignored the questions of minorities, who may also be subjects of exclusion. Does working with minorities require yet a further 'domain' specific to it, which differentiates it from the 'general teacher' and 'the good school'? The cultural issue of difference and how this is managed within 'majoritarian' responses to education is elided in most discussions of inclusion, but is represented in discussions of social exclusion: 'A multidimensional view of social exclusion holds that social exclusion is constituted by a layering of conditions, one upon another, generated by an interaction of economic, social, cultural and political circumstances' (Malloy and Gazzola, 2006, p 9).

To what extent schools can reduce social exclusion at a societal level (as a practice) is questionable in that these are circumstance beyond the control of schools, but if the factors underpinning social exclusion are recognised (economic, social, cultural and political circumstances), then inclusion becomes a concept of 'full inclusion' (Gallagher, 2007). This requires structural and cultural change in the school and school system, and cannot be restricted to a set of special education practices targeted at 'activity restrictions' alone. Where inclusion is different from a good school, the specific domain of reference for inclusion has been ignored, and the fundamental question of *what* inclusion is, and can be, has been replaced with practices of effective inclusion that operationalise and reduce to a technical act the process of what should be viewed as a holistic practice (Allan, 2008). But this is not just a case of *how* questions replacing ideas of *what* inclusion is; as Allan commented, we are increasingly questioning the *why* of inclusion:

Questions about *how* we should include appear to be displaced by questions about *why* we should include and under what conditions. The exclusion of certain individuals from mainstream schools has become legitimate and acceptable, especially if it can be argued that they would have a potentially negative effect on the majority of children within the mainstream. (Allan, 2008, p 4, emphasis added)

We assume that the 'we' Allan refers to are professionals engaged in the practice of education. Questions relating to the *what* and *why* and a move towards qualitative understanding of inclusive teaching will be explored in our later chapter on professionalism (Chapter 11), but the negative effects of inclusion can only be understood from the perspective of personal experience.

Inclusion as personal experience

The final standpoint on inclusion presented by Ellis et al (2008) was that of the 'consumer'. In all of the discussion so far, the psychological effects of the road from exclusion to inclusion (Andrews and Lupart, 2000) have not been addressed. In Ellis et al's analysis of inclusion, the final section addressed the psychological aspects of inclusion as they relate to personal experience. How do pupils (and their parents) experience inclusive education? How does their experience relate to the concept of inclusion?

Non-professional stakeholders (particularly parents) see inclusion as being linked to care, security, social acceptance and wellbeing (Yssel et al, 2007; Runswick-Cole, 2008); others (not least children and young people themselves) see it in terms of friendships and positive peer relationships (Woolley et al, 2006) or of the negative impact of bullying (Norwich and Kelly, 2004). However, in contemporary drives to reduce inclusion to measurable indicators, some commentators claim that 'the views of disabled youngsters and their parents regarding what the desirable consequences of inclusion should be, have been disregarded' (Allan, 2004, p 419). This quote from Julie Allan again begs the question of what the 'desirable consequences of inclusion' *are*.

There are links between education and psychological wellbeing and health (WHO, 2004), but very little comparative research into the differences between inclusive and segregated (special) education. Early research (Wade and Moore, 1993) produced generally negative results about pupils' experiences of special education. More recently, Heiman

(2000, p 1) noted that pupils with learning difficulties in special schools 'felt lonelier than students in other groups'.

Other research, which focused on inclusive education (Meyer, 2001), demonstrated how difficult it was to provide any strong understanding of the social impact of placement decisions for vulnerable children. On balance, she presents data to suggest that disabled children's experiences of inclusive education can be described as 'helper-helped'. Bayliss (1995) showed that interactional behaviour could also be described in this way. The lack of comparative research in this area makes drawing any kind of conclusion highly problematic.

These studies relate to the quality of interpersonal relationships, other studies, which looked at a broad range of factors (relating to achievement and self-reports), presented different findings. For example, in 2006, OFSTED reported that the most important factor in determining the best outcomes for pupils with learning difficulties and disabilities (LDD) was not the type, but the quality, of the provision (OFSTED, 2006). This followed the 2005 OFSTED report on *Promoting Emotional Health and Well-Being in Schools* (OFSTED, 2005), which examined the vital role played by schools in promoting the emotional wellbeing of their pupils. These reports explored the psychological effects of education with respect to mental health (OFSTED, 2005) and inclusion (OFSTED, 2006) in terms of placement. The second report's full title is *Inclusion: Does It Matter Where Pupils Are Taught?*, and both reports emphasised the qualitative aspects of schooling that impact on achievement and wellbeing. The link between wellbeing and education is well attested to. A positive school environment can lead to greater wellbeing (Ravens-Sieberer et al, 2004).

The OECD's (2004) review of children's wellbeing across Europe claimed that if the experience of children and their parents/carers was focused on physical, emotional and social wellbeing, then these factors impact on both achievement and health. The strong interdependency between learning and wellbeing argues that educational processes need to be inclusive. Where schools are working with groups that do not exhibit solidarity or belonging, exclusivity can break the link between learning and wellbeing and result in disaffection, alienation and ill-being. Thus, inclusion becomes a complex phenomenon:

> The processes [involved in inclusion] are psychosocial in that they encompass the sociology of group composition and change, social roles, interpersonal understanding, friendship, social stratification, and the dynamics of social justice, as well as the psychology of human development and behavior,

ecological interactions, attitude change, exercise adherence, motivation, traits and states, and numerous other processes. (Phelan, 1996, p 331)

A different analysis: complexity

Phelan (1996) emphasised the complex nature of psychosocial wellbeing, learning and the quality and nature of the educational environment. Here, the understanding of inclusion moves well beyond simplistic notions of setting suitable learning challenges. The government's policy framework provides the opportunities (functions), from which capabilities emerge. If the capabilities that emerge are restricted to material or economic wellbeing, then the opportunity to develop wider capabilities (linked to concepts of *paidiea* – including sociality) is missed.

If this analysis is correct, then the 'substantive goods' obtained through inclusion are contingent goods, not goods derived from opportunities. This distinction underpins the general debate as to whether inclusion is a state or a process. In the terms we are discussing, if inclusion is a process, then it can be seen as an opportunity to develop capabilities (in Nussbaum and Sen's terms); if it is state, then it is defined by the achievement of the substantive goods that the opportunity (function) provides. This view, derived from the wellbeing arguments, is different from the generally accepted views surrounding the inclusion debate. These ways of seeing inclusion, as either a process or a state, are circular: in this view, inclusion is a process of achieving the state of inclusion, or the state of having achieved inclusion, that is, in both cases, itself.

Earlier chapters noted a variety of theoretical or philosophical positions relating to the concept of wellbeing, and in this chapter we have explored these different positions with respect to educational standpoints as they relate to inclusion. We argue that an educational process ought to result in some form of good life determined through the different levels of embodiment explored in Chapter 2. If we follow Scheper-Hughes and Lock's (1987) formulation of the phenomenological lived body, the social body and the body politic, then both education and wellbeing operate at these different sites. This formulation mirrors a model of 'ecological development' proposed by Bronfenbrenner (1979). He understood development (as this relates to educational, social or psychological development as an emergent property of a system) as differentiated between the *micro-systemic* (phenomenological lived body); the *meso-systemic* (social body): and the *exosystemic* (body politic). Within this model, the interrelationship of the different systemic levels (called the macro–system) results in physical, psychological and social/educational development – these are not separated, but are interdependent. The models of Scheper-Hughes and Lock and Bronfenbrenner are predicated on the lived body, the social and the political (exosystemic factors) and are pragmatic.

Where micro and macro levels are seen as distinct, both inclusion and wellbeing are seen as functions of the individual or of society. This dualist approach creates both those who *lack* wellbeing and may be *excluded*, and those who possess wellbeing and are *included*. A pragmatic approach is thus determined by ascertainment of lack and the determination of a process whereby the lack can be amended, ameliorated and compensated, or if the possession of wellbeing as a *good* is determined to have existed, then the process of reinstatement of wellbeing is a return to normalcy. *Normal* (and its recent derivative normalcy) has a complicated history, but within the content of educational practice, it has come to present one side of a binary opposition between the *normal* and the *abnormal* (one who has and one who lacks). The systemic pragmatism of the essentialist subject and the constructed society creates the boundary between the normal and the abnormal; between those *inside* and those *outside*; between *self* and *other*. Having defined *other* (abnormal), the systemic response is to improve the phenomenological lived experience of the essentialist self, through amending or changing the social circumstances of the self through changing the social body or the body politic. Bringing in those outside is called *inclusion*.

A different view proposed by Woodill et al (1994) presents an existential-humanistic approach whereby a 'person' comprises an embodied identity ('Being') – which is experienced in a particular context, certain time, place and culture. Further, being a fully functioning healthy human is to be rooted (and accepted) in a community, an aspect of life referred to as *Belonging*. Further, action in the world depends on choice: 'the things people choose to do in their lives make them who they are, and who they will become. This unfolding aspect of life is referred to as Becoming' (Woodill et al, 1994, p 62). If this linear concept is reformulated as a dynamic process, then 'Becoming' feeds back into 'Being' as a spiral of growth of embodied identity. This non-dualist approach to understanding identity does not create boundaries between the phenomenological body and the social body; they are interdependent.

If there was no outside, no division between the body and society (as a remnant of the Enlightenment), and we understand the complex nature of education as interdependencies between the three 'bodies'

(Scheper-Hughes and Lock, 1987), which are in turn co-constitutional (Bayliss and Dillon, 2010), then inclusion as a concept no longer stands on its own. Instead, it becomes a vector on the plane of consistency (smooth space: Deleuze and Guattari, 2004) in which *Being* (including wellbeing), *Belonging* and *Becoming* intersect. On this plane of consistency, wellbeing as a concept becomes part of a school process, seen as an assemblage (Deleuze and Guattari, 2004). Inclusion does not *promote* wellbeing as a functioning, in order to develop a capability. It *is* wellbeing. If the argument linking inclusion and wellbeing stands up, then the need for wellbeing in schools (as a bolt-on process to mend, make better, ameliorate ill-being) is negated.

Notes
[1] The Special Educational Needs and Disability Tribunal (SENDIST), established under the Education Act 1993.

CHAPTER 7

Accessing minority voices – implications for wellbeing

Introduction

In this chapter, we explore a number of attempts in the literature to access children's voices concerning their wellbeing. This review includes approaches with very young and disabled children, as well as child-focused research in development studies. We hope that a focus on the most marginalised groups of children and young people will highlight the methodological and conceptual barriers present in wellbeing research with *all* children. It is worth noting that there are very few empirical studies that specifically focus on children's social and emotional wellbeing, so some of the studies discussed have a more general focus on children's voices in research.

The specific focus of the chapter is to consider if children's voices can be regarded as generally 'minoritarian' (Deleuze and Guattari, 2004), and then explore what methods are appropriate to bring these to visibility (Foucault, 1983a) in order to understand their wellbeing experiences. As such, this raises questions of authenticity, representation and power and the importance of understanding the multilayered, embedded and contextual nature of children's wellbeing.

The right to be heard?

The United Nations Convention on the Rights of the Child (UNCRC), developed internationally, was ratified by the United Kingdom in 1991 and includes all UN countries with the exception of the USA, Somalia and East Timor. It contains 54 rights for the world's children, which included an Article specifically relating to the right to be heard (UN, 1990, Article 12); while another reflected the right of the child to freedom of expression: 'either orally, in writing or in print, in the form of art, or through any other media of the child's choice' (UN, 1990, Article 13).

The arguments linking 'listening' and 'rights' are pervasive and persuasive as they support liberal views of children as competent social actors who have the right to talk about things important in their lives. As has been noted: 'the subject is constructed as a rational autonomous individual, with the consciousness to formulate his or her own wishes' (Kjorholt et al, 2005, p 175). But, as these authors suggested, a rights-based account of listening needs to be problematised on three counts: first, there is a danger that in linking listening and rights, we prefigure dichotomous constructions of the child 'as either vulnerable and dependent or as autonomous and independent' (Kjorholt et al, 2005, p 175). Second, rights discourses often exclude the 'being' aspects of childhood, that is, they ignore the embodied nature of the child as a rights-holder and the complexity of emotions involved in exerting one's rights (particularly where there are some basic human needs, such as the need to be loved, which cannot be reduced to a legal right). Third, they argued that a rights-based account of listening and children's voices can oversimplify the difficulties faced by children in negotiating the relationships and emotions necessary to hold rights, and the challenges of the 'taken-for-granted' authenticity of children's voices.

Listening and vocalising

Chapter 2 outlined an argument for accessing minority voices on experiences of wellbeing. In this chapter, we explore this proposition further, and consider in what ways children's and other minority voices are heard in research, policy and practice that consider their wellbeing. That is of course not to presume that all children are 'minoritarian', but given the widely presumed power imbalances between adults and children, this may be an acceptable assumption. Giving people a voice is not just about rights and entitlements to talk and express views, nor is it solely concerned with an acceptance of children's rights to voice opinions and be heard. Rather, it is an active process of communication involving hearing, interpretation and construction of meanings that is not limited to the spoken word. It is also a necessary stage in participation in daily routines and in wider decision-making processes (Clark, 2005).

Listening involves skilful active participation, particularly on the part of adults, to receive the information that children and young people convey. This is no more the case than in work with very young children, as Cathy Nutbrown summed up:

> adults with experience who respectfully watch children engaged in their process of living, learning, loving and being are in a better position to understand what it is these

youngest citizens are trying to say and find ways of helping
them to say it. (Nutbrown, 1996, p 55)

Listening is the process of bringing voices into visibility and allowing
them to be acknowledged and understood. The process of making the
invisible visible demands that the observer engages in multi-sensory
information gathering. In *Birth of the Clinic*, Foucault described the
importance of the observer's gaze in a clinician's ability to piece together
information concerning patients:

> The observing gaze manifests its virtues only in a double
> silence: the relative silence of theories, imaginings, and
> whatever serves as an obstacle to the sensible immediate;
> and the absolute silence of all language that is anterior to
> that of the visible. Above the density of this double silence
> things can be heard at last, and heard solely by virtue of the
> fact that they are seen. (1983a, pp 132–3)

The medical gaze is composed of different sources of information:

> there is a local, circumscribed gaze, the borderline gaze of
> touch and hearing, which covers only one of the sensorial
> fields, and which operates on little more than the visible
> surfaces. But there is also an absolute, absolutely integrating
> gaze that dominates and founds all perceptual experiences. It
> is this gaze that structures into a sovereign unity that which
> belongs to a lower level of the eye, the ear and the sense of
> touch. (Foucault, 1983a, p 203)

While Foucault was writing in a medical context, his ideas related
to the medical gaze as comprising information from all the senses
have resonance in work and research with children. Indeed, the
acknowledgement of the need to access multi-sensory information
in order to better hear and understand children's voices underpins
many attempts, particularly in early years contexts, to access children's
voices. An example is the 'Mosaic' approach developed by Clark and
Moss (2001). This was developed with three and four year olds in
English early years pre-school settings and was inspired by participatory
appraisal methods that allow communities to have a voice, but do not
privilege the spoken word, and therefore is seen to be more egalitarian,
particularly when working with non-literate communities. The aim was
to find ways of developing services that were responsive to the voice

of the child. The approach was based on the metaphor of a mosaic whereby all the pieces are required in order for the picture (voice of the child) to be revealed. It drew inspiration from the 'pedagogical documentation' (Dahlberg et al, 1999; Rinaldi, 2006) methods in the Reggio Emilia pre-schools of Northern Italy, where children, parents and practitioners together collect evidence in order to document children's learning and development.

Mosaic is *multi-method* and recognises the different 'voices' or 'languages' (Edwards et al, 1998) of children and hence supports the tenet of Article 13 of the UNCRC that recommends children should be able to communicate in any media of their choice. It is *participatory*, as it recognises children as experts and agents in their own lives (Clark and Moss, 2005) with capacities and capabilities to communicate about their lives; it is *reflexive*, as it includes children, practitioners and parents reflecting on meanings and takes account of their interpretations; it is *adaptable*, as it can be applied in a variety of early childhood institutions; it is focused on children's *lived experiences* and can therefore be used for looking at a range of experiences, not just knowledge; and it is *embedded* into practice as it is used as a framework for evaluation and assessment and informing early years practice (Clark and Moss, 2001).

These characteristics of Mosaic can often be identified not only in direct practice with young children, but in more general child-focused research, as will be outlined later. What is clear in the writings of Clark and Moss (2001, 2005) is that they perceived that the barriers to listening and hearing children were located in adults' inabilities to be adaptable to hearing the ways in which children communicate.

Minority voices and the child as subject

Chapter 2 raised the possibility that in revealing the 'minoritarian fictions' of children, families and practitioners on their wellbeing, we might attain different perspectives and insights. 'Majoritarian' theory is a form of hegemonic reproduction whereby the dominant knowledge (of wellbeing in this case), traditionally known from a white, male, heterosexual, Western perspective, takes priority. Consequently, the 'minoritarian' is in binary opposition and is only revealed as that knowledge which is 'abnormal' or 'different' to that held to be 'true' by the dominant in society.

To be described as 'minoritarian' does not suggest a permanent label or positioning for individuals. Earlier work with learning support staff who were generally deemed to be 'minoritarian' in respect of school hierarchies and power structures suggests that people move in and out of more and less 'minoritarian' subject positions (Watson et al, 2011) according to contexts and relations with others. The proposed strength of revealing 'minoritarian' fictions is that they have the potential to reveal novel explanations and accounts of experiences that challenge 'majoritarian' theories about concepts. Once a 'majoritarian' perspective is adopted, the holder's thoughts operate in ways that support the hegemonic reproduction and this is fuelled by the desire for status within the ruling discourse. Minoritarian theory works in opposition to this, in that:

> One's perspective is determined by one's site in the social assemblage, together with its preconscious interests. This time, however, one's perspective is immanent in the theoretical field, for the signs and events one encounters may directly affect the unconscious assemblage of desire. One's own perspective becomes a part of the machine that is consumed as the process takes place. (Goodchild, 1996, pp 54–5)

This is a dynamic and intersubjective perspective of knowledge and theory reliant on encounters with people, narratives (or fictions) and the presumption that knowledge of any given concept is constantly in flux and situated. This perspective permits novelties, difference and surprises to emerge, and could be used to deflect normalising master-narratives of children and wellbeing. But it demands that we find ways of accessing children's voices, and that we can interpret their multiple meanings, as 'by recognizing how children's voices are multi-layered we can move beyond the often misguided assumption that voice research with children is by definition good, valuable, or of high quality' (Spyrou, 2011, p 157). There is a need to be critical in research with children and not presume authenticity in children's accounts. Children's voices are not univocal or fixed in time or place. Unfortunately, universal theories (of wellbeing) are easier to operationalise and do not create the methodological confusions, lack of clarity and sheer messiness that the more subjective approaches perpetuate. This is one of the reasons why 'majoritarian' accounts of the world have such a strong hold on our consciousness.

In advocating for voice research with children, it is also important to be reminded of the problems inherent in accessing children's voices, as MacNaughton (2005, pp 130–1) asked:

- Which children's voices will come forward?
- What will the consequences be for each child who participates?
- How might one child's voice silence that of another?
- What can and should I do when the voices are sexist or racist?
- How might intervening as one child voices their knowledge enable another child to speak?
- How will I honour those children who struggle to make their voices heard?

Children's silences in encounters with adults also warrant greater attention (Lewis, 2010).We may be so consumed by the need to include children's voices in research and practice that we forget that there may be 'a preference by children for silence' (Lewis, 2010, p 18).Thus, there is also an opportunity to 'go beyond verbal communication to examine other than surface meanings' (Spyrou, 2011, p 157). Children and adults use and perceive silence in a multitude of ways and the match between adult and child perceptions of silence may differ greatly. Children may be silent because they do not know the answer, do not understand the question, do not want to respond or cannot respond as the question is too emotionally or socially damaging, or they lack the language to articulate their response.The adult may respond to the silence as only being about poor understanding and hence miss the nuances in the exchange. Adults sometimes also use silence in discussions with children to exert pressure on them to respond (by providing an awkward gap in the conversation), or they may feel obliged to fill the space of silence themselves too quickly and pre-empt, interrupt or put words into children's mouths (Lewis, 2010). Hence, there is a health warning to accessing children's voices (and silences) in childhood studies generally, but particularly in consideration of very young or disabled children's voices in research, where there are calls for disabled children to lead the research agendas more overtly and for adults to provide children with the space required to define and understand their experiences in their terms (Watson, 2012).

Methodological challenges

Chapter 5 raised criticisms of attempts to measure wellbeing based on 'majoritarian' perspectives on children's wellbeing.This chapter is the antithesis of the measurement approach and builds upon the criticisms raised. If we believe that wellbeing as an (inconsistent) concept cannot be measured, then what other information is it possible to access about wellbeing in order that we might better support children and young people in social and emotional capabilities and capacities?

The need to access 'minority' voices in research and policy generally is a well-understood ambition; albeit one that is increasingly attracting critique (Lewis, 2010). There are many studies across the world with children and young people that include children's accounts of their experiences (see eg Crivello et al, 2009). Such approaches include the use of methods such as photography (Percy, 2003; Newbury and Hoskins, 2010), drawing (Punch, 2002), mapping (Young and Barrett, 2001), focus groups (Hill et al, 1996; Barnes, 2009) and role play/performance-based activities (Conrad, 2004; Kaptani and Yuval-Davis, 2008), and most use a combination of methods (Crivello et al, 2009), particularly in development studies. Examples include explorations of poverty with children in Vietnam, the impact of violence on children in Rwanda and the impact of poverty on wellbeing in Ethiopia (Crivello et al, 2009). These are deemed to be more 'democratic' than other approaches to data collection as they can enable access to 'the question of how people experience well-being – the analysis not of subjective components of well-being, but the subjective, socially and culturally constructed experience of well-being as a whole' (White and Petitt, 2004, pp 4–5).

The founder of the Social Indicators Research Society, Asher Ben-Arieh, is also a recent proponent of the importance of children's voices in research about their wellbeing. Although it must be acknowledged that this is only partial:

> even if children are granted only partial legal and civil rights and the partial ability to participate in decision making about their lives, then they should participate at least in the same proportion in the study of their well-being, especially since it bears so much influence on them. (Ben-Arieh, 2005, p 575)

In the context of children's participation, this might be deemed to be rather tokenistic, although the suggestions for how children could be involved in wellbeing research do include them contributing to the study design, being the source of information, data collectors, contributing to data analysis and being partners in utilising data (Ben-Arieh, 2005).

Most participatory studies tend to work with older children (aged eight onwards) and little is said about the inclusion of children with disabilities in research that access 'voice'. Contemporary research has started to emerge in childhood disability studies raising questions of how, and using what methods, disabled children can be brought into research (Wickenden, 2011; Goodley and Runswick-Cole, 2012). Although, as some of this suggests, for children and young people generally, but particularly for those with disabilities, it is often difficult to untangle their voice from those of parents and carers who habitually talk for them in what has been termed an 'enmeshed voice' (Abbott, 2012). Issues of researcher's interpretations of children's voices become even more profound when children do not use speech (Simmons, 2009; Clarke and Wilkinson, 2011; Wickenden, 2011) and this is often the case for very young children, as well as those with particular disabilities. Such observations start to address the questions posed earlier from MacNaughton (2005) about which voices are heard and which are silenced.

There are also concerns for validity in child-focused research on wellbeing. White and Petitt (2004) offer the challenge that in claiming to reveal 'authentic knowledge' about people's wellbeing experiences, many participatory and creative approaches can fail and make onerous claims, whereby 'it may be that the formulation of "the good life" does not adequately capture the deepest values of what people consider well-being' (White and Petitt, 2004, p 18). Perhaps research should not be so tasked with defining authenticity of voice and more concerned with other judgements of quality in respect of children's (and others') participation and validation of the outcomes of research.

The ability to capture what it is participants define as contributing to their experience of 'wellbeing' is an epistemological and a methodological challenge that seems to be the crux of the 'majoritarian problem' in wellbeing research; that is, researchers are usually reliant on prefigured conceptions of 'what' wellbeing is and then find ways of researching people's experiences. By offering dominant knowledge on a seemingly intangible concept, which is arguably experienced in a tacit way, are we in danger of only ever giving people (children) a tokenistic voice in respect of validating our hegemonic take on wellbeing? Does this reinforce the 'gap between the promise and practice of participation' (Graham and Fitzgerald, 2010, p 3)? Our ambition in this book is for research into children's wellbeing to start with no prefigured conception of what wellbeing may be; but, rather, to allow children, young people, practitioners and families the opportunities to create 'minoritarian' fictions concerning what they understand to be wellbeing in their local contexts and circumstances. This means that the priority must be to access these fictions or narratives; it is not about asking individuals to rank, score or measure against prefigured categories of what others decide is 'wellbeing'. This rests on an aspiration to reveal complex, situated and novel insights into children's wellbeing and to not just pay lip-service to minority voices in order to 're-confirm rather than challenge the dominant hegemonies' (White and Petitt, 2004, p 18).

Studies that have attempted to access voices on wellbeing

There are a number of studies specifically with children and young people that have attempted to access their wellbeing (as opposed to experiences generally). These include the *Good Childhood* inquiry from the Childhood Society in England (Layard and Dunn, 2009); the *Childhood Wellbeing* report commissioned by the Department for Children, Schools and Families (DCSF, 2008b); and the Young Lives research programme based at the University of Oxford. It is to a review of these projects that we now turn.

The *Good Childhood* inquiry

> *The Good Childhood Inquiry* was commissioned by The Children's Society and launched in September 2006 as the UK's first independent national inquiry into childhood. Its aims were to renew society's understanding of modern childhood and to inform, improve and inspire all our relationships with children. (The Children's Society, 2006)

On the basis of this inquiry, the research team elicited the following category headings of: friends, family, learning, lifestyle, health and values (Layard and Dunn, 2009). But this was not a consideration of children's 'wellbeing' in any clearly defined sense (although it has regularly been used as evidence in discussions of wellbeing). The report paints a bleak picture for children living in the UK, with a claim that adults' excessive focus on their own lives and happiness is leading to excessive individualism, which causes 'a range of problems for children including: high family break-up, teenage unkindness, commercial pressures towards premature sexualisation, unprincipled advertising, too much competition in education and acceptance of income inequality' (The Children's Society, 2006).

The *Good Childhood* inquiry has since moved into a national survey of children's wellbeing (Rees et al, 2010). This comprised a large-scale survey of 9,000 children and young people between the ages of 10 and

15 years old, where the authors acknowledged that 'due to the time of school year when the survey was conducted most young people were towards the upper end of these age bands' (Rees et al, 2010, p 25). This concentration of age groups to older children reinforces the concerns we raised earlier, and it is also worth noting that only 2% of the participants recorded having a disability (118 young people), while 13% of them reported having a long-term illness (although there is no qualitative understanding of what these might be). The methodology draws very much from wellbeing measures approaches, in keeping with Ben-Arieh's view of children's perspectives on wellbeing noted earlier (Ben-Arieh, 2005), and there are claims made concerning wellbeing that suggest it can be quantified and comparisons between children drawn: 'some small sub-groups within the survey such as disabled children and young people not living with parents had substantially lower than average levels of well-being' (Rees et al, 2010, p 81). It is also interesting to note that findings focused on 'the primary importance of relationships, particularly with family, for young people's wellbeing' (Rees et al, 2010, p 84).

Childhood Wellbeing, Qualitative Research Study

The *Childhood Wellbeing* study was commissioned by the DCSF (DCSF, 2008b) to access children, young people's (8–16 year olds) and parents' constructions and perspectives on wellbeing. Children and young people were set tasks before family interviews were conducted, such as recalling times when the children have enjoyed or not enjoyed life, and parents were invited to bring along artefacts that prompted memories of their own childhoods. The appendices of the report revealed that the researchers used photo-elicitation methods with children that comprised 'happy children/young people images' and 'images of children not in a state of happiness' (DCSF, 2008b, Appendix 5), which were used to prompt discussion and in card-sorting tasks. While the report represents seemingly 'authentic voices' on wellbeing, and there are some headline conclusions drawn concerning children's resilience and the correspondence between parents' and children's concerns and issues relating to wellbeing, their uncritical conflation of wellbeing with concepts of 'happiness' and 'good childhoods' – an issue discussed in Chapter 5 as 'convergence' of concepts (Warnick, 2009) – raises questions over the conceptual validity of the findings. There is also no problematisation of what 'authentic voices' are or how these are validated with the children and families.

Young Lives

The *Young Lives* research programme is an ongoing international longitudinal study of childhood poverty in Ethiopia, India, Peru and Vietnam. The study follows the lives of two birth cohorts (12,000 children) and involves the collection of a range of different data sets, including quantitative questionnaires as well as participatory methods (drawings, activity diaries and timelines of significant life events), for example, with 11- to 13-year-old children in Ethiopia to understand their wellbeing. Their approach to children's wellbeing 'focuses on children in the social contexts they inhabit and for this reason accessing children's views, in the context of their communities, is of central importance' (Camfield and Tafere, 2009, p 1).

Data from children were used to establish context-specific and gendered lists of 'well-being' and 'ill-being' indicators, which bring into sharp focus the extent of inequalities for children based on their geographical location and their gender. This was particularly acute in respect of girls' access to education:

> a common saying in the remote rural site in relation to education is that 'a girl never finishes her journey', which may mean that she never completes her schooling, or even having completed it she is unable to go any further. (Camfield and Tafere, 2009, p 18)

Findings emerging from the *Young Lives* study highlight in particular the importance of embedded understandings of wellbeing that take regard of social, economic, geographical, familial and educational circumstances. Understandably, access to education was not raised as a concern in the DCSF (2008b) study in the UK, and this therefore raises questions as to the efficacy of generating universalising OLT approaches to the wellbeing of the world's children.

Subjective–objective dilemma in wellbeing research

Other studies that have used mixed or creative methods in order to access children's voices on wellbeing (rarely is this defined as social and emotional wellbeing [SEWB]) have attempted to do so using a range of methods as outlined earlier and using a variety of research questions that address 'what life is like' for the children, particularly those living in poverty. Examples include studies with: street-based children in Kampala that utilised four different creative approaches to capture the children's lives (Young and Barrett, 2001); poor children in America understanding what is 'special' to them (Percy, 2003); children in South Africa exploring their views on an acceptable standard of living (Barnes, 2009); or children in Scotland understanding their emotional experiences (Hill et al, 1996). Arguably, much of this research is not concerned with wellbeing in any prefigured manner, as the concept of wellbeing is not defined and explored directly with the children. The agenda is very open and subjective and one could argue that the merits in these studies are that they reveal detailed and illuminative insights into a small number of children's lives, which clearly has value and takes positive regard of children's participation and voices as subjective narrators of their lives.

The alternative approach has been to accept predefined Objective List Theory (OLT) domains of wellbeing and then attempt to measure and describe how a particular group of children 'fit' the prefigured concept. This method can be seen in a study with street children in China (Cheng and Lam, 2010) that used a Student Life Satisfaction Scale and a Chinese Positive and Negative Affect Scale for Children. This approach does not take account of children's constructions of wellbeing – just their interpretation of the 'given' concept.

Other approaches have involved children defining the domains of wellbeing to develop indicators for later measurement. A study in Australia involved children in interviews and task-based methods including journal keeping and collage making in order to facilitate children's perceptions of the concept of wellbeing (Fattore et al, 2007), from which were derived wellbeing indicators. These comprised: defining wellbeing (through feelings of happiness); autonomy and agency; keeping safe and feeling secure; self; material resources; activities and being active; and the physical environment and home. While the authors recognised that there was a great deal of specificity and contextuality to these domains derived with 126 children in New South Wales, they also suggested that 'the development of indicators which relate to the experiences of some children may reflect dimensions and domains valued by children more generally' (Fattore et al, 2007, p 25). There are questions of generalisability, as well as a concern that the child-centric work was developed into adult-led measures.

Three different approaches to researching children's wellbeing present themselves in these examples, yet arguably none of them attend to the approach to 'minority voices' we would wish to support and feel is possible in research about wellbeing.

More than just listening?

As many writers on the subject of children's voices and participation acknowledge, listening is not just about being attentive to the voices (even the multiple voices and languages) of children. This is our criticism of the studies we recognise as reflecting more subjective constructions of children, as while they may 'listen', they do not actively engage children in collaborative examination of their conditions and experiences. There is a sense of 'creative/fun data taking' on the part of the researchers, with the ethical considerations attended to because children have task-based research activities to engage them. Listening is also about reciprocal *meaning making* and about engaging in a dialogic process that has an outcome where children genuinely feel their views have been regarded: 'when framed as a dialogic encounter, participation can be seen to have a far broader focus than just "listening" to children's voices since its potentiality is *change*' (Graham and Fitzgerald, 2010, p 4, emphasis in original).

There are claims that rights-based perspectives on voice perpetuate dichotomies of competence and dependence. We need to move beyond such binaries and view listening to children and other minority voices as part of a discourse of care, interdependence and ethics (Kjorholt et al, 2005). This would focus on the relational nature of children's self-reporting and experiences of wellbeing, contextualised in family and other ecological niches (Bronfenbrenner, 1979). Child-centred approaches cannot be 'child-only'. As has been noted in development research with children: 'social and economic justice for poor children must be tackled in the context of their families and communities' (Jones and Sumner, 2009, p 43). More widely, it is acknowledged in voice research that children's experiences, and their voicing of these, are culturally and historically mediated by the contexts they inhabit and thus can never be unique or individual. Instead, children's accounts need to be viewed as located in the 'discursive fields of power which produce them' (Spyrou, 2011, p 161) and which allows us to overcome an 'overly romantic notion of children's voices as unique in a way that neither exoticizes them nor ignores children's perspectives' (Alldred and Burman, 2005, cited in Spyrou, 2011, p 161).

The study by Graham and Fitzgerald (2010) in Australia reviewed a social and emotional learning programme called Seasons for Growth, a loss and grief programme aimed at 6- to 18-year-olds to develop social and emotional wellbeing in children as they deal with separation, divorce and death. They concluded that the relevance of 'having a say' in matters that are of importance to children has four dimensions:

- 'children yearn recognition' (Graham and Fitzgerald, 2010, p 8). This claim is framed within Honneth's (1995) work on the struggle for recognition, as Graham and Fitzgerald (2010, p 4) stated: 'acts of recognition envisage interpersonal, intrapersonal and social change';
- 'children's identities and experiences cannot be generalised or universalised' (2010, p 8);
- 'the intergenerational nature of children's participation should not be overlooked' (2010, p 9) – this is concerned with the emotional and interpersonal dynamics of the adult in facilitating children's voices and in enabling their status as adult to be de-privileged and power differences challenged. Adults need to find ways of dealing with the lived complexities of the child, which can of course be unpredictable, messy and confusing; and
- the value of dialogue, which is not just concerned with 'listening' to children, but which 'focus[es] predominately on the outcomes of the participatory encounter for *children*, and invites us to reflect on how *we, ourselves*, have been "changed", "converted", "altered" or "refreshed"' (2010, pp 9–10, emphasis in original).

Conclusion

This chapter has reviewed a number of published approaches to accessing children's and young people's voices on wellbeing and considered some of the methodological and epistemological difficulties. What is clear is that there is a need to find ways not only of accessing minority voices, but of engaging with children and other minority voices about wellbeing in a dialogic way that does not exacerbate dichotomous ideas, that contributes to real change processes for children and that enables 'genuinely alternative understandings of well-being to emerge' (White and Petitt, 2004, p 20). There is a need to address methodological and ethical issues in wellbeing research in order that minority voices can be placed in context, and embodied in all their messy complexities. This is imperative if we are to understand and improve the condition of children's wellbeing and explore wellbeing as embedded in the multiple contexts of people's lives. Very few examples exist in the literature that truly foreground minority voices and attend to issues of power and participation for children. This requires a reflexivity in research with children that 'accepts the messiness, ambiguity, polyvocality, non-factuality and multi-layered meaning in "stories" that research produces' (Spyrou, 2011, p 162).

CHAPTER 8

Children's peer relationships in schools

Introduction

In this chapter, we consider a range of approaches to address children's difficulties in their peer relations in schools. In particular, we voice criticism of teaching conflict resolution (CR) skills to schoolchildren. We do so not because we do not share CR practitioners' hopes of harmonious and enriching school environments, but in order to examine whether evidence demonstrates the effectiveness of this approach, and to explore and deconstruct the methods of CR in schools to see what unintended consequences and hidden agendas may be in play in regard to wellbeing. 'Conflict resolution' is a broad term and, like 'wellbeing', a contested concept (Isenhart and Spangle, 2000). According to Cohen (1995, p 15) 'conflict is a discord of needs, drives, wishes, and/or demands'. Mack and Snyder stated that conflict 'is for the most part a rubber concept, being stretched and moulded for the purposes at hand' (Mack and Snyder, 1957, p 212). This quote applies also to 'wellbeing'.

Less contested is the recognition that conflict can be intrapersonal (within the individual), interpersonal (between two parties) or intergroup (between groups) (Cohen, 1995), and that it has both a conceptual (internal/psychological) and a behavioural (external/activity) property (Sellman, 2003). In schools, CR is built on a social learning model (Groebel and Hinde, 1989; Bandura, 1997) according to which techniques for resolving conflicts can be learnt, and modelling influences behaviour, as does the environment. The idea that CR skills are readily learnable fits comfortably with Goleman's (1995) model of emotional intelligence, which is the foundation for the Social and Emotional Aspects of Learning (SEAL) programme and much of the social and emotional wellbeing (SEWB) practice delivered in UK schools. CR skills are taught in schools, generally by external training organisations, to support pupils in peacefully resolving conflicts in school and to develop an understanding of its causes and impact.

Most school-based CR practice sees conflict as a natural part of everyday school experience (Tyler, 1998). However, school CR rarely includes consideration of societal structures, class relationships or cultural forces (Sellman, 2003). Like much of the social and emotional learning agenda (see Chapters 4 and 5), school CR sees the locus of control as individuals in relationship with others. In this chapter, we consider three types of school CR and relate them to the school wellbeing agenda: peer mediation (including buddying); anti-bullying initiatives; and restorative approaches (RA). This is not a comprehensive picture, but covers some of the most widespread approaches.

Wellbeing and conflict resolution

UK schools have an operationalised model of wellbeing (see Chapter 4). In this context, CR has two purposes: the promotion of pro-social behaviours (positive behaviour change, social competency, resilience and peer support); and the prevention of problematic behaviours (bullying, violence, aggression and victimisation). Both these purposes tick boxes in the lists of wellbeing indicators and measures that schools are working towards.

The appropriation of CR as a tool for promoting SEWB has high-level endorsement, for example, public health intervention guidance in 2008 advocated CR training for promoting pro-social behaviours in the short term, and the use of peer mediators for creating longer-term outcomes (NICE, 2009, p 31). School CR is one forum through which the *Every Child Matters* outcomes are pursued, particularly 'staying safe' (from 'bullying and discrimination' and 'crime and anti-social behaviour in and out of school') and 'making a positive contribution' ('choosing not to bully or discriminate') (DfES, 2004a, p 9).

It is hard to quantify CR in UK schools, as information is held region by region and school by school, but CR is clearly an established part of schooling. CR schemes were often referred to in early American Social and Emotional Learning (SEL) reports (Wells et al, 2003) and this linking of two different disciplines has translated into UK practice. The rapid introduction of SEAL across UK schools entwines the two approaches. National SEAL guidance advocates CR, describing it as a key area of learning (DCSF, 2009, p 6). Language used in both primary and secondary SEAL outcomes explicitly names CR skills, for example: 'I can resolve conflicts to ensure that everyone feels positive about the outcome' (DfES, 2005b, p 43); 'I can use a range of strategies to solve problems and know how to resolve conflicts with other people, such as mediation and conflict resolution' (DfES, 2007a, p 56); and 'I understand the impact of bullying, prejudice and discrimination on all those involved, am moved to want to make things better for them and can use appropriate strategies to do so' (DfES, 2007b, p 11).

An interesting aside here is why this merging of CR and SEWB has occurred. One factor may be recognition on the part of UK CR practitioners that SEL could widen participation and interest in CR programmes. Although somewhat difficult to prove due to the informal nature of much CR school practice, one does wonder how many CR schemes in schools were promoting social and emotional health and wellbeing *prior* to the publication of Goleman's (1995) *Emotional Intelligence*. The partnership between SEWB and CR gave SEL proponents access to a body of work and theoretical practice through which the new field of SEWB could be authorised and evidenced.

Peer mediation and buddying

In schools, 'buddying' sometimes denotes literacy, work apprenticeship and other schemes, but we are using the term here to mean peer mediation, probably the commonest school CR tool. A study by Houlston et al (2009) estimated that 62% of UK schools used peer support in some form. Baginsky (2004) cites Tyrrell's definition of peer mediation as:

> A very matter-of-fact, logical, linear process, whereby children help each other to deal with their conflicts, playground disputes, and so on. It is a structured process, managed by two mediators, who are children. They introduce the process, establish ground rules, listen to the story from the perspective of each of the disputants and offer to each of them a summary of what he or she has said. They then provide the opportunity for both sides to voice their feelings, help them identify the problems, brainstorm solutions, and, ideally, agree a solution. (Baginsky, 2004, p 9)

According to Baginsky, peer mediation took off in schools in 1992, the commonest form being buddying, where groups of older primary school children are selected by staff to act as mentors intervening in or pre-empting conflict: 'Their [the buddies'] main aim is to help everyone have an enjoyable lunchtime' (Oundle Primary School, 2009). Ideas of what is enjoyable can of course be adult-centric. One school's guide states:

> All over the country schools face the same kinds of problems at playtime, with children having a limited repertoire of games to play, unsafe playing habits, bullying, boredom and other forms of inappropriate behaviour which can lead to chaos and difficulty for the teachers or lunchtime supervisors on duty. (Kingston upon Hull City Council, 2003, p 1)

This paints a rather bleak and problematic picture of a dysfunctional arena requiring management and facilitation of children for adults' benefit. The guide is typical of buddying texts in explaining that the job of buddies is to 'set an example and encourage children to make positive behavioural choices', although not to police the playground (Kingston upon Hull City Council, 2003, p 2). Claims made elsewhere for the success of buddies in achieving such aims are superlative. According to one Welsh online student voice magazine: 'all students show the effects of being surrounded by emotionally intelligent peers who diffuse aggression and provide role models for success' (PupilVoice Wales, no date). Which model of emotional intelligence (Payne, 2009) is being referred to here? As we have argued in a recent paper (Watson and Emery, 2010), academics and practitioners should nuance their understanding of 'emotional intelligence' (EI) based on an informed challenge to EI and related concepts.

Generally, buddies wear some sort of identification: 'peer mediators at East Hill have donned their bright red fleece jackets and watched for conflicts they may be able to help resolve' (CRESST, 2011). What effect this visual demarcation has on non-buddies is not clear, although some reports on UK school practice mention stigmatisation (Challen et al, 2011).

The evidence on peer mediation

In 2004, William Baginsky, on behalf of the National Society for the Prevention of Cruelty to Children (NSPCC), produced a guide to peer mediation for schools that included a wide-ranging review of evidence regarding peer mediation (Baginsky, 2004), which we draw on here. Bitel and Roberts (2003) found no systematic evaluation of the effectiveness of peer mediation and many schools did not record the number of mediations that take place. Baginsky quotes Tyrrell as finding that peer mediation was 'often ... neither structured nor analysed; and rarely is a control group established to verify that any changes have come about because of peer mediation'. Similarly, Sellman

(2003) found little research in the UK on the effectiveness of peer mediation schemes and maintained that there was little systematic monitoring that could add to the evidence linking peer mediation with successful outcomes. The European report on conflict prevention (European Platform for Conflict Prevention and Transformation, 2000) acknowledged the importance of 'scientific evaluation studies', but found these to be 'relatively scarce' for peer mediation. As one UK city council report stated:

> the difficulties of carrying out an experiment in a school setting, however, make the results inconclusive, and more research is recommended, in order to understand the links between peer mediation, humanistic practices in the classroom, and the, apparently, central role of the headteacher. (Baginsky, 2004, p 22)

A 2009 study by the National Institute for Health and Clinical Excellence (NICE) reviewed evidence that peer mediation programmes were effective in promoting social and emotional wellbeing (wellbeing undefined) and found that 'although peer mediation can be effective in reducing bullying and disruptive behaviour it is not always successful'. Moreover, 'there are no clear patterns to define interventions which were effective or those which were not' (NICE, 2009, p 32).

Anti-bullying

Definitions of bullying vary. According to Dan Olweus (2002, p 9), being bullied involves being 'exposed, repeatedly and over time, to negative actions on the part of one or more other persons'. The Department for Children, Schools and Families gave the following definition: 'behaviour by an individual or group, usually repeated over time, that intentionally hurts another individual or group either physically or emotionally' (DCSF, 2007e). Kidscape, a UK charity providing anti-bullying advice, resources and training, considers bullying to be attacks that are: physical, for example, pushing, kicking, hitting, pinching and other forms of violence or threats; verbal, for example, name-calling, sarcasm, spreading rumours, persistent teasing; and emotional, for example, excluding, tormenting, ridicule, humiliation. In practice, definitions of bullying are often based on self-reporting, with resulting confusions regarding the frequency of it. Since the School Standards and Framework Act (HM Government, 1998), schools in England, Wales and Northern Ireland have been legally required to have anti-bullying strategies, while in Scotland schools are only strongly recommended to have one. There have been many government anti-bullying documents and initiatives including, *Safe to Learn* (DCSF, 2007e) and 'Bullying – a Charter for Action' (DCSF, 2007a). There are also a range of websites on the subject – for example, Kidscape, Anti Bullying Alliance, BullyingUK, Bully Free Zone, Childline and The Anti Bullying Network. Charities have historically played a big role and there are some examples of cross-organisational cooperation, for instance, Beatbullying, which is an alliance of over 70 organisations ranging from self-selected local councils, to Barnardo's and the Association of Teachers and Lecturers. Since the 1990s, interest in anti-bullying has grown (Samara and Smith, 2008). In schools, approaches range from disciplinary sanctions to programmes such as the No Blame Approach, which arguably 'only reinforces the idea that actions, including bullying, have no consequences. It is a charter for bullies and a recipe for disaster for victims' (Elliot, 2010).

Measuring the extent of bullying in UK schools is difficult. In 2010, the National Children's Bureau (NCB) published the paper 'Bullying' (Smith, 2010a), which summarised recent surveys and discovered that measurements of bullying varied. The *Tellus 4* survey (DCSF, 2010) found that 8% of children had been bullied at school; a 2007 Birmingham study (Shaughnessy and Jennifer, 2007) found that 15% of primary and 12% of secondary school children had been bullied; while a 2009 Welsh study (Lloyd-Jones et al, 2010) discovered victimisation rates of 6–19%.

Anti-bullying is one of SEAL's seven themes. An individual school may highlight this in a publicly available self-description: 'safeguarding the wellbeing of our students is the first priority at Bradford Academy. This anti bullying policy forms an essential part of our Safeguarding Policy Portfolio and demonstrates our commitment to ensure that our learners feel safe in school' (Bradford Academy, no date).

The anti-bullying charity Beatbullying, in conjunction with the consultancy New Philanthropy Capital, surveyed the impact of bullying on the self-esteem and emotional wellbeing of pupils, with the aim of measuring these impacts (Nevill, 2009). Alongside anti-bullying, the National Strategies website guidance for SEAL offers details of how pupils can take part in peer mentoring schemes to develop self-awareness and empathy, two of the five key aspects of SEAL. A typical approach by a school to forming an anti-bullying policy is described here:

The School decided to update its Anti-Bullying Policy, and pursue an anti-bullying accreditation, awarded by the local authority so it set up an interest group of young people, staff, parents/carers and governors to look at the issue. As a result of this, a group of peer mentors were trained, to offer support to children and young people who had been victims of low-level bullying in the school. There was also training for Year 12 volunteers in restorative justice approaches and how to set up 'conferences' to allow both the perpetrator and victim to discuss how their behaviour had influenced each other. The new system was advertised through assemblies and posters and Year 7 young people were asked to contact the peer mentors directly or by email. (DCSF, 2007d, p 38)

The evidence on anti-bullying

Bullying as an activity is not now understood as an individualised phenomenon, putting it at odds with SEAL individualism, but as a whole school phenomenon, since peer interactions are key; but even whole school interventions are inconsistent in their outcomes (Andreou et al, 2008). In primary schools, the evidence is mixed. One review found good evidence that multi-component programmes that combine curriculum-based social skills development, teacher training and parenting education are effective in managing problem behaviours, sometimes over the long term (Adi et al, 2007). This review noted that the Olweus Anti-bullying programme was effective with regard to reducing victimisation and reports of bullying and improving peer relationships in the shorter term. A programme called PeaceBuilders, which aimed to incorporate pro-social behaviour among pupils and staff, demonstrated effectiveness in enhancing social competence and reducing aggressive behaviour (Adi et al, 2007, p 11). Curriculum-based programmes, such as the Second Step programme and the Good Behaviour Game, have been shown to be effective in reducing violent behaviour in the short term (NICE, 2009). When considering the effectiveness of peer programmes, in particular the role of young people, NICE (2009, p 32) found 'mixed evidence of varying quality regarding the role of young people as peer educators/mediators'.

Restorative approaches

The word 'restorative' in 'restorative approaches' (RA) refers to restoring relationships between wrongdoers and those affected by their actions. Restorative approaches are epitomised by circle time, widely used in primary and secondary schools. The circle can act as a metaphor for the restorative approach where the aim is to 'keep everybody in'. Restorative approaches have gained ground in schools parallel to their use in wider society where they have also been trialled in the criminal and youth justice system. Within and outside school, they remain a minority interest, although with staunch proponents. The application of RA to discipline and punishment issues is sometimes called restorative justice (RJ). The following is a typical definition of RA in schools:

> The restorative approach is to challenge those who behave inappropriately to find a solution that is meaningful and meets the needs of those harmed. It is solution focused, personal and aims to build constructive and empathic bridges, rooting it firmly in SEAL. The restorative approach becomes a 'way of being', once all members of the school community see incidents where harm has occurred as 'teachable moments' to be learnt from and seek opportunities to facilitate conversations in which harm can be repaired, thus empowering all those involved to own the situation, and find the solution. (Flanagan and Clark, no date, p 7)

As this quote shows, RA prioritises emotional expression by victims to perpetrators. Some of its most experienced commentators are cautionary in recommending it unless the wider context in which it is being applied is also considered. Cremin recently wrote: 'we need to be very careful about the context in which young people may experience shame. Restorative approaches need to be used with skill and insight' (Cremin, 2009).

The evidence on restorative approaches in schools

In the Youth Justice Board's *National Evaluation of the Restorative Justice in Schools Programme* (2004), 92% of interventions resulted in the successful completion of outcome agreements between parties; 89% of participants reported a high degree of satisfaction; and 93% of those harmed reported that the process was 'fair' and that justice had been done (Flanagan and Clark, no date, p 18). In the experience of one of the authors as the manager of a mediation service, although during the 'post-mediation high' on completion of agreement parties would say wonderful things about the service, within six months, a case was often either back on the mediator's desk or another intervention such as court or council proceedings had taken precedence.

Conflict resolution and power

Foucault (1995) recognised that power is exercised and operates in all directions rather than from the top down. Our education system, however, tends to a post-war perspective of top-down totalitarian power: education is 'done' to children. Foucault was concerned with places where the recipients, perhaps 'clients' in modern parlance, have little say as to what happens to them. This is a good description of most schools, where students have no real control over the curriculum, teaching, learning or organisational systems (Harber, 2002).

Adult relationships are complex entities with a variety of dynamics and adults are free to develop their own ways of managing this, which can include periods of non-contact with either individuals or groups. In schools, by contrast, an institutional norm demands that young people continually 'get on' with all their peers so that the group atmosphere can be maintained as harmonious and conflict-free – a blueprint many adults would recognise as utopian and not a description of reality. The introduction of CR within the top-down power structure of a typical school, therefore, inevitably operates as much to control behaviour as to teach skills. And behaviour that adults define as problematic may be natural for young people (Stephen and Squires, 2005). Even bullying can be an example of this. In the following case study, the incident of bullying between two schoolgirls is augmented rather than resolved by the institutional response:

> Like she would say really horrible stuff to me and Elizabeth like, make us feel all small.... It probably would have blown over, it probably would have been just a little fight and we wouldn't have talked for a few days and then make friends. But then her mum got involved and like rang up the school and said that we were bullying her. (Ringrose and Renold, 2010, p 586)

In this case, once the adults – parents and school staff – became involved, things moved out of the range of the girls' autonomy into a space heavily overpopulated by authorities. The research paper continues:

> By discursively framing the incident as 'bullying', the school then calls a meeting with the girls (now 'bullies') and Katie (now 'victim')…. Our concern is that the bully/victim binary offers few material or practical resources for the girls to articulate or address the actual social content of meanings of their conflict. It also has a very problematic discursive effect of engendering heightened defensiveness, anger and anxiety. (Ringrose and Renold, 2010, p 586)

The power to deal with and manage this incident within their own context and in their own way was removed from these girls. It would be interesting to know what meanings they put on their school's response. Have they learnt that they are not trusted to take responsibility for managing their own relationships? Or that the 'authorities' will step in to manage any future conflicts they experience? The fixed binary pair bully–victim is unrealistic. One can be both a bully and a victim at the same time, or indeed transfer between these roles.

Stephen and Squires (2005) believe that children and young people are often seen as a problem demanding increasing measures of control. Do school CR schemes such as peer mediation play into the creation of what Foucault (1995) called the 'panoptic society', where the eye of a superior is brought into everyday interactions? The panopticon was originally conceptualised by Bentham and elaborated by Foucault in *Discipline and Punish*:

> All that is needed, then, is to place a supervisor in a central tower and to shut up in each cell a madman, a patient, a condemned man, a worker or a schoolboy. By the effect of backlighting, one can observe from the tower, standing out precisely against the light, the small captive shadows in the cells of the periphery. They are like so many cages, so many small theatres, in which each actor is alone, perfectly individualized and constantly visible. The panoptic mechanism arranges spatial unities that make it possible to see constantly and to recognize immediately. In short, it reverses the principle of the dungeon; or rather of its three functions – to enclose, to deprive of light and to hide – it preserves only the first and eliminates the other two. Full

lighting and the eye of a supervisor capture better than darkness, which ultimately protected. Visibility is a trap. (Foucault, 1995, p 198)

In Sellman's (2003) thesis, he reported that, 'significantly, 81% of conflict occurred on the playground, 15% in the classroom and 4% in the school hall. This suggests that the playground is an arena for conflicts' (Sellman, 2003, p 212). The playground in these instances is an arena for free expression and, at the time when these figures were recorded, a relatively surveillance-free zone.

Sellman further found that 'the inadequacy of outside spaces already discussed may be a factor but it is more likely that the reduced surveillance and different types of activity that characterise school playgrounds allows pupils greater freedom to enact conflicts' (Sellman, 2003, p 212). Here less surveillance equals more conflict rather than more freedom of expression or, more simply, 'being'. Peer mediation responds by rendering pupils 'constantly visible' to one another, yet not quite sure when they are being observed. A recent report on the effectiveness of anti-bullying strategies in schools stated baldly: 'in the primary sector, peer supporters can be the "eyes and ears" of the staff in the playground' (Thompson and Smith, 2011, s 3.1.4).

CR in schools is managed by and accountable to the school hierarchy. It has characteristics of the model of discipline conceptualised by Foucault in his writings on disciplinary technology. CR, particularly within a SEL context, exemplifies a movement away from a confinement model of discipline to a corrective one. CR schemes, in particular peer-based programmes, directly instruct students to survey one another. The greater the number of pupils involved, the longer the reach of the surveillance. Such surveillance has a double advantage when viewed from a school's perspective. It requires little adult time, and it looks into areas that adult observation cannot reach.

The CR codes of behaviour with which children are asked to govern their peer relationships at school are not required of peer relationships among school staff. It is unusual to see schools employing CR techniques as part of their staff policies and practices. Conflict between staff, staff and pupils, staff and parents, or the school and the local community are still dealt with in traditional manners with the authority and power remaining with the school leadership. A policy of 'do as I say but not as I do' reigns. CR programmes are perhaps built on the philosophy of adults wishing to apply skills to children that they do not practise themselves. We are, through many of these programmes, asking children to follow a prescribed model of relating to their friends at times and in spaces that traditionally have been unstructured, thereby arguably reducing the amount of time and space in which children can be children. Konu and Rimpela (2002), exploring wellbeing in Finnish schools, identified social relationships within a 'loving' category as vital to wellbeing. In this context, they recognised that children need a range of loving, supportive relationships. Yet one could question the 'loving' basis to the prescribed and at times controlling CR programmes operating across many UK schools. Konu and Rimpela's work also advocated 'being', which can be expressed through opportunities to be creative and influence school decision-making; such opportunities are not generally part of CR in schools.

Friendship mediated

On the theme of friends, one study exploring childhood wellbeing with parents and children found that 'friends were most often cited as the second most important influence or component in a good/content childhood' (DCSF, 2008b, p 43). By creating groups of mediators and buddies, CR programmes could be seen to formalise and attempt to control children's friendships. Buddies often have a specific remit to 'befriend' those children on their own. The authorities are intervening to 'create' and maintain friendships for more vulnerable children. But are friendships not, and should they not be, freely chosen? This process reflects concerns of a therapeutic culture (Ecclestone, 2004; Ecclestone and Hayes, 2008).

There is a danger that an inadvertent consequence of the good and 'peaceful' aspirations of CR in schools may be to stop 'children being children'. We should question deeply the possibility that this model is built on the therapeutic discourse identified by Ecclestone and Hayes because expansion of this model will inevitably problematise those children who do not fit in with it or are unable to follow its codes, rules and language. In one of the rare pieces of research literature in which children themselves were asked what they did with friends, the response was described as 'one of the things they liked about hanging out with their friends was that they needed very few props, they did very little, except live in their own world' (DCSF, 2008b, p 44).

Why are we seeking to control children's emotional lives and relationships? Perhaps our confusion as to how to repair the problems we see leads us to apply this action 'because we can'. Adults generally do not have the opportunity to direct or control other adults' actions, unless perhaps in a senior managerial position. Our frustrations can be placed on children whom we can control, and this reflects the paternalism raised in Chapter 2. Maybe we are also fearful of children's energy, impatience and their dissatisfaction with what they are being presented with, as reflected in the international wellbeing reports referred to in earlier chapters, whereby:

> There is a climate of fear and confusion surrounding children and young people: preoccupied with protecting our own children from harm, we often fail to reach out to those who need attention most. And all the while our young people are continually subjected to pressure to achieve, behave and consume like adults at an ever earlier age. (DCSF, 2008b, p 5)

Adult actions have perhaps gone beyond behaviour management and into the realms of psychosocial adjustment or policing. Rather than traditional and overt 'hard power' telling pupils what to do (Boulding, 1989) with an unwelcome consequence if they do not, this new model of 'soft power' is more persuasive and psychological: 'I need you to behave differently, I will teach you how to think differently and then you will choose to behave in a way which is more convenient for both of us and contributes to wellbeing'.

If SEAL teaches a blueprint for 'self'-management, the CR aspect of the SEAL curriculum teaches 'other' management, with CR representing the 'social' half of the phrase 'social and emotional'. Optimistically stated, this may defuse and de-escalate conflicts. A more critical interpretation might see CR as a template for behaviour regulation intended primarily to create compliance with the school regime or what Foucault (1995) described as 'docile bodies'. Because of their social orientation, CR skills merge with schools' behaviour management strategies. Indeed, many of the CR initiatives discussed in this chapter were implemented and funded through the Behaviour and Attendance Strategy.

Conflict resolution: promoting, co-opting or stifling pupil voice

Chapter 7 of this book explored in more detail the issue of accessing children's and other minority voices through and for research and decision-making processes. In this chapter, the accessing of pupil's voices we discuss is not for the purposes of research, but in the context of school life and in light of the question: 'What difference does the presence or absence of pupil voice in schools make to pupils' wellbeing?'

Recent guidance from the Office of Standards in Education (OFSTED) has directly linked pupil voice to the wellbeing agenda, and grades as outstanding schools in which 'pupils from a wide range of groups have a strong voice in decisions relating to their learning and wellbeing' (OFSTED, 2011, p 24). But if CR gives pupils a voice, it is a therapeutic voice, a voice that explores and reflects on emotions first, and issues second. In regard to pupil voice, Fielding (2001) has asked, among other things, '*Who* is allowed to speak? *To whom* are they allowed to speak? *What* are they allowed to speak about? What *language* is encouraged/allowed?' (p 100; emphasis in original).

Chapter 7 argued for a dialogic encounter with children and young people concerning their wellbeing, that is currently absent in wellbeing research. In the context of CR in schools, two dialogues take place: that between untrained pupil and trained pupil; and that between trained pupil and school staff member. The first dialogue, although between pupils, is guided by rules that differentiate it from the informal vernacular language generally adopted in pupil to pupil communication. These rules maintain, for instance, that 'the disputants will at least agree that there is to be no swearing or name-calling, no interrupting, and no blaming or accusing one another' (Baginsky, 2004, p 9). The voice that is accessed through such controlled channels is necessarily not a free voice. This power dynamic is worth reflecting on. It raises the spectre of informal social disputes finding themselves wrapped up in pseudo-professional jargon, rules and formalities that may well, if only by accident, 'professionally' problematise everyday experiences. In Gee's (1999) terms, the meaning of the discourse between two pupils engaged in a peer mediation is socially constructed around a clear discourse community: conflict resolution with its attendant roles and knowledge. Adult concepts and constructs are placed on children's dialogue and actions and the process is rarely determined by the children and young people themselves.

The second dialogue taking place is the communication between the trained pupil and the school staff member. The situated language of this dialogue is different to the previous one as both parties are trained and in agreement with the principles and practices of CR. However, the power dynamic within this dialogue still replicates the hierarchical order of the school system. The trained pupil can engage in dialogue, but there are clear limits and boundaries regarding decision-making processes, change and the themes discussed. For instance, it is the school staff member who will make the decisions regarding which conflicts merit the use of CR, what the limits of the process are, what the rules are for taking part and what are to be classified as positive outcomes.

Where pupil voice is in conflict with adult voice, adult power will win out. Peer mentors tend to be seen as the 'emotionally intelligent' within a school community. In effect, therefore, those filtered out as emotionally intelligent by adults have been chosen to be granted a voice. Clements and Clements (2000) acknowledge these issues and assert that the people to benefit most from a peer mediation scheme are those who are trained as mediators, followed by those who take part in mediation.

The issue of selection, particularly in peer programmes, is a challenging topic. Most programmes in the UK operate on a basis where pupils go through an interview or selection process to become a mediator, mentor and so on. As training can be both expensive and time-consuming, it is unlikely that many more than a handful of pupils will initially complete the training. Tyrrell (2002) presented findings from the Education for Mutual Understanding (EMU) project, which asked children who should become mediators: they found that they chose 'the nicest and best, most academically able and suitable characters' (Baginsky, 2004, p 11). Could one interpret this as the pupils most likely to conform, promote the school rules and succeed in ways acceptable to those in control?

Conclusion

This chapter has attempted to expose the current model of CR as delivered across UK schools to a perhaps harsh critique that evaluates its impact on pupil wellbeing. One of the key themes to emerge for CR is the gap between the hugely positive self-reported experiences of the practitioners, and objective, reliable research to support this. At times, an almost evangelistic message emerges from those engaged in CR programmes, yet this message generally comes only from adults and trained pupils. The voices of those to whom CR is 'done' remain for the most part 'minoritarian' and hidden. The practice of CR in UK schools supports a 'majoritarian' discourse in two ways. First, SEAL as a dominant school discourse has normalised a range of personal, social and cultural activities and CR is used as a tool through which this list of activities can be pursued or operationalised. CR is a dominant discourse and a prescribed process for dealing with conflict, controlled and authorised by the school hierarchy and implemented by those pupils meeting the controllers' conditions. The image and mission of the programmes is the peaceful resolution of conflicts, and teaching children techniques to resolve their own conflicts. These are worthy aims and unlikely to be opposed when stated in those terms. The term 'hurrah words' has been coined by White and Petitt (2004) when considering usage of the terms 'wellbeing' and 'participatory'. Hurrah words describe 'good things, engendering a warm glow and drawing people to them' (White and Pettit, 2004, p 4) – and CR certainly fits this criterion.

Second, CR practice is in itself 'majoritarian'. The concept of the 'body politic' used by Scheper-Hughes and Lock (1987) refers to the regulation, surveillance and control of bodies (individual and collective). CR schemes do indeed regulate, survey and control pupils' bodies. The controlling authority extends its *surveillance*. Sellman (2003) described the power tools of traditional approaches to discipline as mutually exclusive with peer mediation, although in practice most schools operate both frameworks concurrently. A traditional school framework is likely in his opinion to ensure that 'new tools are not reproduced and distributed. Consequently, pupils move between activities ... that are based upon different power relations and are characterised by distinct discourses and outcomes' (Sellman, 2003, p 291).

What is described here is the incongruence of the school experience as a whole if different discourses are permitted to govern different areas of school life, weakening the coherence of all discourses in play. Peer mediation is another face of the body politic that also disciplines. The challenge or dilemma for CR practice is also reflected in the work of Goodchild (1996), who noted that 'education is a process of incorporation into the dominant reality, so whatever face one may have, one is forced to think like a "majoritarian", even if one has a grievance against the majority' (Goodchild, 1996, p 110). Ultimately, how conflict is defined, what it means and how it should be interpreted and addressed has not been determined by the children and young people participating in these CR schemes. Perhaps this is a result of CR being subsumed within SEAL. If this is the case, then one would hope that in the future CR, as a discipline, breaks out of the SEAL shackles and finds itself a position where fluidity, debate and discussion are at the heart of it rather than predetermined outcomes. Ideally, such a process would be owned by the young people taking part as well as their families and communities, rather than the school authorities.

Looking to the future of CR in schools in the UK, the picture is uncertain. Up until the beginning of the Conservative–Liberal Democrat Coalition government in 2010, it could have been confidently stated that CR was set to continue to gain ground, but all such predictions are now problematic. What would happen to CR in schools if SEAL fell out of favour? In November 2010, we wrote to the Department of Education asking them about their approach to CR in schools and received the response that schools were free to make their own decisions about this, many commercial options were available and that the government did not wish to dictate policy of this kind to schools.

CHAPTER 9

Opportunities for playful expressions of wellbeing

By Karen McInnes

Introduction

This chapter considers the links between wellbeing, children's development and education in an early years context from a perspective of playfulness. It challenges traditional ideas of the value of play from an adult perspective and the consequential benefits play and play-based curricula are claimed to have for young children (which include claims relating to wellbeing and learning). **Playfulness** as a **disposition** and an **attitude** is offered as a more nuanced way of understanding how the activity of playing could be argued to underpin children's reported social and emotional wellbeing experiences. The chapter argues against objectifying the observable act of playing (and definitional or categorical accounts of what play is), instead arguing for the importance of the individual child's experiences as a player. This is a challenge to the long-held assumption that all play is of value and meaningful to children. The foregrounding of children's preferences and experiences is in keeping with the motivation to bring children's voices to visibility in Chapter 7. In a wellbeing context, this also offers a challenge that human flourishing is concerned with 'enjoyable feelings' or 'enjoyable activities' (White, 2011, p 44) and that both need to be present. A focus on playfulness helps to escape the adult-defined presumption that play activities are always enjoyable and synthesises the need for both enjoyment in respect of children's feelings and of the activity itself.

Recent research underpinned by my PhD studies of playfulness[1] will be presented to show that this alternative construct allows for opportunities for playful expressions of wellbeing. This builds on my research, and as an individual author this chapter will adopt the first-person singular pronoun.

Wellbeing and play

Play is a universal activity shared by humans and animals and is viewed as a vital and necessary aspect of life (Piers and Landau, 1980; Burghardt, 2005). Play is a fundamental human right for all children as articulated in Article 31 of the United Nations Convention on the Rights of the Child (UNCRC) (UN, 1990) and is seen as an essential mode of being for children (International Play Association, 2010). It was included within the *Every Child Matters* framework under the outcome 'Enjoy and Achieve' where it was stated that 'children should achieve personal and social development and enjoy recreation' (DfES, 2004a, p 9). It was also seen as an important part of childhood in submissions to the *Good Childhood* inquiry, which repeatedly emphasised the value of play for children and the need for children to have opportunities to play (The Children's Society, 2006). This has been recognised in policy documentation, with the cross-departmental publication *Time for Play*, which was a strategic approach to play across government departments (Department for Culture Media and Sport, 2006), and a recognition of the value of play for children through sport, for health, for education and within the community.

Explicit links between play and wellbeing were articulated within *The Children's Plan* (DCSF, 2007b), which set out comprehensive plans to make the UK the best place in the world for children and young people to grow up and to secure their wellbeing and health. Play was seen as a key way of achieving this, resulting in the creation of *The Play Strategy* (DCSF, 2008c). This detailed a vision for play until 2020 that valued children's right to play, the benefits of play and the need to develop spaces to play ranging from parks and green spaces to schools and children's centres. In the supporting evidence summary to *The Play Strategy*, the link with wellbeing was clearly stated: 'play is believed to provide the opportunity to develop a sense of wellbeing by allowing children to experience who they are or might be' (DCSF, 2008c, p 1). While wellbeing was not defined, it is clear that there is a subjective view of children and their identities adopted.

As can be seen, therefore, play is not only a mode of being, as recognised by the UNCRC, but is also seen as a part of children's 'becoming'. Wellbeing, development and play are seen as inextricably linked and therefore bound up within education, especially in early years education. Historically, play has been seen as the only mode of education for young children (Dewey, 1933) and has underpinned early childhood programmes since the initial kindergarten developed by Frederick Froebel (1782–1852). Today, early years curriculum guidance across the UK emphasises play-based learning (DfES, 2007a ; WAG, 2008c; NCCA, 2009, Learning and Teaching Scotland, 2010). Within primary education, the place of play is not so secure, although there is a view that a play-based curriculum should be extended into the later years of schooling (Alexander, 2010).

What is play?

The previous discussion of play assumes that 'play' is a concept that is shared and understood by all who use it. However, as discussed in Chapter 2 in relation to the concept of 'wellbeing', this is not the case. Play is a social and cultural construct and a social practice (Wood, 2009) and, like wellbeing, there is much diversity to be explored within the concept. The linguistic diversity associated with wellbeing and exemplified by Ereaut and Whiting (2008) can also be applied to play, which can be used as a noun, verb, adverb or adjective (Moyles, 1994). This affects its meaning and usage and consequently results in virtually anything being construed as play: encompassing such diverse activities as daydreaming, hobbies, partying, performing, competitive sports, celebrations and festivals (Sutton-Smith, 1997).

Unlike wellbeing, however, play can be, and often is, construed in relation to its binary opposite: work. The roots of this binary construct lie with the Victorians and the puritan work ethic that saw work as good and play as evil (Cohen, 1993). This distinction is neither valid nor helpful and it can be argued that play can be work and some forms of work can be play (Schwartzman, 1982). In opposition to the 'work is good' and 'play is evil' dichotomy, play is often construed as being fun, free and involving choice. This presents new dilemmas as not all play is fun or free (Wood, 2010), and although choice is often implied, it is not always clear within play situations with whom the power of choice lies (Ryan, 2005; Ailwood, 2010).

Sutton-Smith (1997) argued that the diversities and ambiguities inherent within play affect how play can be defined. Within the play literature, there have been three distinct ways to define play: by category, by criteria or by a continuum (Howard, 2002). In terms of the theoretical accounts of wellbeing outlined in Chapter 2, these ways of defining play may be construed in the same way as the 'Objective List Theories' (OLTs) of wellbeing. With these definitions of play, the key underpinning principle is to itemise what constitutes play. A categorical definition was first proposed by Piaget (1951) who described a developmental structure of three types of play: practice games, symbolic games and games with rules. However, these categories have been criticised for their stage-like progression and on the grounds of not being inclusive of all types of play, for example, rough and tumble play. Criteria definitions propose that the presence of different criteria denote play or not play and lists have been proposed by Neumann (1971), Krasnor and Pepler (1980) and Rubin, Fein, and Vandenberg (1983), which include criteria such as freedom to choose, intrinsic motivation, pretending, fun and flexibility. Continuum definitions (Pellegrini, 1991) use these criteria on a continuum denoting more or less play. Obviously, these criteria are problematic: not all play is fun, nor does it necessarily involve pretending; and who holds the power over choice? What is apparent from these ways of defining play is that there is a lack of an agreed definition of play and the focus is on theorists or adults looking at the observable act of play – *adults* deciding what is *play* for *children*. Alternatively, it has been argued that play is too elusive to be defined (Moyles, 1989). While this is understandable, it does not provide a clear way forward in attempting to grapple with the complexities involved in understanding the concept of play.

In addition to this definitional challenge, the evidence base for the value of play for development, learning and wellbeing is limited (BERA, 2003; Lester and Russell, 2008; Smith, 2010b). Studies linking play with aspects of development generally show that free play, in particular, offers little in terms of cognitive challenge and contribution to development (eg Jowett and Sylva, 1986; Gura, 1992). There is some correlational evidence for the benefits of pretend play for theory of mind, language and creativity (see Smith, 2010b); but many studies linking play with cognitive development show methodological weaknesses and fail to isolate play from other forms of behaviour such as exploration (Smith and Whitney, 1987).

Curriculum guidance based on play states that the role of the practitioner is crucial in providing an environment that facilitates play, planning play experiences that build on children's spontaneous play and supporting children's play – utilising play as pedagogy. However, this also does not go unchallenged. While most practitioners agree with this and see this as their role, studies have repeatedly shown that practitioners are not comfortable with play, child-led activities and giving children choice (Bennett et al, 1997; Pascal, 1990). It has been shown that the main reason for this stems from the contested nature of play discussed earlier. Generally, practitioners are unclear in their understanding of play because of its diverse nature and the use of adult-led definitions of play and lack of evidence to support play-based practice. Consequently, this has implications for how they implement play in their practice and their own role within children's play (Howard, 2010; Howard and McInnes, 2010).

An alternative conceptualisation of play – playfulness

It has been argued that it is the internal, affective quality of play, or playfulness, that is important for wellbeing and development (Moyles, 1989; House, 2008), although we must also note the contested nature of all of these concepts. Dewey (1933) was the first theorist to argue that the construct of 'playfulness' was more important than play. Having a playful attitude is linked to the concept of freedom and this accords with the 'flow state' identified by Csikszentmihalyi (1988, 1990). Such freedom is characterised by internal affective qualities of pleasure, involvement and deep concentration. This playful attitude or state of mind affects the approach taken to an activity (Schwartzman, 1982) and is characterised by enthusiasm, motivation and willingness to engage (Moyles, 1989). Utilising a construct of playfulness is useful because it moves the debate away from the binary construct of play and work, as playfulness may encompass both play and work activities – an individual may take a playful attitude and approach to their work and experience positive affect. It has also been argued that many of the activities that are viewed as play actually lack playfulness (Youell, 2008). The concept of playfulness also moves the definitional debate away from adult interpretations of the observable act of play. Playfulness is instead concerned with internal feelings, which affect the attitude and approach taken to an activity. However, these motives and feelings are not accessible to the observer, and what looks like play to an observer may not feel like play to the player (Parham, 1996). A post-structural definition of play should, therefore, take into account the child's view of play and take place within the context of children's play (Howard, 2002; Goncu and Gaskins, 2007; Brooker and Edwards, 2010). By doing this, it should be possible to gain an insight into not just what play looks like, but also what it feels like to approach an activity as play. This then enables the separation of play – the observable act – from playfulness – the attitude or approach taken to an activity.

It has traditionally been thought that children do not differentiate between play and 'not-play' (Manning and Sharp, 1977), but a number of studies looking at children's views of play show that children can, and do, differentiate between the two (eg Karrby, 1989; Robson, 1993; Wing, 1995; Howard, 2002; Howard et al, 2006). Using a variety of methodologies, all of the studies have shown that children use cues to differentiate between play and not-play situations. The most recent studies have used an experimental methodology – the Activity Apperception Story Procedure (AASP) (Howard, 2002; Howard et al, 2006). This employs a game-like, photographic categorisation method whereby children sort photographs of their own educational environments into play and not-play. The photographs were paired according to cues, for example, children on the floor completing a puzzle, children at a table completing a puzzle (for an in-depth discussion of the procedure, see Howard, 2009). This methodology was based on the idea of perceiving cues from the environment and was derived from the ecological approach to perception and the theory of affordances (Gibson, 1979; Gibson and Pick, 2000). This theory proposes that what is perceived when looking at objects are not their dimensions or properties, but their affordances – what they can provide or offer. Affordances may be physical such as smooth surfaces affording cycling and running, or social and emotional affording emotional closeness during feeding time between a mother and infant (Kytta, 2002, 2004; Good, 2007). The affordances offered within a given situation are also embedded within the context and frame of reference of the situation; that is, affordances are constrained by what is happening, who is participating and previous experiences of similar situations.

From these studies, it has been shown that the cues children use to differentiate between play and not-play situations include: adult presence, space and constraint (where an activity takes place), and choice. Play situations tend to be ones where the adult is not present, take place on the floor and where the child has choice, as one child said: 'they're playing because they can choose, they've finished their work' (Howard, 2002, p 498). Not-play situations tend to be ones where the adult is present, occurs at a table and the child has little choice; as this child in Wing's (1995, p 236) study said, 'if you're playing, then you're not really doing anything sitting down'. Cues of fun and pretending are ambiguous. According to children, play activities are fun, but so are not-play activities, and activities do not have to include pretence to be considered play. This is in marked contrast to the adult definitions of play and justifies conceptualising play from children's perspectives. This echoes claims made about the importance of attending to children's voices and engaging them in constructive dialogue in Chapter 7. Children are also able to see play and not-play activities on a continuum, often stating that activities are 'a little bit working' or 'a little bit playing' (Wing, 1995, p 237). Furthermore, it has been shown that cue use is often dependent on experience or type of educational setting (Karrby, 1989; Howard, 2002). Cue use is generally more defined in settings that are more structured and teacher-directed, whereas children in more play-oriented settings tend to view more activities as play.

The use of these cues may also be explained in terms of their affordances. The cue of adult presence may be viewed as a social and emotional affordance. Studies have shown that teachers tend to take control away from children and reduce their participation in an activity (Linklater, 2006; Payler, 2007). Therefore, the cue of adult presence may be viewed as affording a lack of freedom, control and participation in activities. However, these affordances may be dependent upon how practitioners interact with children during their play activities. In settings where practitioners work alongside children participating in and co-constructing play activities, children may be less likely to use the cue of adult presence as a defining feature of play and not-play situations (Howard and McInnes, 2010). In these settings, the cue of adult presence may be seen to afford freedom, control and participation. Choice is a factor in intrinsic motivation (Cordova and Lepper, 1996), and even the illusion of choice has been shown to increase intrinsic motivation and learning (Swann and Pittman, 1977). Therefore, the cue of choice may be viewed as an emotional affordance affording children motivation and enthusiasm and enabling them to feel in control. The cue of space and constraint may be viewed as a physical affordance. An activity taking place on the floor affords movement and physical activity, which in turn has been shown to aid concentration and cognitive performance (Pellegrini and Bohn, 2005).

The affordances just described are all features of playfulness: freedom, control and motivation. White (2011, p 131) argued that 'education for well-being' is 'built around acquiring personal qualities (dispositions) on the one hand and understanding on the other'. He proposed that dispositions were the most important and focused on the characteristics of the becoming child – arguably, a playful disposition lays the groundwork for education and wellbeing. Conceptualising play from children's perspectives, based on their experiences and contexts, allows the separation of play from playfulness and potentially enables practitioners to understand play more clearly. There is also the potential to provide evidence to link playfulness with learning and wellbeing, further supporting practitioners in their attempts to maximise play in the classroom.

The discussion will now focus on evidence from my recent PhD project, which utilised a concept of playfulness based on children's cues to show that children displayed enhanced performance and behaviours conducive to learning when practising a task under playful rather than formal practice conditions. The potential of my findings for a reconceptualised idea of wellbeing is discussed later in the chapter.

Playfulness and learning

My recent PhD utilised the cues children use to define play and not-play situations to look at the links between playfulness and learning (McInnes, 2010). Building on the work of Thomas, Howard and Miles (2006), some of the cues children identify and use to differentiate play and not-play situations were manipulated under experimental conditions to create playful (adult proximal, on the floor, choice) and formal (adult present, at a table, no choice) practice conditions. Children from different types of early years settings (reception class in an infant school, reception class in a primary school and a nursery school) were allocated to one of the practice conditions. The children carried out a familiar problem-solving task during a four-stage procedure: pre-test, practice, post-test and delayed post-test.

Results have shown that children in playful practice conditions tend to perform and behave differently to children in formal practice conditions (McInnes et al, 2009). Children in playful practice conditions usually exhibited significantly improved performance in time taken to complete the task than children in formal practice conditions. In fact, children in these latter practice conditions actually showed decreased performance at post-test stage, although they usually showed improvement by the delayed post-test. Children in playful practice conditions also showed greater involvement in the activity as measured by the Leuven Involvement Scale (Laevers et al, 1994). They tended to display behaviours argued to be more conducive to learning such as leaning towards the puzzle, smiling and greater focus on the activity. In addition, they employed more purposeful problem-solving behaviours using less repetitive behaviours and tried out new ways to solve the problem. As one child in a playful practice condition stated, "I will check if I can do it, but if I can't I will practise". Children in playful practice conditions were also more likely to rate the practice condition as 'play', with children making comments such as, "it was fun, it was play". Whereas children in the formal practice conditions made comments such as, "it was hard work, not play". These findings indicate that children tended to view the playful practice conditions as play-like, which resulted in improved performance and a behavioural approach that is more playful.

The cue of adult presence was particularly important, and so I conducted a series of studies to investigate the role of the adult in more detail. In these studies, four practice conditions were employed: playful and formal practice conditions as before, and then a playful practice condition with the adult present, and a formal practice condition with the adult proximal. The same four-stage procedure was employed using familiar problem-solving tasks with children from two different early years settings. Results from these studies have shown that children assigned to the practice conditions with the adult proximal to the task, rather than present, tended to exhibit superior performance on the problem-solving task. Generally, these children also showed higher levels of involvement during the task and behaviours associated with increased motivation, and rated the practice condition as play (McInnes et al, 2010).

Throughout the studies, the cue of adult presence was used differently by children in different settings. Therefore, the final study in the series looked at how the cue of adult presence might develop in the early years setting by comparing adult–child interactions between children in one setting who tended to use the cue of adult presence to define play and not-play situations and children in another setting who generally did not. Adult–child interactions were compared across different types of activities, groupings and curriculum areas. Results showed that adult–child interactions differed across the children in the different settings (McInnes, 2010). In the setting where children used the cue of adult presence to differentiate between play and not-play activities, practitioners were more likely to initiate interactions with children and to ask more closed and less open questions. In addition, practitioners used language which indicated that control and choice in interactions and activities resided with the adult rather than the child such as "I want you to build something". Practitioners also engaged in less problem-solving with children using sustained shared thinking (Siraj-Blatchford et al, 2002) and used less playful language. In the setting where children did not use the cue of adult presence, initiation of interactions was more balanced between children and adults and more open questions were asked such as "what would you like to choose?" In addition, there was more engagement in problem-solving activities using sustained shared thinking and more use of playful language by practitioners with children.

Furthermore, these differences appeared to be underpinned by differences in understanding about play and its links with learning and development (McInnes, 2010). In the setting where children generally did not use the cue of adult presence to differentiate between play and not-play activities, practitioners seemed more secure and confident in their understanding of play, their role in children's play and how this should be implemented in practice. As one practitioner noted, "sometimes I play alongside them, sometimes they don't want me beside them and they move away, that's okay". In the setting where children tended to use the cue of adult presence, practitioners seemed less secure in their understanding of play, their role in children's play and how this should be implemented in practice. In this setting, practitioners were more likely to focus their attention on adult-led teaching activities and participate less in child-led play activities as exemplified by this practitioner, "we don't plan for play we plan for what we want them to get out of an activity".

Overall, the findings support a conceptualisation of playfulness based on children's cues, which they are able to voice and develop through experience. Using this concept enables practitioners to focus on playfulness, the approach and attitude taken to an activity, rather than play, the observable act. As has been shown, manipulating the cues children use to differentiate between play and not-play activities results in differences in performance and behaviours conducive to learning. Furthermore, the cue of adult presence has been shown to be critical in this conceptualisation and that how practitioners interact with children affects how this cue is used. In turn, how practitioners understand play impacts on their interactions with children.

Playfulness and wellbeing

So far, the discussion has argued for a concept of playfulness that utilises children's rather than adults' voices. It has identified how this concept is concerned with a playful attitude and approach to a task, rather that the observable act of play itself. It has also identified how playfulness as an attitude and approach to a task may be applicable to many situations, be they work or play. In addition, it is argued that playfulness is applicable to children 'being' in terms of their behaviour and their 'becoming' in terms of their development. Using the theory of affordances, it has also been suggested that utilising the cues children generally use to differentiate between play and not-play activities may result in feelings of freedom, control, participation, motivation, enthusiasm, choice and action. However, this may be dependent upon how adults interact with children as adults need to have respect for children's voices, listen to them and allow them to have choice.

The conceptualisation of wellbeing is problematic. However, taking the same standpoint as the conceptualisation of playfulness and listening to children's voices, an understanding of wellbeing may be taken that has parallels with playfulness. There has been limited work on children's concepts of wellbeing, especially very young children. However, research conducted with older children on their understandings of wellbeing (Fattore et al, 2007) indicated that they used words such as choice, control, freedom, a positive sense of self and a good physical environment to conceptualise wellbeing. These words have resonance with the cues children used to define play and not-play activities and with the evidence from their observed attitude and approach taken to a task when they are in situations that they define as playful.

Playfulness and wellbeing within education

From the research cited earlier, it has been shown that a pedagogic approach based on a construct of playfulness has the potential to maximise behaviours that facilitate learning and possibly wellbeing. It is hypothesised that this approach is applicable to a range of activities, whether they are defined as work or play and across all age phases of education. Therefore, playfulness has relevance within the classroom as well as outside of it, and is not just confined to playtimes.

The cues children identify to differentiate between play and not-play activities can be utilised within a school situation. Giving children choice in activities and in materials should enable feelings of motivation, enthusiasm and control, which may facilitate learning and possibly wellbeing. In an early years classroom, children may be given choice over which activities they engage in. They may also be given choice as to the materials they use within a given activity. In one early years classroom in my study, children were given choice as to whether to take part in adult-led group activity or not, and adults frequently used the word 'choosing' with children, thereby making choice explicit for children. In a primary school, children in years three to six were expected to undertake a project over three weeks. Children were able to choose the project within a given topic, one example being a book for younger children. Children could choose what to do, how to do it and organise themselves to complete it. Children excitedly engaged with the topic, were enthusiastic and motivated, and high-quality work was produced.

The environment in which children are taught is important for enabling feelings of playfulness and wellbeing. Children defined play activities as ones that occur on the floor, whereas not-play activities occur at a table and having freedom to move is conducive to concentration and feelings of control. Therefore, teachers need to consider the physical layout of the environment and it is clear that feelings and experiences of wellbeing are *contextual*. In one early years classroom studied, more activities were available on the floor and children were allowed to stand at tables as well as sit. This arguably enabled children to view more activities 'as play' and to take a more playful approach, as evidenced by children kneeling over activities completely engrossed in what they were doing. In a primary classroom, a workshop arrangement enabled children to move around as they selected resources and carried out their activity.

The teacher–pupil relationship seems to be critical in enabling children to feel playful. Therefore, teachers need to consider their behaviour in relation to children's views of play. They need to take their lead from children and co-construct activities with them, this should enable children to view more activities as play and take a more playful approach, thereby affording them greater freedom to be in control. For example, in the early years, this means co-constructing play activities with children (Howard and McInnes, 2010). This may include playing alongside, and with, children in their self-chosen play activities. In the primary classroom, this might result in playful ways of engaging with children by using playful language and engaging in meaningful problem-solving together.

Conclusion

'Play', like 'wellbeing', is a highly challenged and contested concept. Traditional conceptualisations are based on adult views of the observable act of play and this has been shown to be problematic in terms of evidencing the benefits of play and for practitioners' understandings and practice in relation to play. This chapter has attempted to deconstruct the model of play based on adult perceptions and offer an alternative, post-structuralist conceptualisation of playfulness based on children's perceptions of play, which empowers children. Recent research indicates that children identify and use cues in the environment to define play and not-play situations and that this enables play, the act, to be differentiated from playfulness, the approach and attitude taken to an activity. The cues children use afford children greater freedom, control, participation, motivation and movement, which arguably have the potential to maximise learning and wellbeing – if we take the view that wellbeing is *subjectively experienced, contextual* and *relational*.

The role of adults in facilitating playful activity is central to this discussion as they could consider their own playful behaviour and co-construct play activities with children that then facilitate a more playful approach and attitude to be taken. In this way, parallels may be made between children's conceptualisations of playfulness and wellbeing, which allows for playful expressions of wellbeing.

Note
[1] McInnes, K. (2010) 'The Role of Playful Practice for Learning in the Early Years', unpublished PhD dissertation, University of Glamorgan.

CHAPTER 10

'A golden thread' – children's rights and their contribution to wellbeing discourses

By Margaret Boushel

Introduction

This chapter further develops Chapter 9 in that it recognises the importance of children developing personal dispositions and attitudes and the right and opportunities to express their agency, autonomy, choices and concerns. It explores the potential for rights-based perspectives to contribute to discourses on child wellbeing. There are several reasons why this might be a fruitful line of enquiry. A rights-based perspective, because of its focus on contexts, entitlements and relationships, may serve to broaden the focus of wellbeing theories to include greater attention to the 'social body' and the 'body politic' (Scheper-Hughes and Lock, 1987). The embodied nature of wellbeing through this multidimensional approach to bodies will be further explored here. I will argue that attention to a theorised and well-articulated notion of children's rights is an essential element of a holistic discourse of emotional and social wellbeing.

The chapter begins by introducing the concept of rights and considering the attention to children's rights in recent UK legislation and policy and its impact in school settings. This is followed by a brief examination of approaches taken to children's rights in the wellbeing literature. The debates within children's rights discourses in relation to some key concepts – 'rights', 'generation' and 'capacity' – are then examined with reference to empirical research, and their potential contribution to key concepts of children's social and emotional wellbeing is considered.

Two research studies in particular will be drawn on to illustrate the discussion. One is an evaluation of the Rights Respecting Schools Award project (Sebba and Robinson, 2010),[1] the other is based on my PhD study, which explored how adults working in education and other child welfare settings made sense of children's rights and how this impacted on their approach to practice (Boushel, forthcoming).[2] For this reason, as in the previous chapter, this one is written using the first-person singular pronoun.

Legal and moral definitions of 'rights'

'Rights' are usually defined as claims of entitlement against a person or organisation. They are often divided into two types: legal and moral. Legal rights are entitlements enforceable within existing law in a specific jurisdiction. Moral rights are rights claimed under ethical principles, which may or may not be legally enforceable. The development of rights-based theories is often associated with Western philosophy, but they are a common feature of many philosophical and religious traditions.

'Human rights' refer to moral rights underpinned by a broad universal consensus as 'necessary for the person or group to be able to achieve their full humanity, in common with others' (Ife, 2001, pp 10–11). Contested and constructed 'through an ongoing dialogue about what should constitute a common humanity' (Ife, 2001, p 6) and drawing on emerging knowledge from across the social, physical and life sciences, they provide general principles that guide our obligations towards one another. Many commentators identify three generations of human rights. The first two categories to emerge were civil and political rights – developments of liberal political philosophy and concerned with individual freedom of conscience, access to justice and rights to participation in political processes – the third, social rights, came later, arising from the development of social democracy and socialism and identifying positive rights related to how economic and social resources should be distributed. More recently, concepts of social and political rights have been extended to include global issues such as the environment, anti-colonialism and peace (Ife, 2001).

Acknowledgement of the human rights of children has taken a different trajectory, with social rights being the first to be recognised and children's civil and political rights still contested and underdeveloped (Boushel, 2000; Percy-Smith and Thomas, 2010; Quennerstedt, 2010). This is due at least in part to contested understandings of childhood and attitudes to adult power. As a result, the history of children's rights in the UK is a history of struggle, initiated at various times by philanthropists and by children and those working with them, through direct action, creative legal challenges to laws designed with adults in mind and, recently, through pressure on the UK government from

European and international bodies. Children's experiences in schools are the focus of many of these struggles.

Children's rights in the UK – the legal, political and policy context

The UK does not have a written constitution setting out aspirations and rights for its citizens. Instead, citizens' legal rights are enshrined on a piecemeal basis in individual pieces of legislation and in the case-by-case decisions of common law. The Human Rights Act 1998 (HRA, 1998) is the most comprehensive legislation in relation to rights in the UK. It obliges UK courts to interpret UK legislation in compliance with the European Convention on Human Rights (ECHR) (CE, 1950), which has had a significant influence on UK legal judgments about children's rights (Fortin, 2005; Lyon, 2007a), for example, ensuring that young people continue to receive confidential contraceptive and sexual advice and banning the indiscriminate use of 'stop and search' police powers.[3] In addition to the HRA, specific legislation has had an impact on children's rights, such as improved anti-discrimination laws and, in a negative way, the Anti-Social Behaviour Act 2003, which gave police power to curtail freedom of movement and assembly.

The United Nations Convention on the Rights of the Child (UNCRC) (UN, 1990) is not, of itself, legally enforceable, although increasingly it is drawn on in reaching judicial judgements. Its strength lies in its success in codifying wide-ranging universal aspirations about the rights and needs of children and using these as a basis for regularly monitoring worldwide public state accountability. In its most recent review of UK implementation, the UN committee pointed to the need to improve children's rights in several areas including increased attention to child poverty, mental health services, bullying in schools and by addressing the 'low' level of rights awareness among children, parents and the child welfare workforce (UN, 2008, p 5).

There is no systematic approach to children's rights in the UK and increasing differences in the approach of the four UK 'nations'. Recent attempts to situate the Children Act 2004 – the legislation underpinning the English *Every Child Matters* (ECM) (DfES, 2004a) policy developments – within a rights-based framework and include a full ban on smacking were unsuccessful (*Hansard*, 2004). The Coalition government has not yet declared its policy on either ECM or children's rights. It is perhaps not surprising, therefore, that in my study I found that professionals across a range of education and welfare settings shared no common understanding of children's rights. For two thirds, ECM policy seemed to function as their 'objective list' in this area.

Within schools, attention to pupil or student 'voice' has begun to reshape children's participatory rights.[4] To date, meaningful participation is variable, with limited impact on key aspects of school life such as the curriculum and relationships between pupils and teachers (Whitty and Wisby, 2007).

By 2010, 1,600 primary and secondary schools throughout the UK had registered with the Rights Respecting Schools Award (RRSA) pilot project, funded by the Department for Children, Schools and Families (DCSF) and developed by UNICEF UK. The RRSA project 'takes a whole-school approach to children's rights, using the UNCRC as a "values framework"' (UNICEF, 2010). The project evaluation found that 'for the majority ... the RRSA has had a significant and positive influence on the school ethos, relationships, inclusivity, understanding of the wider world and the well-being of the school community, according to the adults and young people in the evaluation' (Sebba and Robinson, 2010, p 13).

In almost all schools evaluated, staff and pupils reported experiencing 'a strong sense of belonging' and 'a strong finding to emerge was how positively pupils talked about their school life' (Sebba and Robinson, 2010, pp 19, 37). Indeed, 'for some school communities, there is strong evidence that it has been a life-changing experience' (Sebba and Robinson, 2010, p 13). The evaluation reported a 'clear overlap' between the wellbeing dimensions in the *Innocenti* overview (UNICEF, 2007) 'and the indicators of success in the RRS' (Sebba and Robinson, 2010, p 37).

So, despite political ambivalence and lack of consistency, there is evidence to suggest that where a rights-based approach has been developed in a holistic way, children's relationships and self-reported happiness have improved. The next section will consider evidence of children and young people's views of rights-based approaches and the rights they consider important in their lives before exploring some of the challenges presented by rights-based perspectives.

Children and young people's views on rights

In a fascinating oral history of working-class childhood and youth from 1889 to 1939, Stephen Humphries (1995) explored children's understandings of and reactions to perceived inequalities in their lives. Their concerns included aspects of the school syllabus that were viewed as hypocritical, class-biased or unfair, particularly religious instruction, support for imperialism and 'competitive individualism' (Humphries, 1995, p 52), coercive practices including corporal punishment, and structural issues like the timing of holidays and the school leaving age. Their reactions included disenchantment, disengagement and distrust, as well as energetic resistance through both individual and collective action. Humphries identified over a hundred strikes by pupils across the UK, lasting from a few weeks to many months.

One hundred years later, public protests by school pupils about the increased cost of university education provide a current example of young people's perceptions of their education rights and their willingness to engage with 'the political body' to assert their views. Consultations undertaken by the Children's Commissioners and others give a clear message about the high value children place on their civil and political rights and their views on the areas that need addressing in school settings. The most recent consultation (Chamberlain et al, 2011, p 9)[5] found that 'the most important priorities for children and young people to improve their school life and education were preventing bullying and having good teachers'. In addition, 'only about one in seven children and young people felt that (long-term or permanent exclusions) were "always" used fairly', and 'a majority reported that they would like to be involved' in choosing new teachers, but only about one fifth reported currently being involved in this area (Chamberlain, 2011, p 8). 'Having a say' in the decisions made about them was the single most important issue to children in Northern Ireland and Scotland (Kilkelly et al, 2005; DCSF, 2007c) and this echoes the sentiments of the Australian study reported in Chapter 7 (Graham and Fitzgerald, 2010). Age restrictions, negative attitudes towards children and young people, and safety from violence and crime were issues for English children (DCSF, 2007c).

In a report for the UN committee prepared by children and young people supported by the Children's Rights Alliance for England,[6] nearly half thought bullying was a problem in their schools, too much schoolwork and insufficient time to relax were issues for 40%, and lack of support for underachieving pupils and lack of privacy were also mentioned (CRAE, 2008). They too wanted more involvement in decision-making in all aspects of school life, action to stop bullying, greater respect and fairer treatment by teachers. Children from discriminated-against groups were more likely to experience bullying and disrespect (CRAE, 2008, p 55).

In 2010, the Children's Rights Director for England published two reports on the views of children living away from home in a variety of settings[7] and those in receipt of family support services. The first related to 'Rights and responsibilities' (OFSTED, 2010a). A large majority (70%) of the 1,834 contributors thought it a good idea to have rights and responsibilities written down. The main reasons given were that 'it was important to know what rights they have and what is expected of them'; it 'would help people to have their say and be listened to'; and it 'would help things become more equal and fair' (OFSTED, 2010a, p 8). Within the top 10 rights identified were 'not being discriminated against', 'not being treated or punished in a way that is cruel or meant to make me feel bad about myself', 'to have privacy' and 'not to be bullied' (OFSTED, 2010a, p 15). The second report was about 'Fairness and unfairness'. The 268 children who contributed interpreted 'fairness' as 'getting your rights, having a say and being listened to' (OFSTED, 2010a, p 7) and they 'feel more angry and upset about being treated unfairly than almost anything else we have ever asked them about over the nine years we have been consulting children' (OFSTED, 2010b, p 4).

A Canadian study (Raby, 2008) connected rights discourses with a sense of agency. In a study of pupils' participation in school rule-making, it found that the perspective children (and by implication their schools) take to children's rights has implications for their attempts to explore and take action on issues of concern to them – affecting both their 'functionings' and their 'capabilities' (Sen, 1985): 'it was when they identified themselves as social actors and rights holders in the present that they were most able to challenge school rules they found to be unfair' (Raby, 2008, p 77).

Conversely, Whitty and Wisby (2007, p 91) found that young people, 'often because they are simply not used to being asked for their views ... can be unsure about their right to have a voice', with potentially severe consequences for their sense of agency. Indeed, as a recent overview of consultations with children found: 'If a child or young person believes that they have no rights to act or voice, and no channels to express their views, they feel frustrated about how the workforce works with them and believe they can do nothing about it' (DCSF, 2008a).

Taken together, these reports powerfully attest to the importance of rights-based perspectives in discourses around wellbeing. Yet it is noticeable how rarely UK reports of consultations with children use rights-based language. Instead, terms such as 'views' and 'wishes' dominate. It is unclear whether this reflects unacknowledged cultural ambivalence with this discourse or a conscious decision by some or all of those involved.

Rights-based theories in wellbeing discourses

Given their potential contribution, rights-based theories have received limited attention in discourses of children's wellbeing. The most recent systematic review of the literature on children's wellbeing, focusing on the period from 1991 to 1999, made no mention of children's rights (Pollard and Lee, 2003). Statham and Chase, authors of a short overview of childhood wellbeing literature (DCSF, 2008b), primarily refer to an article by Morrow and Mayall (2009) to substantiate their view that a children's rights perspective within wellbeing initiatives is likely to 'focus more on factors which provide opportunities and help them reach aspirations, and which focus on the quality of their lives now rather than just in the future' (DCSF, 2008b, p 5), whereas initiatives based on a developmental perspective are 'more likely to adopt measures associated with deficits, such as poverty, ignorance, and physical illness', which they seem to distinguish from rights-based approaches.

The focus of the Morrow and Mayall article is on attempts to measure children's wellbeing using secondary data sets. Their concerns are about the adequacy of the measures used and the 'deficit lens', which they argue is often employed. In a wide-ranging discussion of the UNICEF *Innocenti* report (UNICEF, 2007) , they show how the media hype following the report's publication reinforced negative cultural constructions of children and young people. They pointed out that children and young people 'have very clear ideas about how they are represented' and that their portrayal 'as "thugs" and "yobs" and a group to be feared directly impacts on [them] and contributes to making them feel unhappy and unhealthy' (11 Million, 2008, p 7, cited in Morrow and Mayall, 2009, p 226). They argued that childhood cannot be decontextualised and 'disconnected from adulthood' (Morrow and Mayall, 2009, p 226) and that cultural problems and processes need greater recognition in the development of wellbeing measures, so, for example, 'we need to hold a mirror up to adult worlds and see how they reflect back upon children' (Morrow and Mayall, 2009, p 226). Morrow and Mayall were critical of the individualistic nature of the wellbeing debates, asking whether it risks 'depoliticising children's lives': 'is the focus on well-being inherently individualistic and, thus, is it a way of NOT talking about welfare and responsibilities of governments towards children?' (2009, p 221, emphasis in original).

Nick Axford (2008) takes a very different view. His main interest is in arriving at measures of wellbeing that can be used to identify children who need additional state support – a deficit model. He identified rights as one of five wellbeing domains (the others being need, poverty, Quality of Life [QoL] and social exclusion), but is wary of rights-based perspectives. Rights-based measures, he posits, 'arguably betray a fundamentally negative view of human nature' (Axford, 2008, p 143). His criticisms seem to be based on a predominantly legalistic interpretation of rights-based practice, where, he argued, 'respect for due process ... may take precedence over rectifying deficits of care and meeting client's needs' (Axford, 2008, p 162). In his analysis of case records, he takes account only of 'serious infringements' of children's rights to provision, protection and participation, which can be identified, he believes, using objective measures (Axford, 2008, p 36). He found in the records examined that 'the child's perspective is glaring by its omission' (Axford, 2008, p 203), but did not see this as a 'serious infringement'. Axford's approach seems in sharp contrast to the perspective taken by the RRSA project.

Studies focused on children's perceptions of wellbeing imply that children tend not to use the term 'rights' when discussing this topic. There are no direct references to children's rights in a large Australian study undertaken by Fattore and his colleagues to explore with children their understandings of wellbeing (Fattore et al, 2007), nor in the DCSF-funded study on childhood wellbeing (DCSF, 2008b), although sociological theories related to concepts of generation and power are central to the research design and analysis of the former. What comes across strongly from both of these studies and from others is the importance children and young people attach to being treated with respect and to having a sense of agency – fundamental elements of human rights discourses. For example, Fattore et al found that children's concepts of wellbeing included feeling safe, feeling valued, the capacity to 'act morally' and 'to act freely and to make choices and exert influence in everyday situations' (2007, p 18), adding that 'fundamental to what activities associated with well-being are about is having power and not feeling powerless'(2007, p 20).

Children's rights – theoretical and professional challenges

Children present particular theoretical challenges to 'rights' discourses because of culturally defined attitudes towards them and because of their varying and developing capacities. In exploring these challenges, a broad 'human rights' perspective is a helpful starting point. This invites us to question taken-for-granted perceptions of children and childhood. It also offers a moral reference point, drawing on ethical discourses but 'more outwardly focused' (Ife, 2001, p 105), and thus is particularly useful in revealing relationships of power.

Theories of critical social justice underpin human rights discourses. In a series of debates aptly entitled *Adding Insult to Injury*, the philosopher Nancy Fraser and others identified redistribution, recognition and rights to representation as essential dimensions of a critical theory of social justice sufficient to meet the theoretical challenges presented by an unequal, globalised world (Olson, 2008). Axel Honneth (1995) drew attention to the importance of *recognition*, a theory that sees social recognition as an essential aspect of human identity and the struggle for recognition as key to social change. Honneth defined recognition as having three elements – self-confidence, self-respect and self-esteem. The first he associated with positive regard, the second with entitlement to legal rights and the third with the public acknowledgement of a person's capacities. Recognition theory, discussed earlier (see Chapter 2), is making an important contribution to the analysis of children's participation in civil and political life (Graham and Fitzgerald, 2010).

Alexander and Pia Lara (1996), in a positive but critical analysis of Honneth's recognition theory, introduced the concept of 'mediations'. They point out that 'confidence (in seeking recognition), and its lack, can be articulated *culturally* and regulated *institutionally*' (Alexander and Pia Lara, 1996, p 4, emphasis in original) and they draw attention to the mediating role of 'surrounding cultural ideals' and 'surrounding social structures' (1996, p 4). These linked concepts of recognition and mediations are helpful in conceptualising the contribution of rights-based perspectives to theories of social and emotional wellbeing.

The nature and type of rights children can, or should, have is contested. In Figure 10.1, three intersecting axes, focusing on concepts of rights, generation and capacity, illustrate three central aspects of these contested areas. It is important to explore these in a critical, reflexive manner, for, as Fielding has discussed in relation to student voice, the way in which the concept of rights is understood will have an impact on responses to related questions about how, by whom, where and when rights are identified, acknowledged and acted upon (Fielding, 2001). These concepts and their relationship to discourses on wellbeing are considered in more detail later.

'Rights'

The first axis relates to concepts of 'rights', with 'justice' at one end of a continuum and a broader moral ethic of 'care' at the other. The concept of 'rights' provides a language with which to discuss, acknowledge and determine individual and universal legal and moral claims in relation to each other and the state. As far as children are concerned, the concept is contested in particular ways – hence the inverted commas.

Figure 10.1: Children's rights – theoretical and professional challenges

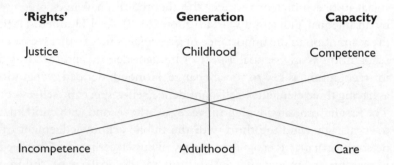

Interpreting 'justice' as based on concepts of universal human rights, such as are partly included in the UNCRC, uses the language of rights to serve a broad purpose. As the children's rights theorist Freeman (2007) points out, it 'make[s] visible what has for too long been suppressed' and 'lead[s] to different and new stories being heard in public'. In doing so it allows also for the promotion of the individual and collective demands of those whose rights are legally unacknowledged. Freeman also points out that rights, 'without remedies', are 'of symbolic importance, no more' (Freeman, 2007, pp 7–9). Theorists with a legalistic interpretation of justice agree. They argue that 'some of the economic, cultural and social rights' contained in the UNCRC 'are not rights at all but merely claims based on ideals regarding children's needs in a perfect world' (Fortin, 2005, p 12) and serve a limited purpose (Lyon, 2007b).

From a different perspective, some feminist theorists are wary of rights-based discourses because of concerns that such discourses undervalue interpersonal interactions motivated by a sense of care rather than justice. They suggest that an 'ethics of care' (Gilligan, 1982) is a more appropriate paradigm as it reflects the interconnectedness of human beings (Kleinig, 1982, cited in Freeman, 2007, p 11; see also Arneil, 2002), and this discussion is developed further in Chapter 11. This approach, however, can be criticised for its lack of attention to the power dynamics in the relationship between carer and cared for. This criticism can also be applied to the 'needs-based' discourses that so often dominate the child education and welfare fields. Indeed, the sociologist Martin Woodhead urged caution in the use of needs-based theories because 'needs' 'are not a quality of the child but reflect the views of stakeholders who believe they have the wisdom to shape children's futures' (Woodhead, 1997, p 80).

'Human rights' are moral rights seen as universally relevant, unconditional and inalienable. They do not depend on the rights-holder undertaking particular responsibilities before they can be invoked. As Howe and Covell (2010, p 93) point out, the UNCRC 'makes no mention of the responsibilities of children'. Rights do make claims on others (including children) who have the responsibility to respect them, but this is a separate issue. This confusion of rights and responsibilities is evident in much public policy and is 'a way of de-politicizing claims about rights' (Howe and Covell, 2010, p 93).

A further criticism of rights-based perspectives is that they reflect the increasing individualisation of minority world neoliberal societies by emphasising the autonomy of the child, often in tension with the rights of parents (Reynaert et al, 2009). The UNCRC manages some of these tensions by circumscribing children's rights in several ways. Article 3(1) sets out the overriding principle that 'the best interests of the child shall be the primary consideration' and explicitly identifies 'the special rights of parents and those in loco parentis'. This approach has been criticised, as has what is seen as the Convention's limited conceptualisation of children's citizenship rights (Woodhead, in Percy-Smith and Thomas, 2010). All of these criticisms have some merit and indicate the complexity of the concept and the potential for confusion within and between various discourses.

The RRSA project emphasises the universal and moral aspects of rights-based perspectives as they are enshrined in the UNCRC (Sebba and Robinson, 2010). This is clearly a major strength of the approach, which is seen as 'a way of being' in school and in relation to the wider world (Sebba and Robinson, 2010, p 4). It has encouraged recognition of potential inequalities, contributing to 'uniformly positive attitudes to diversity' and 'very positive attitudes of inclusivity' (Sebba and Robinson, 2010, p 5) reported by pupils from a range of minority ethnic backgrounds. Economically disadvantaged students 'reflect[ed] on their own difficulties in a more global context', which, it was observed, 'helps them feel as though they have something, they are not that badly off' (senior manager of a primary school, cited in Sebba and Robinson, 2010, p 24) and students' sense of agency in responding to abusive experiences increased: 'we always get some disclosures when we talk about rights at the beginning of the school year ... they feel empowered to tell someone and that is something that probably wouldn't have happened if it wasn't for this [RRSA]' (senior manager of a primary school, cited in Sebba and Robinson, 2010, p 20). The language of rights and responsibilities increased children's capacity to discuss complex concepts: 'It gives us a language, a vocabulary to talk about difficult things; a set of concepts that we can articulate' (Sebba and Robinson, 2010, p 18).

Interestingly, the RRSA evaluation found that over three years, 'there was an increasing emphasis on responsibilities as well as rights' by pupils interviewed (Sebba and Robinson, 2010, p 13). This finding was not explored, but it is noted that in a small number of schools, a focus on responsibilities led to more authoritarian practices. Howe and Cavell evaluated part of the RRSA project in a local authority that engaged all its schools in an adapted version of RRSA, called Rights, Respect and Responsibilities (Howe and Covell, 2010). Arguing that an emphasis on responsibilities is 'the miseducation of rights', their evidence suggested that 'when children's rights are respected by teachers and when children are provided with systematic opportunities to practice their rights, they come to realize the importance of respecting the rights of others' (Howe and Covell, 2010, p 101).

The findings of my study illustrated many of the conceptual challenges outlined earlier. I found little common understanding of rights or common source of 'rights' knowledge. Most participants rarely used rights-based language and only one third mentioned the UNCRC. For some, children's rights were 'a golden thread' underpinning their work, but many were confused about or suspicious of rights-based approaches. Some understood child protection as intrinsically different to 'children's rights', and an area where adult authority took precedence: "because if this is a neglect issue it doesn't matter whether they've got a right to or not there needs to be supervision". Some viewed participation rights as potentially self-seeking – "having their say and getting their way" – and likely to encroach on the rights of others; what Hill and colleagues in their review of children's participation have termed 'a zero-sum assumption' (Hill et al, 2004, p 82). The findings suggested that professionals were often confused about the relationship between rights and responsibilities and the role of both in children's lives. Several saw responsibility as a *quid pro quo* for rights. Many saw it as a necessary training for adulthood and a minority perceived it as a threat to a notion of a carefree childhood. The majority included some notion of responsibilities as part of the fabric of the relationships that supported family and community life. To explore further why concepts of 'rights' in relation to children might be so contentious and confused, I turn now to the concept of generation as it is understood and experienced in relation to children.

Generation

The second axis in Figure 10.1 relates to the concept of **generation**, with childhood/children at one end and adulthood/parents/teachers and so on at the other. In the literature on childhood, the concept of 'generation' is used primarily in a sociological sense, to identify childhood as a social construction, differentiated from adulthood, with children as active agents who are likely to have different perspectives and interests. This differentiation also makes possible the identification of children as a 'rights-bearing' group in relation to adults, a group whose experiences are framed both by generational differences and by adult power. It is this perspective on generation that underpins the UNCRC and which is of particular interest here.

Theorists who take a children's rights perspective (Holt, 1975; Federle, 1994; Archard, 2004; Valentine, 2004; Freeman, 2007) highlight generational power differentials and emphasise the need to create 'zones of mutual respect for power that limit the kind of things that we may do to one another' (Federle, 1994, p 366). Others, such as O'Neill, suggest that the focus should be on adults' obligations rather than children's entitlement, believing that children have 'interests' rather than rights (O'Neill, 1998, p 25). The latter resonates with perceptions of children as objects of concern, rather than subjects in their own right; perceptions that are changing but still evident in UK law and policy and in the attitudes of child welfare professionals. Indeed, adults' reluctance to reduce intergenerational inequalities is a consistent finding of many studies of school (Devine, 2000; Fielding, 2001; Lundy, 2007; Robinson and Taylor, 2007; Whitty and Wisby, 2007), child welfare and community settings (Hill et al, 2004).

When those working with children explicitly acknowledge children's rights and try to minimise generational imbalances of power, this can contribute to a sense of 'recognition' (Honneth, 1995). There is evidence of this in the RRSA evaluation. In many schools, the UNCRC was drawn on to reframe school cultures and structures, a 'way of being' (Honneth, 1995, p 4), leading, in the majority of schools, to positive rights–respecting relationships in classrooms that supported pupils' enjoyment of learning and their contribution to one another's learning. This was empowering for the children in the schools studied, especially 'the kids who have been brought up to think they have no rights' and those who lacked confidence as 'it helps the less confident to explain themselves (Sebba and Robinson, 2010, pp 16, 14). It helped develop their sense of agency 'as they understand that they have rights and the right to make choices about their lives' (Year 3 teacher, cited in Sebba and Robinson, 2010, p 16). Rights-based approaches also proved a useful mediator for both children and school staff in their negotiations with parents.

The RRSA was not always sufficient to shift intergenerational power imbalances. In two schools, it was interpreted 'as a mechanism for adults to manage children, with charters being quoted punitively and the language of rights being used by adults to exercise greater control' (Sebba and Robinson, 2010, p 22). Howe and Covell (2010, p 97) also found that in some schools staff were 'much more comfortable in teaching responsibilities' and 'more reluctant to educate children about their rights in a systematic and comprehensive way'. The RRSA evaluation suggests that for many staff, re-envisioning adult–child relationships is not an overnight development, but a journey of discovery: 'I'd say the last five years has been the most significant in my life, it's given me an opportunity to re-evaluate how I relate to young people, and probably how I run my own life to an extent' (secondary school teacher, cited in Howe and Covell, 2010, p 14).

In my research study, the majority of participants identified children as a rights-bearing group, but, for most, attention to imbalances of power between generations was limited. The evidence suggested that many did not actively involve children in decision-making. Children's views were explicitly recorded in only one third of cases. Some participants expressed concern that rights-based language would increase intergenerational conflict and reduce parents' engagement: "most people are wrestling with that, parent's rights, keeping parents happy" (headteacher). This fear, or unwillingness, to change the balance of power is often linked with a belief in adults' capacity to use power more wisely and cited as reasons for the continuance of intergenerational inequalities on such a large scale (Lundy, 2007; Robinson and Taylor, 2007). Therefore, it is to the concept of 'capacity' that I now turn.

Capacity

The third axis in Figure 10.1 focuses on the concept of **capacity**. On the one hand, capacity determines a person's ability to stay safe and feed and care for themselves – the focus of social rights. Perceptions of capacity are used to determine a child's civic and political rights, the more usual and controversial sense in which it is discussed in the literature (Reynaert et al, 2009).

A rights-based perspective encourages the maximisation of children's participation in all aspects of their lives without ignoring rights to protection from abuse and harm, but there are significant differences between theorists in how children's capacity is conceived and should be treated . Federle (1994, p 344) argued that 'capacity remains central to rights talk because it advantages powerful elites' and that concepts of rights should focus on redressing power imbalances, regardless of capacity. Others see children's capacity as relevant in the exercise of rights, but differ on how it is conceived and assessed. For example, Eekelaar drew on developmental psychology and described society's task as 'bring[ing] a child to the threshold of adulthood with the maximum opportunities to form and pursue life-goals which reflect as closely as possible an autonomous choice' , what he calls 'dynamic self-determinism' (Eekelaar, 1994, p 53). From a more sociological perspective, others understand children, and adults, both as 'beings' and as 'becomings' with related and variable competences that should be recognised. For both Lee and Cross, these include the knowledge and experiences of children and adults as service-givers as well as service-receivers (Cross, 2011; Lee, 2001).

The unmet demands of UK children and young people for greater participatory rights suggest, among other things, that our attitudes to children's capacities need re-examination. Cross-cultural (and some UK) studies illustrate the diversity in children's experiences and draw attention to the impact of context and culture on children's perceived and achieved competence (Beauchamp and Childress, 2001, in Freeman, 2007; Alderson et al, 2006; Percy-Smith and Thomas, 2010). Meaningful participation has been shown to increase social, emotional and practical competences by encouraging a sense of belonging, expanding skills and experiences, providing opportunities to make new friends, increasing self-confidence, and 'build[ing] a sense of their own agency' (Fitzgerald et al, 2010, p 302), all important for a sense of wellbeing. Conversely, initiatives that merely pay lip service to children's participation encourage disengagement and frustration (Hill et al, 2004).

The RRSA evaluation noted that 'pupils' participation in school life had increased since the introduction of the RRSA (Sebba and Robinson, 2010, p 28) over the three years of the evaluation, but their opportunities for involvement in central issues such as teaching appointments and the evaluation of teaching and learning were still limited in many schools, which may at least in part be a comment on beliefs about their capacity. In my study, most participants made a link between children's competence (as perceived by adults) and their participatory rights using age and intellectual development as the most usual markers. Many frequently expressed concerns about the perceived dangers of overestimating children's emotional capacity to be involved in decisions affecting their lives.

Conclusion

The evidence reviewed here shows that 'rights' is a contested concept and that the meanings applied to it in particular situations need exploration, which indeed may be an aspect of its usefulness. Rights are 'a matter for moral reasoning and for the application of values' (Ife, 2001, p 48) and in relation to discourses around children's social and emotional wellbeing, it can be argued that rights-based perspectives provide an essential lens on the structures, processes and relationships that support and govern children's lives. The evidence considered reminds us that as far as children's 'social body' and 'political body' are concerned, we live in an adult-dominated and individualistic culture in which the concept of 'rights' is easily separated from its connection with moral and universal codes, and where children's rights are frequently seen as threatening to adult order, a danger to children themselves or, as Lee (2005) suggests, an uncomfortable challenge to familiar notions of attachment. However, although a causal link cannot be assumed, at an operational level, the RRSA evaluation suggests that rights-based approaches situated within a universally acknowledged ethical code and used as a framework for school behaviours and relationships make a positive contribution to children's happiness, self-esteem and sense of agency.

The chapter draws attention to some overlapping and intersecting elements in the concepts and discourses around children's rights and children's wellbeing, which I suggest can help to illuminate and strengthen the contribution of these elements to both discourses. The most obvious is the relevance of recognition theory. The RRSA evaluation illustrated how the language of rights and the ethical basis of the UNCRC 'guide for living' may make transparent universal mutual obligations and support Aristotelian ideas of living well and virtuously. The universal nature of a rights-based code provides conceptual 'spaces' that encourage reflection, awareness and understanding about the social and political 'body' and the possibility of including this understanding in defining the 'self' and group (Scheper-Hughes and Lock, 1987). In doing so, it encourages attention to the social relationships and community aspects of Konu and Rimpela's (2002) model of wellbeing. Its potential to underpin collective activity and claims-making merits further attention.

A rights-based perspective adds other dimensions implied, but not made explicit, in wellbeing discourses. In particular, it addresses issues of power and challenges taken-for-granted perceptions of adult roles and authority. It takes as given children's entitlement to participate in social and civic society and can challenge unexplored perceptions of children's capacity and adult responsibilities. It has the potential to lead to new understandings and initiatives as children reconceptualise 'rights': perhaps challenging the boundaries of that 'intermediary space' between home and public spheres that is the school, and their relationship to it (Cockburn, 2007).

Alexander and Pia Lara (1996) draw attention to the potential that contexts and behaviours have in contributing to the recognition of rights. Publicly acknowledging and modelling rights-based structures and relationships can act as positive 'mediations' and encourage exploration of the concepts of justice, responsibility and entitlement. This in turn seems to strengthen children's sense of self and others and their confidence in drawing on rights-based theories to take action in their own lives. Helpful approaches may include: critically challenging our own understandings of adult power and children's rights and capacity; learning from and working with children to create structures and relationships in which rights-based ethical codes are valued and renewed; modelling rights-respecting language, behaviours and relationships; creating opportunities to support children in expanding their capacities; and challenging negative and disempowering depictions of children and childhood.

It would be foolish to underestimate the challenge of effective engagement with rights-based discourses in education and welfare settings. The challenges faced by staff in developing rights-based approaches identified in the RRSA evaluation are borne out by other studies in the education and child welfare fields (Maguire and Marshall, 1999; Alderson, 2002, p 1; Howe and Covell, 2010). There is also the danger that rights-based discourses will be hijacked by forces inside and outside the school setting in the pursuit of school and organisational performance targets, or confined to the realms of 'citizenship' or Personal Health and Social Education classes; that they will be poorly implemented; or, for other reasons, that they will not achieve their potential to encourage reflection and transformation (Robinson and Taylor, 2007). My PhD study found that a common language and understanding of children's rights among child welfare professionals cannot be assumed and opportunities for professionals to explore the concept are limited. Nevertheless, rising to these challenges and developing more egalitarian and respectful learning contexts and relationships may have considerable benefits for children and for all of us: not least because the evidence suggests such contexts may be more creative and enjoyable.

Notes

[1] The evaluation was undertaken over three years through annual visits to 12 schools, plus once-off visits to a further 19 schools using a combination of focus groups with pupils identified by a purposeful sample of schools, interviews with staff and analysis of data provided by the schools.

[2] The study drew on interviews with 39 professionals and para-professionals working with children in the 5–13 age range and using the *Every Child Matters* Common Assessment Framework (CAF) processes in one Children's Trust area. In addition, CAF records for 30 children were tracked for one year. Using focus groups, children and parents who had used interprofessional services helped frame the research and professionals, para-professionals, parents and children commented on initial findings.

[3] See http://www.crae.org.uk/rights/hra.html

[4] In the past couple of years, three education journals have devoted special issues to the topic, with many examples of school-based projects.

[5] Reference to a survey of nearly 2,000 children aged eight to 17 undertaken by the National Foundation for Educational Research for the Children's Commissioner for England. Available at: www.childrenscommissioner.gov. uk/content/press_release/content_397

[6] An online survey was completed by 1362 children and young people and a further 346 children and young people (from groups identified in the 2002 UN report as needing further protection of their rights, including gay and lesbian, black and minority ethnic, traveller, looked-after children, and children and young people with additional needs) took part in focus group interviews.

[7] For example, boarding schools, residential special schools, further education colleges, children looked after by the state.

CHAPTER 11

Professionals supporting wellbeing in schools

Introduction

This chapter considers concepts of care and support and the role of adults in providing for the social and emotional needs of children in schools: who they might be and how they can contribute to a reconceptualised notion of children and young people's wellbeing that foregrounds subjective understandings and the importance of relationships. In particular, we challenge notions of support for children with special educational needs (SEN) and disabilities, as well as for all children and young people, and this builds on the critique of inclusion in Chapter 6. There are, however, some general messages here for how all professionals in schools could support *all* children's social and emotional wellbeing.

In the same way as we have challenged wellbeing and its conceptual basis, we also need to ask what does support (for learning, wellbeing etc) look like and how can we theorise this? That is, how can adults impact upon children's experiences in schools and how can these be understood? We write this from the belief that 'social support is something you do, not something you give' (Taylor et al, 1998, p 1) and illustrate this with data obtained with school teachers and teaching and learning support staff, which challenges policy and occupational standards that seek to normalise the practice of professionals in schools.

The next section begins with a Foucauldian deconstruction of the concepts of 'care' and 'support', which while drawn from his analysis of medical practices, has resonance for this discussion of wellbeing support.

Care and support

'Care' and 'support', like 'wellbeing', are concepts that serve a function to name a phenomenon or problem. Linguistically, both care and support are nominalisations (noun forms derived from verbs), which provide objective ontologies of what may be presumed as something you can *give*. Can we negate these verbs? To 'uncare'? To 'unsupport'?

These are grammatically unacceptable forms, in much the way we argue 'ill-being' as not functioning in the English language; but if we create adjectives (uncaring, unsupported), then these reflect states of subjects and objects. Indeed, if we revert to verb formulations of to care and to support, then the transitive verbs reflect activities (with human subjects and human objects): to care and to support is something we *do*. Such actions are reflective and reflexive.

To understand the propositions here, we start with nominalisations, as defining the concept as an object allows it to be understood through a set of characteristics that can be taught (pedagogy of the concept). In this case, the act of providing support to children can arguably be objectified and taught to those in the role of provider. This permits the assertion of a discipline, which develops *doxa* (both orthodoxies and heterodoxies) or training regimes and curricula. The *doxa* is inscribed through the concept of obtaining a degree (which originally meant to master a discipline). Through the mastery of the discipline, we can attempt a Foucauldian conversation of '**spatialisation**' (Foucault, 1983a). Foucault argued in *The Birth of the Clinic* (1983a) that medical epistemes construct medical 'objects', as objects of care and support – let us call this 'inadequacy' (note the noun). Such objects transcend the visible; they become abstractions, which are located in the body. The results are as follows.

Primary spatialisation: there exists a disease entity, which can be described (in terms of genetics, bodily difference, social deviance). Primary spatialisation is a process of conceptualisation/abstraction. Here, *inadequacy* exists as an abstraction, which transcends the body to explain functional incapacity. In this case, in accounts of children who are described as in need of additional support in schools to compensate for home circumstances, 'inadequacy' lies in the abstracted and generalised child–family nexus, not in the school organisation or society generally.

Secondary spatialisation: there exists a body in which the disease is located with 'an acute perception of the individual' (Foucault, 1983a, p 16). The body is 'abnormal', described in terms of functional anomaly. In social and emotional wellbeing (SEWB) terms, this suggests that it is possible to identify individual children for whom support is required, and the 'inadequacy', or disease, is a function of that child's wellbeing. But function can be seen in terms of Deleuze's 'brick' (Deleuze and Guattari, 2004), where concepts can be determined at different levels of connectedness, or as different connections within a semiotic network. What level of analysis is appropriate? The objective or the subjective? The ideational or the relative? Inadequacy is realised through diseased bodies. Bodies here are not singularities, and what is being argued is that in objectifying children's bodies as in need of care and support, we engage in a view of bodies as inherently individual and ultimately pathologise children. Scheper-Hughes and Lock (1987) argued instead for a multiplicity of body(ies) whereby the body(ies) is (are) a lived phenomenal experience, which has a(n) (auto)biography that is realised materially and is subject to social norms – the 'social body'. The concept of social body(ies) refers to:

> The representational uses of the body as a natural symbol with which to think about nature, society and culture.... The body in health offers a model of organic wholeness; the body in sickness offers a model of social disharmony, conflict, and disintegration. Reciprocally, society in 'sickness' and in 'health' offers a model for understanding the body. (Scheper-Hughes and Lock, 1987, p 7)

Tertiary spatialisation: there is a requirement for a social space in which the body may be located and looked after, such as hospitals and (in the case of wellbeing) schools. Functional incapacity defines guardianship and trusteeship. Foucault argued in *Power/Knowledge* (1980a) that discursive practices create regimes of truth; people (children/ professionals) are subject to 'the concepts of *strategies, technologies* and *programmes* of power' (1980a, p 246, emphasis in original), which exercise power–knowledge relationships. In *The Birth of the Clinic*, Foucault (1983a) proposed that primary spatialisation of the objects of care and support occurred by reformulating people (ie the objects of the verbs) as *objects* of care and support. Through the disciplining of bodies (both bodies of knowledge and agentive and objective bodies), the subjectification of those in need of care and support (through the negations 'uncaring', 'unsupported'), and their resulting objectification of a set of *needs* (the reason why they need care and support) (Foucault's secondary spatialisation), we arrive at the tertiary place (spatialisation) of the social space of care and support. This is provided through the professionalisation of the social space (schools) through its regimes and practices: that is the policy and practice of wellbeing agendas in schools.

This Foucauldian narrative is pessimistic and gloomy. But if we reframe the objectification of care and support (Foucault, 1983a) as a set of verbs, then care and support become encounters between people (Deleuze and Guattari, 2004) located in a set of circumstances. The circumstances are driven by *eudaimonia* (happiness), not normative ethics, and located in *kairos* (the timely). As a result, 'care' and 'support' become related to concerns of mutuality, reciprocity, recognition (in a Hegelian sense) and an emergent sense of humanity located in the deconstruction of the binaries to care—to uncare and to support—to unsupport. The subjective and timely encounters of support will be developed further in this chapter. In particular, we address the question of who *does* social and emotional care and support in schools. This question leads us to a consideration of those staff described in a *support* role.

Support staff in schools

Over the last 50 years, there has been a massive expansion in the number of adults in UK classrooms who are not teachers. Recent figures confirm increases year on year as the number of support staff in England (full-time equivalent) rose by 8,800 (4.9%) to 190,400 between January 2009 and January 2010 (DfE, 2010a), as compared to just over 60,000 in 1997. Recent initiatives, under the rubric of remodelling the workforce, have sought to legitimise the role of support and to provide clear pathways of professional development (qualifications), pay and status (DfES, 2002, 2003). *The National Agreement* (DfES, 2003) on workforce remodelling in schools began through consultation, and latterly through the publication of standards (LLUK, 2007; TDA, 2007) that set out the expectations for a support role in schools and colleges.

Increasingly, in England, support workers are utilised to cover for teachers to allow them planning, preparation and assessment (PPA) time (Cajkler et al, 2006). There has thus been a strong focus on professionalising the workforce in schools to ensure a more highly skilled workforce (Whitby, 2005) and this agenda has been supported by concerns to develop more integrated children's workers (Cameron, 2005) in order to meet the five *Every Child Matters* (ECM) (DfES, 2004a) outcomes.

The term 'support' (generally stated as classroom support) appears in many government publications, yet the concept of support itself is as ill-defined and fuzzy as wellbeing. Social support has been used to refer to the encouragement, assistance and reassurance available to individuals from their network of recurring relationships with other people (Campbell, 1994). There has also been recognition that high levels of social support protect people from the adverse effects of stressful life events and chronic life strains (Cohen and Hoberman, 1983) and there is overwhelming evidence underscoring the significance of social support in maintaining effective psychological adjustment (Wills, 1991). Social support, however, is not a unitary phenomenon. For example,

Cajkler et al (2006), in their systematic literature review, identified 12 different formulations of support in schools, which included: caring-only support for those with physical disabilities; academic support for those with intellectual or other diagnosed disabilities and conditions; supporting bilingual learners and those for whom English was not their first language; as well as general classroom and behaviour management support for small groups of learners with SEN and whole classes.

What's in a name?

The adult in the classroom has various labels: teaching assistant, learning support assistant, learner support assistant, classroom assistant and more. Within each of these identifiers are implicit models of what the role of the adult in the classroom *is*. Our recent research with teaching and learning support assistants suggests, however, that professional identity is far from singular, and is marked by individuals managing a number of professional identity 'positions' (Davies and Harre, 1999) concurrently (Watson et al, 2011). A teaching assistant assists teachers/teaching; a learning support assistant, supports learning; a learner support assistant supports learners (Bradley, 1994); while a classroom assistant supports classroom organisation. Arguably, the predominant role in the literature is that of *teaching assistant*, and more recently the Higher Level Teaching Assistant (HLTA).

The label of teaching assistant underlines the developing professional role of 'pseudo-teacher'. This pedagogically focused role sits alongside the emergent whole child focus in schools driven by the ECM agenda, which highlights a humanistic understanding of children that assumes that learning is predicated on wellbeing (deriving from a Maslowian Objective List Theory [OLT] understanding of child development and motivation). This presumes that in order for a child to be a good learner, they must be safe and well-fed, and have emotional security, positive self-esteem and a sense of belonging. Where these psychological determinants of educability are in place, the child will learn.

Psychological determinants of educability are matched by the 'sociological determinants of educability' (Levinger, 1992) that contribute to a psychosocial analysis of learning. Levinger reviewed the literature of what is termed the 'Active Learning Capacity' (ALC) model:

> ALC was defined as a child's propensity and ability to interact with and take optimal advantage of the full complement of resources offered by any formal or informal learning

environment. *As a child's ALC increases, the child's school achievement will also rise* (assuming that the school does not penalize or discriminate against children with high ALC). (Pollitt, 1990, cited in Levinger, 1992, p 4; emphasis added)

Psychosocial support is also dependent on the quality of interaction between children and carers and on cultural issues related to parental expectations of education for their children. The assumption underpinning the concept of ALC is that unless the child has the *precursors* to learning, they will not learn effectively. We suggest that the ECM agenda explicitly supports a notion of learner support that attempts to ensure ALC in children as part of the process of education.

There appear to be tensions, however, in the reconciliation of these agendas (achievement/learning and wellbeing). The recent Select Committee Report on Special Education (HM Government, 2006) criticised policy directions arguing that the social agenda of ECM was at odds with the agenda for achievement and driving standards upwards within the government's initiatives towards professionalising the workforce. We proposed in Chapter 2 that ECM has been the OLT of wellbeing for children in the UK (and implicitly criticised this model of wellbeing); however, we do not disregard the potential benefits of a focus on wellbeing in schools per se – preferably in a holistic and embedded manner that is not dissimilar to White's (2011) aspiration for a 'well-being school'. Our criticism resides in the inconsistent use of the concept of wellbeing and uncritical acceptance of predefined operationalised lists of wellbeing goods that are deemed essential for children's flourishing and well-living.

The Select Committee report (HM Government, 2006) was similarly supportive of the importance of a focus on wellbeing in schools, but suggested that the prevailing pedagogical discourse of professional development for support staff had ignored the ECM agenda, together with the lack of any recognition of, or coherent strategies for, extending training in the field of SEN and disability. This is particularly evident in the content and foci of the HLTA qualifications, which are viewed as progression routes into teaching. If social and emotional wellbeing of children is increasingly not viewed in policy as a priority for support staff, it is equally the case that it is not a priority of teaching and teachers. As has been reported in research with teachers: 'teachers are supposed to teach, they are not social workers' (Avramidis et al, 2000). This reflects the views of Craig (2009, p 16) cited in Chapter 1, where she argued for teachers to return to being good teachers 'not as surrogate psychologists or mental health workers'. So we might question: who takes responsibility for the social and emotional wellbeing needs of children in schools?

The role of policy

Training regimes result from policy and construct professional knowledge. The occupational standards for support staff provide the normative regimes through which the 'para-professionals' may be observed (hierarchically) and examined (Foucault, 1991a). Thus, the docile body of the para-professional is constructed through the programme of professional development exercised through normative structures, determined by the authoritative voice; that is, the objectification of para-professionals (as people) is brought into being by the exercise of power, which determines the nature of the object itself brought into being (resulting in 'para-professionalism' as a concept).

Where they are docile and can demonstrate competence (through successful completion of tasks and assignments), they may be accredited with the status of para-professional. The status so accorded allows authoritative voices to legitimise the practice so objectified and brought to vision. The standards contain 'truth', against which the experience of professional lives can be determined and corrected when seen to be in error. This truth impacts on children in that it, in itself, also contributes to a programme that brings into being/vision a set of corrective practices to order the 'docile bodies' (Foucault, 1991a) of the client groups in question. But this is not just at the body phenomenal level, it is at a collective level, as there is an assumption that support staff and teachers are part of school communities with:

> a shared set of normative and principled beliefs; ... shared causal beliefs; ... shared notions of validity; ... and a common policy enterprise – that is, a set of common practices associated with a set of problems to which their professional competence is directed, presumably out of the conviction that human welfare will be enhanced as a consequence. (Haas, 1992, p 3)

Such communities have been described as **epistemic**, and epistemic communities are regarded as *normative* (O'Brien, 2003, p 326). An epistemic community is used to refer to a dominant way of looking at social reality as a set of shared symbols and references and mutual expectations, whereby political actors develop ideas and norms that underlie an issue area. The actors, moreover, are conscious of the construction of these ideas and norms. Put differently, an epistemic community creates a discourse that develops and implements standards of *normal* behaviour. In defining some behaviour as normal, the discourse also suggests that other behaviour is *abnormal* and in need of correction. The shared (professional) meanings contained within an epistemic community define the boundaries between *normal* and *abnormal*, or between (in this case) those who *have wellbeing* and those who *lack it*.

The policies and occupational standards for teaching and learning support assistants (TLSAs) frame the normal behaviours expected, yet a critical discursive reading of the policy related to support staff in schools suggests an absence of a conception of expected *quality* in the provision made by these adults in teaching and learning support. This is particularly evident in the published occupational standards for teaching and learning support in England. The Training and Development Agency for Schools (TDA) have seven published units, with 69 sets of standards to be achieved; whilst Lifelong Learning UK (LLUK), who oversee further and lifelong education, have three standards and 32 separate performance criteria. How such fragmentation of role can possibly support holistic professional development, career trajectories and portability of qualifications is questionable. Beyond this, it is not clear how fragmenting the job of support into objectified acts or 'competencies' (Eraut, 1994) can realistically prepare workers for what is essentially focused on human interaction and connections (Watson et al, 2011).

By reducing occupational standards to a discrete set of *competencies*, we posit the child as *object* and the *subjectivity* is lost. Learning is objectified away from the lived (phenomenological) experience of the child (of her/his self and of others). The role of the support worker, it seems, is thus to support the child through the processes of observation, judgement and examination in a manner that should approximate that of the qualified teacher. Rather than being viewed as 'supporting' the teacher, we argue that teaching assistants should instead be seen as 'semi-autonomous supporter[s] of learning' (Cajkler et al, 2006, p 51). This is in accord with recent government standards for teachers that see the teaching role as a 'manager of learning' (Cajkler et al, 2006, p 51) and would foreground their role in *support of learners* (as opposed to teachers). This also has some parallels with European models of social pedagogy and the role of the *Pedagogue* in many European countries (Petrie et al, 2009). This is a discussion we will return to in Chapter 12.

Evidence from practice

A recent study[1] with TLSAs[2] involved interactive workshops and interviews with teaching and TLSA staff in six schools in Devon drawn from primary, secondary and special educational settings. The project focused on the *role* of the TLSA in schools and sought to better understand their *practice*, as opposed to policy rhetoric. The details of the project are written up elsewhere (Watson and Robbins, 2008; Watson et al, 2011); here we explore the participants' experiences and perspectives on social and emotional support that emerged in the project.

'Good' TLSA practice

Through the workshops, we co-developed with participants a set of broad constructs against which they believed TLSA practice could be judged as 'good'. These were: Ethical Practice, Personal Qualities, Communication, Managing the Social and Learning Environment and Knowing the Child. While these headings have been populated with further properties, we do not intend to present the detail of these here.

Given the discussion of standards and policies for TLSAs earlier, it is interesting to note that the participants identified a very clear cluster of constructs of 'good' practice, which were solely focused on knowing children/learners, with specific illustrations of this related to wellbeing, for example, further properties of this construct included: 'promote pupil's social and emotional development'; 'contribute to the health and wellbeing of pupils'; as well as 'promoting independence'. Critical appraisal of these constructs confirms that the primary focus of good practice as determined by the group of practitioners was children, with 18 of the expanded property statements relating to support for children/learners. A further three related to support or contact with parents; with seven focused on their professional development as practitioners. Only six related to supporting teachers. The constructs and their properties represent successive levels of data analysis and refinement in respect of linguistic interpretation and many hours were spent with the participants thrashing out underlying meanings and exact wordings in order to capture the concepts appropriately, so the overt focus on children in their accounts was not happenstance, but was carefully formulated and considered.

Above all, the elicitation of the constructs and their properties revealed new understandings of TLSA roles and practices. For example, there were overlaps identified by participants between the role of TLSA and teacher:

"It [the process of research] helped enormously because it has given me more – I feel that I can do it, that I can actually go into a class and several times I've been left in charge of Betty's [teacher] class, which you've just seen is very, very challenging. If it's just for an hour or two, then I have to be able to manage the whole class. If it's something that's quite structured and Betty has left me in charge, I feel able to do it and so I don't think without the project that I could have. The children have got more respect because I feel more confident, so instead of just being in a corner in the classroom and just washing out the pots, Betty has made sure that they know that whatever I say goes as well, so that helps." (Kelly, primary TLSA)[3]

Kelly is seen here operating in *para-educator* mode, fulfilling the professional needs of *teacher support*. In a different role, Kelly performed other duties where pupils were the main focus of her attention:

"Yes, because there are so many more things that you do during your day. You can't even begin to tell people how many different things you're doing, you're just like a juggling act all the time, one person's asking you this while somebody else is coming up to ask you to administer first aid, then somebody's gone running out of school so you have to go and sort that out. There's just so many things that happen all at the same time that to actually have to think about at the end of the day makes you realise what you have to cope with during just a normal day." (Kelly, primary TLSA)

The multiple demands of their role and the moving in and out of different role expectations was a pertinent feature in defining good TLSA practice, which needed to be flexible and responsive to local contexts and child and teacher needs. But the TLSAs were not solely in responsive mode, flitting from role to role; it became clear that they provided a far more ongoing cohesive function in schools that enabled classrooms and children to engage in educational practices – what we have termed 'socio-emotional *glue*'.

Socio-emotional glue

The central category that defined the world of the TLSA was that of *knowing the child*. All of the TLSAs reported that they belonged to the communities from which the most deprived of the schoolchildren came from. Several of them had grown up in the school locality and had personal knowledge of the most troubled families in the area. This was seen as a form of identity affirmation and cultural legitimacy. They described this in terms of being a form of cultural and interpersonal *glue* between teachers, who in their experience were generally middle class and came from outside of the school locality, and the children and families in the school (and sometimes between children and their families) (Watson et al, 2011). The workshops (and subsequent interviews) reinforced the role of the TLSA as providing this glue: "we see the children through different eyes to the teacher. We can see where trouble is brewing in the class and we diffuse it. Often the teacher does not know anything was wrong" (Louise, primary TLSA).

And from Kelly:

> "I would rather spend half an hour just chatting about what they did at the weekend and try to understand what their mood is and gauging that so they've actually got me to come to if they've had a really bad weekend and perhaps the police have been called and they've gone round to the house and stuff like that – if they feel that they want to talk to me about that, and all I've done is make them feel better about going home at the end of the day, then that's what I feel – I would rather be doing that than actually sat round teaching them how to do maths and English. Because how they feel is really important to me, and if they've got no brothers or sisters – one of my mentoring children has got a mum that had a boyfriend who, in his words, didn't like children, so had no brother or sister that he could actually go and chat to, and if I'm the only person in his mentoring session that he feels he can open up to, then I'm more than happy to do that. I feel that my position as a classroom assistant has taken a bit of a turn, becoming from somebody who supports in literacy and numeracy to somebody who actually *supports their life*." (Kelly, primary TLSA)

The comment by Kelly that she "supports their life" was illuminative as it suggested the embedded nature of children's wellbeing not just in school contexts, but in the bridge between home and school, and the role that school professionals can have in ameliorating and supporting familial relationships.

The forms of the constructs generated also stressed the distinctiveness of the role of the TLSA (compared with teachers). If these practice domains are mapped across different forms of support or professional attitudes, then an understanding emerges of the nature of a TLSA 'community of practice' (Wenger, 1998) that is concerned with managing boundaries between the community of practice of teaching and that of the TLSA. The demarcation of the communities of practice of support and teachers was indicated by *knowing your place* (Watson et al, 2011) (this was an agreed narrative/storyline from the working group in the workshops). TLSAs reported a distinct hierarchy from teachers. This place in the hierarchy was concerned to harmonise, rather than conflict, together with providing the glue of the classroom's social environment that enabled learning to take place. Here, we see some parallels with the conflict resolution agendas in schools discussed in Chapter 8.

Communication, as a specific practice domain (eg teamwork, managing learning, mutual support, working with others, glue, interpersonal qualities, consultative, listening, mediation, alternative forms of communication), provided evidence of distinctiveness in practice from teachers. These descriptors of communication provided by teachers and TLSAs are more closely associated with forms of *social support* rather than *pedagogy*. Communication for the TLSA was a social process of managing relationships, where the emphasis was clearly upon relationship building and maintenance, rather than a form of communication prevalent within a practice of teaching, which controls and directs (predominantly) learning and, by implication, learners (children and young people).

Interestingly, the category of 'special educational needs' did not loom large in the workshops or interviews, although the group were very clear about the range and nature of some of the difficulties individual children presented. TLSAs were concerned with 'knowing the child', irrespective of need – they identified more with a discourse of the *person*, rather than a discourse of *need* and viewed their own adaptability to context and individual need as a sufficient resource to support SEN. The institutional discourse (in the sense of a categorical understanding of conditions) of SEN was missing. But the concept of support strongly emphasised a professional discourse that exemplified the community of practice of TLSAs, as the following excerpt from one of the interviews with Kelly emphasised:

Debbie Watson: "We've talked about the two tracks, haven't we, the sort of teacherly support and both of them having equivalence, and what you're doing very strongly it seems is providing strong emotional support and keeping them together."

Kelly (primary TLSA): "I think that's where Betty [teacher] and I get on really well because she knows that I can go and have a chat with someone who's not really concentrating in her lesson, we can come back in 10 minutes' time and they've got it off their chest and talked about it and then they can settle down and do the learning side, allowing her to do the teaching."

Debbie Watson: "[And later] I hear you've been bringing the child to school?"

Kelly: "I've actually done it since last September. Because he was – last year he was climbing the walls – he was swinging from anything he could swing from – he wouldn't do anything he was told. When he moved from Year 4 to Year 5 there was this big thing about him having to come to school in a taxi. The taxi was hardly ever on time, it used to bother him, and then at 12 o'clock he used to have a taxi home again, and used to spend 11:30 to 12 saying 'Is it here yet?'. So just by me going into school and taking him home again took all that worry away from him. Whether that contributed to the fact that he was better behaved, I have no idea, but we put nice music on in the car, we usually have a nice little chat about what happened the day before, if he's got any worries, all that business on the way to school and then hopefully by the time the bell goes at 9 o'clock he feels more prepared and grounded to start work. It isn't what happened today, but you can't have it every time."

Debbie Watson: "There's always going to be one or two days when it isn't right."

Kelly: "Yes. I'm prepared to go out of my way for children who just need a little bit of extra TLC [tender loving care]."

Kelly's practice was corroborated by the teacher (Betty):

"Kelly can tell what mood he is in after about half an hour. And that's interesting because she knows if he can come round. He comes in sometimes in that state he was this morning, and she goes instinctively 'He's not going to settle we need to get him home'. I don't know what it is because he always looks the same to me. I might say 'He's a bit off this morning' and she says 'Mmmmm, give him five minutes and he'll be OK' and she's always right. It's amazing. They have a really good relationship." (Betty, primary teacher)

The importance of interpersonal relationships was voiced in respect of other professionals, teachers and parents, as well as pupils. For example, in the special school context, the TLSA provided a focus for liaison and support for professional teamwork:

"It's got to be teamwork, you can never do something like this on your own. You've got to have the team to get the knowledge of the child. It's not just the child being in the class, it's physically, communication, eating and all that." (Helen, special school TLSA)

While, in a secondary context, the TLSA mediated relations between teachers and families and her standing in the local community was viewed as advantageous by teachers:

Debbie Watson: "In terms of support, we've talked about TLSAs being the 'glue' in the classroom, and supporting emotionally and enabling kids to stay in schools. Is Jenny doing all of that plus the learning support, or do you see the distinction between the two?"

Lesley (secondary teacher): "She [Jenny] does all those things – one can't happen without the other. I think it's all of a oneness, because you're involved in what's going on in the classroom and involved with the children's learning, so you know where they're at to be able to talk to the parent when they're collecting the child ..."

Debbie Watson: "She has that contact with the parents?"

Lesley: "Because they're older, the parents tend not to come to classroom so often, but they often wait at the end of the day. She wouldn't hesitate to go out and say 'I have to tell you your son worked so hard this afternoon in maths, it was really hard work'. She lives in the village, she knows everybody, but she would do that if it was appropriate."

When the forms of support provided were explored with Jenny, she responded very clearly about the importance of knowing the children and young people she worked with:

> "I find it really easy. That must sound very stupid but I think that in the beginning, I think that in October I just work things out and now I can just pick the student out who needs support. I don't have to go and see a teacher or anything I just pick them out quietly…. I found out with one student that his mother had passed away when she gave birth and the baby was about a year old and he had another brother who was about four, and they all had different fathers and the father of that child wanted to adopt the boy and his brother, and the other father was trying to get custody, and he was absolutely devastated and so worried that he was going to lose his brother, and of course losing his mum, he didn't mind coming down and speaking to me, having that opportunity to work out what was best. So with Lesley [secondary teacher] we decided that the best way for him was to register with her support class because the courts had heard that his attendance at school was low." (Jenny, secondary TLSA)

Discussion of TLSA data

The outcomes of the study indicated a strong sense of TLSAs *doing* social support with a clear underpinning of the categories of ECM and wellbeing generally. The workshop and interview data revealed that the role of TLSAs was distinct to that of teachers, but there were elements of overlap. Where boundaries between TLSAs and teachers existed, these were discussed in terms of *knowing one's place* (with the TLSA reportedly being in a subordinate position to that of the teacher) (Watson et al, 2011). The TLSA discourse revealed was unashamedly child-centred, but this was tinged with regret that they lacked the professional skills and status of teachers. The assumption seemed to be that in order to progress in educational settings, the acquisition of qualified teaching status (QTS) was essential. Where such a training process devalues social support (or at least marginalises it as optional), this is to miss the point of what TLSAs *do* – and here, to emphasise the point, support is something the TLSAs *do*, not *give*. This, together with the cultural proximity of the TLSAs to the children in their care, defined a role that was clearly distinct from that of teachers.

The workshop and interview methods engaged in enabled access to the 'minority voices' of the TLSAs. The experiences of people who formed the institution (Foucault's tertiary spatialisation – here, schools) (both in terms of its owners and its clients) did not constitute a homogeneous social body (constrained by the body politic and exercised on the body phenomenal) and nor were the people 'docile' (Foucault, 1991a) and willing to have occupational standards and training regimes inscribed on their phenomenological experience of doing support.

This understanding returns us to the discussion of 'epistemic communities' (Haas, 1992). Schools are based on presumptions of consensual values and practices as 'a concrete collection of people who share the same worldview (or *episteme*)' (Haas, 1992, p 2) and it is this solidarity to collective norms and values that creates boundaries for insiders/outsiders. The TLSAs did not ascribe to the epistemic community of teachers or schools (and there was no evidence that teachers held this singular worldview either). But nor were the actions of TLSAs discrete and lacking in consensus. There was a strong sense of a TLSA community that challenged the hegemonic normalising gazes of children, and which revealed a distinctive (but not unilateral) engagement with children in schools. These accounts were revealed in the 'fictions' (Goodchild, 1996) of the TLSAs and teachers and offer challenges to 'majoritarian' truths of wellbeing in schools.

The operationalisation of concepts such as wellbeing via the ECM outcomes prefigures a school 'community'. A prefigured community of a school requires certain forms of 'membership', which are predetermined. Creating a boundary between 'inside' (those who have wellbeing) and 'outside' (those who do not) is defined through an OLT of what defines membership, where the characteristics of membership, such as policies focused on enhancing wellbeing in schools, 'form the objects of which they speak' (Foucault, 1972, p 118) . A different view by Jean Luc Nancy (1991) sees community as *emergent* (not prefigured) and dependent on the relationships between individuals (as a 'becoming'). As he commented on the danger of a singular predefinition:

> The community that becomes *a single thing* (body, mind, fatherland, Leader ...) ... necessarily loses the *in* of being-

in-common. Or, it loses the *with* or the *together* that defines it. It yields its being-together to a being *of* togetherness. The truth of community, on the contrary, resides in the retreat of such a being. (Nancy, 1991, p xxxvi)

Where systematic reviews (Cajkler et al, 2006; Alborz et al, 2009) still fail to define the role of TLSAs, and where the Select Committee Report (HM Government, 2006) bemoans the lack of child-centredness (and the lack of implementation of the ECM agenda) in schools, it is difficult to understand why the pressure towards QTS for support staff is so prevalent. *Glue* is necessary to facilitate learning, but where this remains implicit, rather than explicit (to quote *Shakespeare in Love*, the 2000 film directed by Sam Mendes) – 'it's a miracle'. More importantly, explicit models of social support, located in the professional development of TLSAs, rather than teachers, actually allow for real partnerships across distinct professional roles that can benefit children.

Conclusion

To return to Foucault's spatialisations, it is clear that the 'minoritarian' insights gained with TLSAs suggest a radically different interpretation of caring and supporting children in schools than homogenised and objectified ideas embedded in nominalisations of the concept of 'giving' support suggest. We have argued here for a different model of care and support based on 'doing' and the verb formulations. This approach highlights the importance of timely and respectful encounters between, in this case, TLSAs and children, which facilitate support in their lives and contribute to their experiences of social and emotional wellbeing.

Teaching and learning support staff are by no means the only non-teaching adults in schools who work in these ways. There is evidence in the literature of many other professionals and para-professionals who do not objectify the acts of support (nor the children they work with). These include school nurses (Kay et al, 2006) and home–school liaison workers (Spratt et al, 2006), although, as the paper by Spratt et al (2006) suggests, the tendency of particular professional groups to remain within their own *habitus* (and effectively work in silos) challenges the potential benefits of joined-up working for, and with, children, in respect of their mental health and wellbeing.

Notes

[1] Directed by Debbie Watson and funded by the Esmée Fairbairn Foundation.

[2] The participants were subject to numerous naming of their 'support' role and requested that all of these be regarded with this encompassing term.

[3] For the sake of anonymity each participant has been given a pseudonym and they are identified as being a teacher or a TLSA.

Part 3
New directions

This part draws together emergent strands of thinking on children's social and emotional wellbeing (SEWB). Chapter 12 explores the context of approaches to supporting children's wellbeing, and this reflects the propositions offered in Chapter 1 of SEWB being *subjectively experienced*, *contextual and embedded*, and *relational*. In Chapter 13, we revisit the policy and practice strands of the book and offer our vision (and predictions) for SEWB in schools under the Coalition government. The concluding chapter pulls together these ideas and propositions and revisits the questions raised in Chapter 1 concerning the nature of wellbeing as a concept.

CHAPTER 12

The space to do something different

Introduction

In Chapter 2, we opened up the possibility that there was a space in wellbeing research and practice with children to understand social and emotional wellbeing (SEWB) differently. Earlier chapters deconstructed traditional and meta-narratives of wellbeing, largely drawn from 'majoritarian' accounts in medicine and economics, and challenged their validity in capturing and describing the wellbeing of children and young people. Chapters 10 and 11 emphasised the importance of valued adult contributions to children's wellbeing experiences in terms of respecting and facilitating children's rights and challenging definitions of social and emotional support and care for children and young people in schools. Chapter 9 exemplified the importance of children exerting choice over activities and balancing enjoyable activities with subjective feelings of enjoyment and this draws on the discussion of children's voices in Chapter 7.

This chapter explores the possibilities available in social pedagogical models, and other approaches, to reframe support for children's SEWB. Such models do not rest on traditional notions of wellbeing embedded in medical or economic discourses, nor on traditional models of operationalising wellbeing in schools, but, rather, on the importance of adult–child relationships (driven from a values rather than ideological basis) (Evetts, 2008); on children being *valued, respected* and *listened to* in ways that can enable 'genuinely alternative understandings of wellbeing to emerge' (White and Petitt, 2004, p 20). Before considering specific approaches that may hold promise, we explore the theoretical bases for approaches to care and support in education that could enable us to think differently about children's SEWB.

Ethics of care as a value basis for working with children and young people

Ethics of care arose as a feminist response in the 1970s and 1980s to traditional liberal theory and critiqued the assumptions behind many ethical theories such as Kantian ethics based on moral reasoning, and Aristotelian virtue ethics. '*Caring* in these accounts refers to care for, emotional commitment to, and willingness to act on behalf of persons with whom one has a significant relationship' (Beauchamp and Childress, 2001, p 369; original emphasisl). Feminist writers were particularly critical of the masculine basis of ethics and the 'justice-based' approaches to moral discussion; rejecting Kantian universal rules and individual rights, which 'ethics of care' writers such as Gilligan (1982) suggests are generally (although not exclusively) gendered ethical assumptions:

> Men *tend* to embrace an ethic of rights using quasi-legal terminology and impartial principles accompanied by dispassionate balancing and conflict resolution, whereas women *tend* to affirm an ethic of care that centres on responsiveness in an interconnected network of needs, care and prevention of harm. The core notion involves caring for and taking care of others, and it is modeled on relationships, such as those between parent and child. (Beauchamp and Childress, 2001, p 371, original emphasis)

Held (2005, pp 9–10) proposed three core principles to an ethics of care, whereby:

- 'the central focus of the ethics of care is on the compelling moral salience of attending to and meeting the needs of the particular others for whom we take responsibility'. As she also stated, 'prospects for human progress and flourishing hinge fundamentally on the care that those needing it receive';
- 'it involves emotion rather than rejects it'. This is not to suggest all emotion is appropriate in caring but that 'emotions such as sympathy, empathy, sensitivity and responsiveness' are valued and seen to be important to be developed in care relationships;
- '[it] rejects the view of the dominant moral theories that the more abstract reasoning about a moral problem the better because the more likely to avoid bias and arbitrariness ... the ethics of care

respects rather than removes itself from the claims of others with whom we share actual relationships'.

These principles describe the actions of the teaching and learning support staff in Chapter 11 and underpin the claims made about the role of adults in children's SEWB as a reconceptualised notion of professionalism that supports the *whole child* (as opposed to *whole school* approaches). Feminist writers such as Carol Gilligan were generally writing about theoretical propositions of care and caring, with reference in particular to parent–child relationships and care for patients. Nel Noddings was similarly regarded as a founding writer of the ethics of care, and made substantial contributions to ways in which an ethics of care can be brought into education and schooling. She viewed education as 'a constellation of encounters, both planned and unplanned, that promote growth through the acquisition of knowledge, skills, understanding and appreciation' (Noddings, 2002, p 283).

'Care' and 'caring' are not easily defined, as we explored in Chapter 11, but what is clear from our discussion in that chapter is that care is not something you *give*; it is a verb and is concerned with *doing* – and this fits well with a feminist ethics of care. Here, caring is determined by the way in which the care relationship is phenomenologically experienced in a care encounter. This demands the carer being engaged in reflection upon their caring practice. This is something we explored with the teaching and learning support assistancts (TLSAs) in the project reported as they kept reflective diaries on their practice. The power of narrative (Bruner, 1973, 1987) in enabling professional reflection (Schön, 1983; Moon, 2000) was starkly represented in one of the secondary TLSAs' journal. In this, she recorded on 14 consecutive days 'sat with "L" today; "L" cannot read'. Becoming hugely disheartened with this, we were thrilled to read her day 15 entry: '"L" cannot read: I need to do something about this'. She then reported several weeks later that the pupil was making progress with her reading and it is this 'receptive attention [that] is an essential characteristic of a caring encounter' (Smith, 2004, p 3).

Noddings argued that education from a care perspective has four characteristics:

- **Modelling** – 'we do not merely tell them [children] to care and give them texts to read on the subject, we demonstrate our caring in our relations with them' (Smith, 2004, p 5).
- **Dialogue** – the engagement in dialogue about modelling care and receiving feedback from recipients of caring practices.

- **Practice** – this relates to the importance of practising and reflection on caring in order to be better at caring.
- **Confirmation** – involving trust and continuity: 'the latter is needed as we need knowledge of the other and the former as the carer needs to be credible and to be capable of handling explorations and what emerges sensitively' (Smith, 2004, p 5).

It is possible to place the narratives of the TLSAs in Chapter 11 in these components of caring. *Knowledge of the child* (as a form of 'confirmation') was a key construct in defining their practice, and elsewhere we have discussed the TLSAs maternal/gendered connections with children (Watson et al, 2011). As one of the primary TLSAs stated: "I'm prepared to go out of my way for children who just need a little bit of extra TLC [tender loving care". This is the 'feminine view' of an ethics of care that is 'rooted in receptivity, relatedness and responsiveness' (Noddings, 1984, p 2). We have also stressed the nature of care and support as evident in what adults *do* for and with children and the importance of reflection on this practice. *Dialogue* was also an important concept in our discussion of accessing minority voices in Chapter 7 and the necessity not just to 'hear' voices, but to engage in meaningful dialogue that brings about change in experiences and situations.

An ethics of care approach to professionalism is no less professional than practices based on logical reasoning, as it involves the interplay of complex interpersonal skills that are reflected upon and challenged by practitioners in their everyday practice. In a social work context, this reflective interpersonal approach has been described as 'relationship-based practice' (Ruch, 2005; Ruch et al, 2010), where interesting debates about the nature of warm, supporting relationships have emerged, such as whether it is appropriate to feel a form of love for those we care for:

> Warmth, affection and even love may all have a place in constructive and empowering professional relationships, and workers should be encouraged to use these emotions in a thought*ful*, rather than thought*less* way (Yelloly and Henkel, 1995) – to be aware of their own emotional responses and reflect on their meaning. (Turney, 2010, p 147)

In respect of work with children and young people, an ethics of care is more than based on virtue ethics, whereby the focus is on the moral agent: the 'paradigm person, real or idealized, who sets the standards of noble conduct for a culture' (Pellegrino, 1995, p 255). A feminist ethics of care is based on relationships and reciprocity, which are messy, complex and multi-directional, and relies on the individual making sense of circumstances and making ethical decisions not based on rules and boundaries, but on human rationality:

> The ethics of care demands reflection on the best course of action in specific circumstances and the best way to express and interpret moral problems. Situatedness in concrete social practices is not seen as a threat to independent judgment. On the contrary it is assumed that this is exactly what will raise the quality of the judgment. (Sevenhuijsen, 1998, p 59)

Emotional practice of professionals/embodied nature of support

There is increasing acknowledgement, particularly in professional practice with young children, of the need to reconnect with professional identities and practices that foreground emotionally sensitive ways of working with children and build on children's needs for secure attachments (Bowlby, 1969), where 'the adult maintains the equilibrium of the relationship with the child (through being caring, sensitive, available and responsive)' (Manning-Morton, 2006, p 47). We have a situation in the education profession, and in teaching and learning support, that is predominately feminine, yet increasingly influenced by the hegemonic, masculine imposition of standards and training regimes:

> the discourses and actions associated with professional institutions and practices have generated disciplinary and regulatory powers over teachers (who are mostly women) and children. Standards have been created through which individuals judge and limit themselves, through which they construct a desire to be 'good', 'normal' or both. (Cannella, 1997, p 137)

Practitioners with, particularly young, children favour emotional connections and experiential wisdom, yet are subject to pressures to replace these knowledges with imposed standards, which can undermine professional identities and replace intuitive knowledge of the child with a focus on performativity and technical, rational models of practice focused on assessment and targets. This is the model of professionalism described in Chapter 2 based on ideology as a 'hegemonic belief system and mechanism of social control for "professional" workers' (Evetts, 2008, p 399). Arguably, this leads to normalised models of professionalism that challenge practitioners' 'natural' (values-based) modes of practice. Thus, there exists a space for critical reflective practice and opportunities to *be professional* that allow for real professional growth, rather than pure conformity (Osgood, 2006). Good professional training with children should not rely on practice experience *or* theoretical knowledge in isolation. There should be acknowledgement of the personal, physical and emotional aspects of learning and practice as work with children connects with our emotional selves, and this should not be diminished or undermined in favour of sterile theory. This rests on the requirement to develop reflexive and reflective practitioners who have a capacity for ongoing learning (Manning-Morton, 2006) and who practice within an ethics of care that respects the emotional and relational dimensions of care and support.

This returns us to earlier discussions and the need to reconnect with a holistic integration of children's and practitioners' beings as comprised of mind, body and emotions, and recognition of the embedded and relational nature of our (well)being in society (Scheper-Hughes and Lock, 1987). Such a view could enable a form of professional 'boundary crossing' (Manning-Morton, 2006) that would allow adults working with children to overcome the binary divisions of children as vulnerable or independent and that viewed children both as active strong agents of their lives as well as in need of physical and emotional comfort and care. As Scheper-Hughes and Lock (1987, p 29) claimed, emotions 'provide an important "missing link" capable of bridging mind and body, individual and society, and body politic ... emotions are the catalyst that transforms knowledge into human understanding and that brings intensity and commitment to human action'.

They also argued that emotions were open to the same binary separations of mind–body, nature–culture and individual–society critiqued earlier in respect of children's bodies 'being' 'well'. That is, they suggested that we foreground public, stylised and distant forms of emotion as cultural forms that are acceptable to display in the social body and neglect the importance of the more individualised, embodied emotions as private passions and desires that are to be kept away from all but our intimate relationships. This dichotomy of emotions (and neglect of individually experienced emotions) is, in their words, integral to the 'epistemological muddle' (Scheper-Hughes and Lock, 1987, p 28) of bodies that we began by critiquing in the book. Writing from a medical anthropological perspective, Scheper-Hughes and Lock (1987) made the observation that the power of emotions embodied and expressed by individuals and collectivities can provide another form of engagement with the world that has the potential to unite the three bodies. In caring for others, much of our communication and act of *doing* care is embodied and emotional in 'essentially wordless encounters … that acts in largely non-verbal and even pre-reflexive ways to "feel" the sick person back to a state of wellness and wholeness and to remake the social body' (Scheper-Hughes and Lock, 1987, p 29).

Model of support based on an ethics of care: social pedagogy

Social pedagogy has attracted a great deal of attention in social work and social welfare as something deemed 'educational, dealing with human well-being' (Hamalainen, 2003, p 78) and where the 'social' and the 'pedagogical' are brought together in order to avoid the 'social pedagogical embarrassment' of failing to reconcile ambitions of social cohesion *and* the celebration of difference and diversity (Vandenbroeck et al, 2011, p 54). In the UK, we have looked to countries such as Denmark and Germany, which have an established history of pedagogues particularly in respect of social work with children in residential care (Cameron, 2004). Increasingly, attention has focused on the potential for social pedagogy in education, as well as care (Moss and Petrie, 2002), with proponents arguing for the holistic benefits of the pedagogue in UK schools as contributing to an inclusive framework and a place where 'care and education meet' (Petrie et al, 2009; Cameron and Moss, 2011).

Social pedagogues can be found in most Continental European countries, and while there are commentators who call for the term 'pedagogies' in order to acknowledge the diversities of practice (Cameron and Moss, 2011), there are some generally understood commonalities. Defining characteristics of a social pedagogue are that they are in a holistic relationship with the child and inhabit the same space as children and other professionals. There is emphasis placed on the importance of reflective practitioners who share in the practical and creative endeavours of child. Many are originally trained in the creative arts and this is viewed as essential in order to enrich children's lives and improve their self-esteem and wellbeing (Petrie et al, 2009).

Pedagogues are trained to view parents as partners and this involves teamwork and valuing others in inter-professional practice and family involvement (Petrie et al, 2009). Pedagogues are careful not to replace, but to foster, a child's group life with their peers and other adults, and the approach builds on children's rights movements and the value of education in children's development. With origins in the thinking of early years educational pioneers such as Frederick Froebel and Johann Heinrich Pestalozzi, who linked poverty and social distress with the importance of education, 'social pedagogy is based on the belief that you can decisively influence social circumstances though education' (Hamalainen, 2003, p 71). This is not just desired at the level of individual children, but is an ambition at a collective level, whereby 'social pedagogy has been concerned with creating societal well-being' (Eichstellar and Holthoff, 2011, p 39).

Social pedagogy in Europe was an emergent field for educationalists who believed that an individual pedagogy was required. Emergent themes in the ways in which social pedagogues support children in these countries include the humanistic balancing of constructions of the child that enable young people to take responsibility and exert rights. There is a strong focus on the physical care of and contact with children, where pedagogues engage in cuddles, affection and close relationships that allow workers to support holistic life development. This is about a vision of practice as *heart*, *brains* and *hands* in combination. 'Heart' is concerned with compassion and empathy; 'brains' is the ability to reject universal explanations of children and to bring multidisciplinary knowledge to bear in finding solutions; 'hands' refers to activities engaged in together – arts and crafts, sports, and outdoor activities (Cameron, 2004). This suggests that practitioners are required to strike a careful balance, whereby:

> what makes the relationship professional in social pedagogic terms is that the professional uses her personality and is authentic, but understands that her personal life experience should only be introduced to the relationship where it would enhance or enlighten the child's own experience – otherwise this should be kept private. (Eichstellar and Holthoff, 2011, p 43)

Caring professionals creating caring pedagogies?

What is the impact of debates on professionals supporting in a caring manner for children's SEWB? To understand this, we return to discussion of the *being* component of wellbeing that began in Chapter 2. From a post-structural perspective, Goodley's (2007) work offers a different challenge to commentators of childhood that view childhood as *being* and *becoming* simultaneously, as he suggested that we were all constantly in a state of *becoming*. He used Deleuze and Guattari's (2004) concept of a *rhizome* to present a thesis on humanity concerned with networks of relations and connections that are ever growing and becoming, where 'becoming challenges the marketized product of being' (Deleuze and Guattari, 2004, p 325) as a singular and individualised bodily experience. He encouraged a multiplicity of experience based upon the social body (Scheper-Hughes and Lock, 1987), where the social connections and relationships were more substantive than the individual embodiment of each child/teacher/parent and where encounters between people created opportunities to 'be' in new and challenging ways:

> thought is the consequence of the provocation of an encounter, with the rhizome of thought shooting in all directions, without beginning or end, but always being in between. It is a multiplicity functioning by means of connections and heterogeneity, through exposure to difference, and constructed not given. (Dahlberg and Moss, 2005, p 117)

A becoming view of childhood equates more to hedonistic/desire theories (as subjective realities) and this conforms with Deleuze and Guattari's views about 'desiring-machines' and the 'rhizome', which opposes the arborescent dichotomies (or Derrida's binary oppositions) of the subjective–objective. 'Desiring' requires that the membership of the community define their own membership and the *good* (as in 'good life') emerges out of that definition as a subjective/intersubjective process. This presents an alternative to models of predefined concepts of wellbeing and SEWB focused on the operationalisation of Objective List Theories (OLTs).

Goodley (2007) described 'socially just pedagogies' as offering a new way of seeing inclusion (and, we argue, SEWB), which includes, among other components:

> *experimentation with a caring pedagogy; not in terms of caring for subjects but caring becomings.* This may well involve elucidating those everyday happenings that constitute social justice: caring, reciprocity in the educational relationship, ordinariness, extraordinariness, intuition and personal shared understandings between the agents of pedagogy. (Goodley, 2007, p 329, emphasis in original)

There are important messages here for how the SEWB of all children can be supported and fostered. The point being that SEWB is an **encounter**: between subjects and objects and concepts, which do not exist apart from each other, and where 'difference' (as an objective categorisation of children) is not foregrounded.

This notion of a caring pedagogy, set alongside *rhizomatic* thinking and inclusive school communities as *emergent*, suggests an alternative way of conceptualising wellbeing. To return to Deleuze and Guattari's (2004) concept of space introduced in Chapter 2, one could suggest that a caring pedagogy in schools can only exist in a 'smooth space' as opposed to 'striated', as 'striation refers to the blocking of possibilities and movements of subjects and objects in the social nexus of power and knowledge, the occupation of terrains of knowledge and the setting of territories by powerful others' (Roets and Goodley, 2008, p 5).

The exertion of power and regimes of truth (Foucault, 1980b) work counter to 'socially just' cultures in schools as they position some children less favourably than others; to be different is to be *abnormal*, and to demand specialist attention. Such a perspective draws upon normalisation tendencies in schools, and society generally, and is predicated on OLTs of wellbeing where items are decided by others and imposed upon children. Smooth spaces allow for the 'fusion of harmony and melody in favour of the production of properly rhythmic values' (Deleuze and Guattari, 2004, p 478) in respect of relationships and practices of social justice and equality, whereby multiplicity is encouraged and a philosophy of difference can emerge that acknowledges and welcomes change and fluidity and offers a realistic challenge to dualist Western thinking. This creates the space for desire fulfilment or *eudaimonic* approaches to wellbeing, which value the perspective of the subjective body in deciding what is good for themself. This is a right that we have excluded children from, where the exertion of desires/hedonism has been viewed as inappropriate by paternalistic practices.

A wellbeing approach: 'crystals of wellbeing'

How might a socially just, inclusive approach to wellbeing that draws on an ethics of care work in practice? What are the features that could contribute to such a school culture? A recent publication from a collaboration of researchers at the University of Lapland (Ahonen et al, 2008) called *Crystals of School Children's Well-Being: Cross-Border Training Material for Promoting Psychosocial[1] Well-Being through School Education* is one of a few attempts found of approaches to SEWB that include a conceptual and theoretical description of what wellbeing might look like in a school context. This book arose out of a working group of the Arctic Council to establish the future of children and youth of the Barents region. The book comprises a range of examples of how 'psychosocial wellbeing' (or SEWB) can be improved among children and young people and attempts to present integrated ideas with a focus on the arts, relationships and the environment to promote wellbeing.

The author of the conceptual chapter, Eiri Sohlman (2008), traced the origins of their psychosocial wellbeing model to the ideas of sociologist P.H. Ray, who, in identifying the characteristics of transmodern culture, noted that we have embedded in our cultures elements of virtue such as 'mutual respect, trust, belonging, neighbourhood, community, love and caring' (Sohlman, 2008, p 17). As Sohlman (2008, p 17) commented: 'education should always be committed to the ideal of a good life. It cannot even be defined without referring to values, the virtues we must seek to communicate to those we educate'. As such, there are elements of Aristotelian thinking (virtue ethics), but also an ethics of care, in the ideas presented, and this is one of the few accounts of children's wellbeing that is not operationalised, utilitarian or reduced to lists of basic needs or capabilities in an OLT approach.

In parallel with the theory offered by Scheper-Hughes and Lock (1987), Sohlman (2008, p 17) also recognised a holistic conception of humanity that comprises three modes of existence: 'bodily existence (existence as an organic process), consciousness (existence experienced as being aware of himself), and situationally (existence as relationships to the world within one's individual life setting or situation)'.

In placing these ideas in a school context, and in consideration of children's SEWB, there is a continuing focus on a holistic and complex, multilayered approach to wellbeing. There is also concern to enable children to 'live in harmony with their physical, social and cultural environment' (Sohlman, 2008, p 18) and this strongly reflects the social body described earlier (Scheper-Hughes and Lock, 1987). We critiqued the controlling ambition of conflict resolution approaches in Chapter 8 as promoting a utopian version of social cohesion and harmony, the ambition in the Barents project seems more palatable on the basis that they foreground *all* children's relationships (not just the 'pathological') and understand the social and cultural mediations in children's wellbeing. Their approach is not to make children behave in ways that are not reflected by wider society; rather, they embed children strongly within adult society, as well as their environment, and there is recognition of children as both 'beings' and 'becomings' simultaneously.

Sohlman drew upon the work of Konu and Rimpela in Finland who have developed a model of school wellbeing (Konu and Rimpela, 2002; Konu et al, 2002). Their model was based upon the theoretical model of welfare developed by Erik Allardt (1976), an ecological model that places children in the contexts of school, home, community and their environmental surroundings. Konu and Rimpela adapted Allardt's model (*having, loving* and *being*) to a school and child context and their model has four dimensions: *School conditions* (having), *Social relationships* (loving), *Means for self-fulfilment* (being) and they added a fourth dimension to Allardt's original three of *Health status* (health). The properties of these have been expanded and a clear focus on the importance of relationships (student–student, teacher–pupil and others) in the psychosocial development and maintenance of wellbeing of children can be seen, and this theme, along with one of empowerment of children through education and learning, permeates the book.

It is interesting, given the earlier discussion in this chapter, that emotions (in particular, love) are explicitly mentioned where, 'the principle idea of love is an I–You relationship that entails a dialogic encounter' (Sohlman, 2008, p 22). This has parallels with Buber's (1996) 'I–Thou' relationship, as opposed to 'I–It', whereby:

> the self … exists and develops *creatively* by acting on the environment and drawing a response from the "other", while the "other" simultaneously acts on, limits and informs the child so that any necessary *adjustment* can take place to keep the self safe. (Harris, 2008, p 370, original emphasis)

An 'I–It' relationship arguably often exists in schools where children are objectified as the 'objects' of learning or other (wellbeing) interventions. 'I–It' relationships are often task- or skill-oriented and result in little change in either member. A reflexive relationship of the child in a wider nexus and based on an 'I–Thou' formulation allows for social growth where 'teachers [and other professionals] discover that they can find shared solutions to emergent problems of learning and living together through dialogic relationships' (Harris, 2008, p 379).

While the dimensions of psychosocial wellbeing in the Barents project have arguably been drawn from an OLT model, and are open to the criticisms of paternalism, elitism and control that have already been discussed, what is interesting is their explicit focus on values and virtues, and of the value and importance of children in their own right, and in their many and varied life contexts. We do not suggest that this model is the panacea to criticisms of poorly articulated or inconsistent concepts of children's wellbeing, but it does afford a different perspective that seeks to unify children's experiences within the contexts of their families, culture, identity and ethnicity, and promotes wellbeing as located in all of these situations. In this respect it points to the embedded and contextual nature of the experience of wellbeing and has parallels with the ecological models discussed in Chapter 6. For some, for example, Sami children in Norway, this may mean a deep connectedness to a sense of culture, community and the physical environment (Nutti, 2008). This is a conception of embodiment that takes account of extensions of the individual into the realms of nature and the landscape (Nutti, 2008; Schjetne, 2008). Rather than focusing on the negative impacts (pathology) that make children unwell, there is an overt agenda to seek the positive aspects of children's lives and their health in order to increase their wellbeing (Kostenius and Nystrom, 2008). Children are viewed as active, full members of the community whose psychosocial wellbeing contributes to the wellbeing of the society as a whole (social body). A clear ambition of the Barents project was to improve the cultural competence of their children and young people in order to combat the growing pressures of globalisation and individualisation and consolidate their sense of identity and place (Schjetne, 2008), with a real sense of 'belonging' (Woodill et al, 1994).

The 'crystals of wellbeing' are *emergent* properties of the coming together of educationalists and children where boundaries between adults and children and within groups of children have been dissolved in a form of *andragogy* (guiding adults to learn) as opposed to *pedagogy* (directing/leading children to learn), and result in a community experienced as more inclusive. The community was not prefigured (in the sense of 'epistemic communities'), but *emergent* and *becoming*, and this foregrounds the subject's role in 'being well' and included in educational experiences. Wellbeing can be viewed as an emergent property, which, following Nancy (1991, ch 10), is also inclusion (emergent membership); and it is here that the crystallisation occurs. As Sohlman (2008, p 22) asked: 'whether, when we are at school, we learn to love or to objectify each other'.

Note
[1] Psychosocial wellbeing is taken to be the social and emotional dimensions of wellbeing that this book focuses upon.

CHAPTER 13

Policy and practice reflections

Introduction

The policy and practice chapters raised issues that deserve further attention. We start with the policy that, more than any other, has driven wellbeing practice in UK schools, *Every Child Matters* (ECM) (DFES, 2004a). ECM uses an objective list model of wellbeing, with Social and Emotional Aspects of Learning (SEAL) and many of the conflict resolution programmes serving as its operationalised arm. ECM, 'warts and all', is the vehicle through which notions of wellbeing are currently addressed in school settings. It sets out a centralised and prescriptive framework within which childhood is viewed. There is, particularly in English schools, a lack of evidence, evaluation or critical debate regarding the actualisation of ECM through Social and Emotional Learning (SEL) activity. While engaging with children's social and emotional development is vital, and the contested nature of the concept of wellbeing in education does not mean that there is not a need for many of the activities taking place on the ground, there remain concerns with the implementation of ECM that derive from the philosophy behind it.

The philosophy of *Every Child Matters*

ECM takes a clear egalitarian philosophical position, *every child matters* as much as the next. This has translated, within SEL, into the universal application of a deficit model of wellbeing to all children, arguably one of the key failures of the scheme. ECM currently covers whole schools, monitoring and measuring the social and emotional development of all pupils. An alternative framework might start from acknowledging the positives many children already have in this field, and offering greater support to children with greater needs, arising from dialogue built upon being known (see Chapters 11 and 12). True dialogue can only arise within relationships that acknowledge the local context and culture of each child (and adult). Every child matters, but no two children matter in precisely the same way.

The status of ECM as state-sanctioned suggests that the state is interested in fixing the deficits it perceives many children to have. ECM implies that we need to be protected from our children, that our children need to be protected from themselves and that all of us need to be protected from poor parenting practices. As Clements and Clements (2000) noted: 'the notion that children are now subject to innumerable risks in greater numbers, and with greater consequence than ever before can only have a corrosive effect on child-rearing'. The rhetoric of ECM arguably corrodes childhood wellbeing.

Hoyle (2008) referred to the 'ECM brand', which brings with it a certain way of thinking, talking and acting – the big D of discourse (Gee, 1999) – which while forging one vision of the world, hides alternative views and the actions associated with them (Morgan, 1986, cited in Hoyle, 2008). ECM aims to help children:

- Engage in decsion-making and support the community and environment
- Engage in law-abiding and positive behaviour in and out of school
- Develop positive relationships and choose not to bully and discriminate
- Develop self-confidence and successfully deal with significant life changes and challenges
- Develop enterprising behaviour. (DFES, 2004a, p 9)

Apart from the enterprising behaviour, itself ideologically flavoured, the picture seems to be that children should be engaging with society in a manner reminiscent of a pre-war shire village, a reality that has never existed outside of Sunday evening television programmes. All engagement with others and the community must be positive, but positive for whom? One could argue that children acting in this manner are very convenient for adults. This nationalised model of children's lifestyles, seemingly drawn from Enid Blyton, is silent regarding challenge, anger, radicalism, protest, creativity, alternative lifestyles, newness or change. It is a model of wellbeing well suited to the perpetuation of a nostalgic past in order that adults can feel comfortable and safe. In 2010, many young people, including schoolchildren, protested on the streets of England regarding cuts in the education budget. Were they making a 'positive contribution' in terms of ECM?

If children are to make the positive contribution ECM outlines, societal structures need to be in place to reflect, support and encourage this. Yet children generally are not invited to take part in meaningful decision-making. Here is one example of what happened when young people took up the invitation to participate:

> Working with pupils to identify factors within school that contributed and detracted from well-being, Duckett and colleagues encountered a number of issues of power and control. For example, *the commissioning local education authority (LEA) vetoed some innovative data collection methods suggested by the pupils*, such as text, video and drama, despite being keen to conduct participatory research. (Evans, 2011, p 347, emphasis added)

Within and outside education, communities face harsh cuts and inherent inequality. Discrimination exists across many of society's mechanisms (Holdaway and O'Neill, 2006) and youth unemployment is high. By what mechanism are children and young people genuinely offered the chance to influence such issues, regardless of their personal levels of self-confidence or desire to take part in decisions? They are literally disenfranchised.

By prioritising its own operationalised world view, ECM has made it more difficult to perceive children's wellbeing as a broad and interconnected concept, both flexible and renewable: not a status to be achieved, but a state to understand and explore. The prescription of positive outlooks and outcomes created by objective list systems blinds us to the stories of actual children and how they engage with the world. Listening to their actual stories entails more risk: what if wellbeing for children demands changes in society that adults are not willing or able to make?

Another concern is that ECM has fuelled surveillance, at a fundamental cost to those surveyed. This issue was well articulated by Hoyle (2008) who believed that children and young people's privacy to explore feelings, experiences and worries away from the gaze of the state is shrinking. The description earlier in this book of the school playground as seen through the eyes of a local authority (Chapter 8) or the 'professionalisation' of friendships in the playground bears witness to this gaze. At a broader level, a visit by a child or young person to a third-sector advice agency to talk about sexual activity, for example, can quickly trigger police intervention. The Office of the Information Commissioner has found that children were concerned about invasions of their privacy, and that they would be reluctant to use 'sensitive services' and may turn away from 'official' agencies and rely more heavily on other sources of help and information (Hilton and Mills, 2006, cited in Hoyle, 2008). The loss of this space is significant. According to *The Guardian*, on 9 June 2009 (Mansell, 2009) even toilets in school are not necessarily a private place for pupils. At Ash Manor School in Aldershot, CCTV cameras were installed, on a temporary basis according to the school, in both the boys' and girls' toilets in order to 'ensure safeguarding'. In the same article, it was revealed that a company called Classwatch, a CCTV firm, promised through its surveillance technology to 'produce dramatic improvements in behaviour'.

Finally, there is a contradiction inherent in making teachers responsible for pupils' wellbeing (this is explicitly the case in Scotland) while at the same time the National Curriculum limits and controls teachers' input into their own specialist subjects. It seems somewhat confusing that a teacher will require three to four years' training in order to enter the classroom, yet once in practice, can be given two days' training in emotional health and wellbeing (EHWB) and be considered able to support and teach this new 'subject'. Would the same standards and expectations be set for the introduction of any other new 'subject'? Perhaps the ECM discourse, and in particular the lack of space it has made available for any alternative views or discourses regarding children's wellbeing, has been key to teachers not questioning or challenging the SEAL or EHWB approach.

Measurement

The ECM outcomes framework includes a series of life indicators and quality measures, for example, 'NI 72 PSA 10/DSO 3' or 'Achievement of at least 78 points across the Early Years Foundation Stage with at least 6 in each of the scales in Personal Social and Emotional Development and Communication, Language and Literacy' (DCSF, 2006). Such scales may reveal a certain set of problems impacting on children's wellbeing, but there are many gaps in this picture and it has no space for localised or cultural and social differences. Some factors may be immeasurable.

As we were finishing this chapter, one of the authors went to his child's choir concert at the Royal Northern College of Music as part of the Manchester City Council School Music Service. On sitting down and browsing the programme for the performance it was fascinating to see that the opening page of the programme had managed to operationalise the music performance and linked it to the five ECM outcomes: 'Stay Safe – Involvement in group music making provides children and young people with numerous opportunities to work in and out of school within a safe environment where they can build trusting relationships with teachers, other adults and peers.'[1]

In order to operationalise and meet standardised national targets, ECM created an agenda of measurement and recording that has dominated English SEL practice over the past decade. ECM requires that practitioners assess and make judgements about the behaviour and actions of children, a process that in itself raises questions regarding wellbeing. Put simply, if one is being weighed and measured all the time, one may start to get a little anxious as to why this is occurring and the results it is showing. Expanding this line of criticism raises the question of whether SEL input is neutral, or whether it may sometimes *reduce* wellbeing. The final report from one wellbeing intervention, the UK Resilience Project, included the caveat that 'schools and facilitators should keep in mind the possibility that the programme could have a negative effect for individual pupils' (Challen et al, 2011, p 6).

The Office of Standards in Education (OFSTED) was in the recent past a key player in the realm of measurement, inspecting schools in order to assess how well they were promoting the wellbeing of their pupils as defined by the five *Every Child Matters* outcomes. School-level indicators included attendance rates, take up of school meals, how safe pupils felt at school and whether issues such as bullying were successfully addressed. Pupils' behaviour and healthy lifestyles were also key elements of this agenda along with the ubiquitous 'economic wellbeing'. Dr Mary Bousted, General Secretary of the Association of Teachers and Lecturers, commented: 'Ministers have readily accepted that important aspects of pupil well-being cannot be quantified, but in the next breath they demand statistics'.[2] Under the Coalition government, OFSTED no longer measures pupil wellbeing, instead focusing on four core areas – pupil achievement, teaching, leadership, and behaviour and safety. However, OFSTED Chief Inspector, Christine Gilbert, insisted that ECM's focus on pupil wellbeing would not be abandoned: 'good schools will be looking after the wellbeing of pupils, which will come through if you're looking at the leadership and the management of the school, if you're looking at discipline and so on'.[3] So, *plus ça change!* The messages of discipline and behaviour continue to drive the agenda of wellbeing in schools.

SEL practice in schools in Scotland includes Growing Confidence, which emphasises community involvement, caring relationships and belonging. The project has designed a staff and pupil wellbeing questionnaire, which is completed anonymously online and intended to be used as a self-evaluation tool for the whole school to enhance its relationships, ethos and culture. The Growing Confidence questionnaire is built around four themes; Self-Regard and Self-Confidence; Resilience and Personal Coping Skills; Respectful Relationships and

Empathy; and Safe, Caring, Learning Environment. These themes could be linked to Curriculum for Excellence (CfE) and used as data within its outcomes framework.

Growing Confidence mirrors the contested debate regarding what is meant by children's wellbeing. On the one hand, it has clear and worthwhile aims, is dedicated to promoting children's positive mental health and emotional well-being, and, according to its literature, makes a positive difference to pupils and staff. On the other hand, its questionnaire format reinforces the measurement agenda, is methodologically questionable and reduces wellbeing to a 'circle the response' message.

In England too, measurement has driven the agenda. SEAL took the lead role, providing many ways of counting and measuring social and emotional skills, with a particular emphasis on behaviour, albeit in ways that demonstrated little methodological rigor. Interviews with practitioners often revealed them to be in the uncomfortable position of having to implement a contradictory model of children's wellbeing supported by misleading and un-evidenced practice research. The impact of this can be seen in the words of a SEAL practitioner interviewed in Manchester who noted that: "behaviour is a key driver in this strategy [SEAL]: behaviour means it gets funding and priority. We need to show programmes will impact on behaviour and promote positive behaviour". The lead officer for EHWB in Manchester acknowledged that even where measurement exists, there is "no one consistent measure and measurement is an issue".

Evidence, evaluation and critical debate

It is our contention that many of the projects highlighted in this book have built their practice on weak research and evaluation evidence that does not meet the claims being made. We have, for reasons of impact, placed a great deal of emphasis on SEAL. However, it is worth turning the lens on another popular UK programme, if only to offer some triangulation to the findings and position presented. The United Kingdom Resilience Programme (UKRP) is a UK-adapted version of the well-known Penn Resiliency Programme for Children and Adolescents, developed by Drs Reivich and Seligman at the University of Pennsylvania. The programme was originally developed to prevent adolescent depression in America. For the UK: 'It now has a broader remit of building resilience and promoting optimistic thinking, adaptive coping skills and social problem-solving in children, with the aim of improving psychological well-being, but potentially also behaviour, attendance and academic outcomes' (Challen et al, 2009, p 4).

UKRP's interim evaluation in 2009 set out the programme's intention and linked 'wellbeing' with 'behaviour' 101 times in a 121-page report (compared with the 30 times it used 'wellbeing'). The rollout of UKRP to all Year 7 pupils in 22 schools across three local authorities (Manchester, Hertfordshire and South Tyneside), along with a three-year longitudinal evaluation, was initiated and funded by the Department for Children, Schools and Families (DCSF) in the academic year 2007/08.

Between 2008 and 2011, the London School of Economics led a longitudinal evaluation of the UKRP. The final evaluation report was published in April 2011 and makes for interesting reading. The rigorousness of this evaluation process is questionable as the aim of the programme appears to have shifted mid-process. The following statement is from the interim report from 2009: 'The UK Resilience Programme (UKRP) aims to improve children's psychological well-being by building resilience and promoting *positive* thinking' (Challen et al, 2009, p 3, emphasis added). However, compare it to this statement from the final report in 2011: 'The UK Resilience Programme (UKRP) aims to improve children's psychological well-being by building resilience and promoting *accurate* thinking' (Challen et al, 2011, p 4, emphasis added). According to its authors, this study is actually measuring different outcomes from those with which it was tasked originally. If 'positive thinking' and 'accurate thinking' are not different things, then why change the text in the first place?

The results of this long-awaited three-year evaluation, irrespective of the evolving nature of its aims, are worth highlighting. At best, they are mixed. According to the authors, there was no measured impact on behaviour scores (bearing in mind this was the dominant discourse for the programme's introduction) or life satisfaction scores, whether measured by pupil self-reports or by teacher reports. By the two-year follow-up in June 2010, no impact had been reported on any of the outcome measures. In terms of balance, it was reported that some impact had been achieved in respect of depression scores, attendance and attainment; however, this was 'small and relatively short-lived' (Challen et al, 2011, p 36). If these findings were not concerning enough, it is the discourse surrounding this programme, similar in nature to the discourse associated with SEAL, which really raises alarm bells.

The Centre for Excellence and Outcomes in Children and Young People's Services (C4EO) is a Department for Education (DfE)-funded project that aims to act as a best practice hub regarding children's services, used by all local authorities across England. Their website states: 'for the first time, excellence in local practice, combined with national research and data about "what works" is being gathered in one place'.[4] The development of the UKRP programme along with the interim report findings are prominently displayed on the C4EO website. When accessed in June 2011, this self-declared forum for evidence-based research carried no mention of, or link to, the final UKRP evaluation report. It seemed the final report had been read by those who update the website, in this case Hertfordshire Council, as they reported 'the evidence of its [UKRP's] positive impact on children's wellbeing is impressive, with impact still being seen 18 months after the end of the programme'. 'Still being seen 18 months after' is perhaps a positive spin on 'no impact after two years'. There is also allusion to the small and short-term positive results with the description of UKRP as 'an evidence-based proactive programme that can reduce depression and anxiety and improve behaviour'.[5] Because no timescale is given, this description of effects grants more credibility to these particular results than is merited by the qualified statements in the original report.

In a recent article, Maggie Evans (2011, p 426) noted that in regard to the UKRP evaluation, many of the researchers were themselves critical of the study's limitations:

> the researchers recognise many of the problems with the UKRP study: self selection and time investment by the facilitators make it likely that they will be positive; the possibility of spill over effects to the control group; the lack of consistency in how the programme was rolled out, whether or not the whole programme was covered; difficulties in getting data from questionnaires.

One wonders how the researchers might react to the endorsement of UKRP by C4EO and Hertfordshire Council. The outcome is a DfE-funded programme report (the UKRP Final Evaluation) that does not appear on a DfE-funded website that has a history of promoting UKRP and a mandate to identify and disseminate national best practice. There is also a local authority, part of the pilot UKRP scheme, actively promoting UKRP, selling its services to disseminate the programme further (Hertfordshire County Council act as the UKRP Teacher Training Agency[6]). The basis for the endorsement for UKRP appears to be a series of pupils' and teachers' beliefs about the programme, with no reference to the overall findings of the evaluation.

As the childhood wellbeing debate grows, what will happen if the evidence emerging is not what people want to hear? Neither SEAL (Humphrey et al, 2010) nor UKRP appear to have provided the positive evidence expected. Whatever one's position in this debate, it needs to be recognised that for all their fundamental flaws and bold claims, actual practice within wellbeing programmes in schools has opened a door to understanding, listening to and working with children in new ways. In our opinion, the SEWB industry is too big to fail. Too many commentators, practitioners, policymakers, educationalists and media sources have invested too much time, money and confidence in the implicit belief that these practices work, despite lack of evidence. If the beliefs are not to be challenged, where does this leave us? Perhaps the emergent SEWB para-profession will be committed to justifying its own existence. In this context, where will a truly holistic (locally contextualised) model of wellbeing – one that places children's voices at the heart of it, not measuring and weighing, but listening and learning – sit? We offered some suggestions in Chapter 12, but there is little evidence that the UK government is minded to implement such radical reforms of staffing roles and expectations in schools.

How can we overcome the barriers, including the vested interests of large organisations and governments, that stop us engaging in a healthy balanced debate regarding children's wellbeing? Where and how can we create spaces for recent programme experiences to be objectively explored and considered? The present position is well articulated by Coleman (2009, p 286): 'it will come as no surprise to find that research provides no clear answer to the question as to whether programmes in schools are able to enhance the well-being of pupils'. One of the core defenders of SEAL, Katherine Weare, when recently interviewed on BBC Radio 4, said:

> I think the time is now right (as is happening in other parts
> of the world who are working in this area) of getting more
> formal – of saying okay, let's look at what practice has been
> effective, what's worked, what hasn't worked.[7]

Her phrase 'getting more formal' may be a euphemism for gathering more evidence, in which case given that SEAL was supposed to be an example of evidence-based policy, the admission is a telling one.

The cost of implementing SEAL has recently been identified as £40 million for the period 2007 to 2011,[8] but this figure should probably be doubled considering the initial time spent on developing materials, establishing the programme and the roll-out in primary schools from 2005 onwards. The future of schools' wellbeing policy is now uncertain under the UK's Coalition government. The future of ECM also appears somewhat shaky. Bearing in mind that *The Children's Plan* (DCSF, 2007b) is in essence ECM's big brother, it is worth briefly reflecting on a report from the influential Conservative think-tank, the Centre for Policy Studies, entitled *Cutting the Children's Plan: A £5 Billion Experiment Gone Astray* (Burkard and Clelford, 2010). This pulls few punches, declaring that: 'it is doubtful whether the programmes in the *Children's Plan* can ever achieve the high ambitions set out for them. Most are flawed both in concept and in practice' (Burkard and Clelford, 2010, p 6). The report concluded: 'the centralised approach, where a Whitehall department creates and funds an endless stream of new programmes, is a model which must now be questioned' (Burkard and Clelford, 2010, p 44).

One can see within this report a series of clear philosophical messages, many of which are reflected in Coalition practice: the reduction of the state's role; the placement of responsibility for behaviour onto the parents and children; and the belief that it is not the schools' role to manage or intervene in mental health/emotional wellbeing issues. This fits nicely with the Coalition government's drive to implement the 'Big Society' plan, a programme concerned with 'helping people to come together to improve their own lives. It's about putting more power in people's hands – a massive transfer of power from Whitehall to local communities'.[9] This perspective alongside the radical cuts in public expenditure, and the changes in the OFSTED Inspection Framework, make it highly likely that ECM will find itself slowly watered down and ultimately a redundant strategy. The result of this would likely be a drastic pulling back of the taught SEL programmes such as SEAL and a move away from universal delivery of SEL to a more targeted approach.

At present, it is hard to identify just where wellbeing in schools will fit into the Coalition's education agenda. With Amartya Sen having the ear of Downing Street, it is likely that any wellbeing policy developed will reflect the capabilities model and most likely continue down the operationalised road. David Cameron has stated that 'from April next year we will start measuring our progress as a country not just by how our economy is growing, but by how our lives are improving, not just by our standard of living, but by our quality of life'.[10] Although this initiative is far distanced from the schools arena, it does indicate a continuation of the objective list model of wellbeing and the government's interest in this aspect of our lives.

One area of interest within schools is the new legislation (the Education Act 2011) allowing teachers to search children's bags and confiscate items (mobile phones etc), as well as giving greater disciplinary powers to teachers and schools. Increased surveillance and tighter discipline may not turn out to be tools for promoting and encouraging wellbeing in schools. Shami Chakrabarti, Director of Liberty, stated: 'Asking teachers to play policeman to their students risks destroying a sacred relationship of trust. Confiscating mobile phones and looking through the phone records, text messages and address lists is proportionate for terrorism investigations, not breaches of school rules'.[11]

The Coalition's 2010 Schools White Paper, *The Importance of Teaching* (DfES, 2010b), appears to have stripped the debate of the term 'wellbeing' (only two mentions in the whole report), instead returning to the old ground of 'behaviour' as the driver fuelling policy. Mention is frequently made to bullying, pupil behaviour, safety and personal responsibility. Where wellbeing is used, it is presented in the context of the World Health Organization (WHO) model of health-promoting schools, rather than a coherent or holistic model of pupil wellbeing. In the White Paper, Bill Holledge, head teacher of Culloden Primary School, offers an indication of where Coalition policy towards SEWB in schools is going:

> supporting pupils' health and wellbeing is something we are committed to at Culloden Primary School – because this is the right thing to do. We don't need the government to tell us that we should be doing this, or how we should do it. (DfES, 2010b, p 29)

It appears that the future direction for wellbeing in UK schools will be at the moral discretion of head teachers and staff.

Notes

[1] Music Showcase 2011 Programme, Manchester Music Service, Manchester City Council.

[2] Quotation from: http://news.bbc.co.uk/1/hi/education/7661236.stm

[3] Christine Gilbert in interview with *Children and Young People Now*, 8 February 2011. Available at: http://www.cypnow.co.uk/news/1053492/Ofsted-exclusive-interview-Savings-reinvested-help-councils-rated-inadequate-says-Christine-Gilbert/?DCMP=ILC-SEARCH

[4] Available at: http://www.c4eo.org.uk/about/default.aspx

[5] Quotation from: http://www.c4eo.org.uk/themes/schools/vlpdetails. aspx?lpeid=176

[6] Report to Hertfordshire County Council Schools Forum on 20 January 2010 by Lucy Bailey. Available at: http://www.hertsdirect.org/docs/pdf/s/ agen5sf200110 (accessed 14 July 2011).

[7] Katherine Weare in interview for *Analysis*, BBC Radio 4, 7 March 2011.

[8] *5 Live Investigates*, 28 November 2010.

[9] Quotation from: http://www.cabinetoffice.gov.uk/big-society

[10] *The Independent*, 25 November 2010.

[11] Quotation from BBC News website, 4 February 2011.

CHAPTER 14

Conclusion

Chapter 1 posed a number of questions regarding wellbeing as a concept and its intersections and surrounding fields and concepts, which were proposed in Figure 1.1. We asked to what extent the concept of social and emotional wellbeing (SEWB), as operationalised for children in schools, was consistent and the extent to which we could observe the practice and effects of the concept. Lastly, we asked whether in deconstructing wellbeing, we were either rearranging the plane, articulating a new plane or forcing an intersection of that plane with others.

The book has addressed these questions and raised new ones about the concept and practice of wellbeing in schools, and with children. We have revealed the *inconsistencies* inherent in the concept and explored ways in which wellbeing is operationalised in schools and the role of educational professionals and educational discourses in perpetuating a belief in the need to make all of our children 'well' with universal agendas, policies and programmes. In deconstructing and tracing the genealogy of wellbeing, we are rearranging the 'plane of immanence' (Deleuze and Guattari, 2009). In interrogating concepts of education, welfare, law, childhood, philosophy, politics, health, psychology, anthropology and cultural studies (as they intersect and relate to the concept of wellbeing; see Figure 1.1) we have foregrounded and examined these complementary concepts in ways that allow new light to be shed on wellbeing:

> Philosophical concepts are fragmentary wholes that are not aligned with one another so that they fit together, because their edges don't match up. They are not pieces of a jigsaw puzzle but rather the outcome of throws of the dice. They resonate nonetheless, and the philosophy that creates them always introduces a powerful Whole that, while remaining open is not fragmented: an unlimited One-All, an 'Omnitudo' that includes all the concepts on one and the same plane. It is a table, a plateau, or a slice; it is a plane of consistency, or more accurately, the plane of immanence of concepts, the planomenon. (Deleuze and Guattari, 2009, p 35)

Many theories of wellbeing acknowledge the deeply embedded nature of the concept, but they also try to 'fit' the pieces of the jigsaw together, see associations and build theoretical models that enable predictions and hypotheses about wellbeing to be posited. We have *rearranged* the plane of immanence and gazed anew at the concept of wellbeing from multiple perspectives – and this 'rhizomatic' approach is what we intended with Figure 1.3. This is not about a (re)making of wellbeing as a concept, but a deep realisation of the complexity of wellbeing:

> Concepts are concrete assemblages, like the configuration of a machine, but the plane is the abstract machine of which these assemblages are the working parts. Concepts are events but the plane is the horizon of events, the reservoir or reserve of purely conceptual events: not the relative horizon that functions as a limit, which changes with an observer, which makes the event as concept independent of a visible state of affairs in which it is brought about. (Deleuze and Guattari, 2009, p 36)

If we follow this 'plane of immanence', then it is only possible to reveal the *effects* of concepts on *embodied* people (children) (see Figure 1.2), where such issues as rights, social responsibility, happiness, flourishing, capabilities, functions, participation, respect, positive engagement, educational achievement, social and educational inclusion, choice, self-esteem, positive behaviour, and social development can be observed. These 'effects' constituted the subject of many chapters throughout this book as 'what interests us are the circumstances' of wellbeing (Deleuze and Guattari, 1980, p 16).

Throughout, we have emphasised the subjective nature of wellbeing and the importance of revealing embodied experiences. The narrative that this book tells is as follows:

- We have an uncritical acceptance of the need to improve wellbeing – which is poorly defined and *inconsistent* – this includes a simplistic understanding of children, their bodies and their social and cultural milieu.
- *Every Child Matters* (ECM) (in England and Wales) is the current vehicle for wellbeing. In order to operationalise ECM, we have 'bought into' wellbeing programmes such as Social and Emotional Aspects of Learning (SEAL), United Kingdom Resilience Programme (UKRP), conflict resolution and other approaches with little critique or evidence base. Mental health concerns have largely

been subsumed in universal wellbeing approaches – this approach does not support those with genuine mental health problems, and normalises emotional fragility and social inability for *all* children as something that adults have to ameliorate.

- Care and support are poorly defined and objectified with the result that we pathologise children as *lacking* in wellbeing and focus on adults in schools as *giving* support. This does not legitimise support practices (or ECM generally) as they are deemed to be secondary in importance to achievement agendas. Social and emotional support is not about *giving*, it is about *doing*.

- Wellbeing is not about *giving* (programmes, policies in schools), it is about engaging with children and young people in meaningful *dialogic encounters*.

- Childhood wellbeing approaches should be concerned with accessing minority voices, engaging in dialogue that foregrounds children's choices and rights and encourages their playful expressions of *being* 'well'; developing complex and embedded constructions of wellbeing; re-engaging with all 'bodies'; and challenging stigmatising notions of difference.

- 'Epistemic communities' (Haas, 1992) in schools and a practice of professionalism based upon 'ideology' (Evetts, 2008) that operationalises hegemonic ideas and practices in schools do not create the 'smooth space' (Deleuze and Guattari, 2004) required for inclusive wellbeing practice. There is a need to support practices and a form of professionalism that constitutes an 'emergent community' (Nancy, 1991) based on a *relational ethics of care* for, and with, children.

- If we achieve this, then wellbeing, inclusion and education would become synthesised into positive experiences of 'being', 'becoming' and 'belonging' for children that do not demand bolted-on policies and agendas of wellbeing. In the deconstructive process, in unpacking wellbeing as a concept, **wellbeing disappears**; that is, it becomes subsumed in other concepts and concerns (positive attitude towards education and care of all children), rather than being a therapeutic and pathologised 'agenda' layered onto educational discourses to compensate for the deficits of the few (who become a growing number).

This is a relational and embedded view of wellbeing that acknowledges the phenomenological body in experiencing and reporting wellbeing; but it is also a deeply social view of the human body that acknowledges the importance of others in the project of human flourishing. Children and adults do not flourish in isolation from others; they form and maintain relationships and these provide a platform for wellbeing experiences (social body). Wellbeing is not just concerned with an analysis of human nature, needs and even capabilities, it is deeply interrelated with questions of intersubjectivity and inter-relationality in all human encounters. This returns us to the three propositions articulated in Chapter 1and exemplified through the visual heuristic that framed the book (see Figure 1.3): SEWB is *subjectively experienced, contextual and embedded,* and *relational.*

The 'body politic' in respect of children's wellbeing is experienced at the level of how a society treats and understands its children and young people. The prominence afforded to subjective accounts of experience is essential and requires methods that bring minority voices to visibility in innovative and genuinely exciting ways because:

> if individuals are not authorities on what a flourishing life is for themselves, who – if anyone – is? No one can lay down in detail how a person will best flourish in the future. There are simply so many ways of thriving, so many forms of wellbeing goods. (White, 2007, p 22)

This demands an approach to listening to minority voices based on:

> a relational ethics – such as the ethics of an encounter – [which] accommodates greater complexity. It understands children's voices and perspectives as multifaceted, changing and conceptualized. Rather than authentic, "children's voices" are spoken from particular positions within an intricate web of relationships with others. (Kjorholt et al, 2005, p 178)

As:

> by telling and listening to different narratives, listening practices may gradually contribute to increased consciousness of what it means to be *that particular embodied child* in the particular context. Emotional as well as cognitive experiences are thereby recognised and made visible. (Kjorholt et al, 2005, p 184, emphasis in original)

There is a need to challenge 'majoritarian' perspectives on children's wellbeing that normalise what wellbeing should be, and consequently pathologise and problematise other ways of being well. We need to find new ways to break out of Cartesian dualist thought that permits mind–body (and emotion) separations and go beyond the objectification of children's wellbeing as a *medicalised* concern to be *operationalised* through targets, outcomes and measures. Connecting with the social body in all its permutations may be one way forward for children's wellbeing to emerge as a concept over which they and their families have control. Wellbeing is something to be achieved by individuals and collectivities in society – to be embodied and owned. We need to recognise children simultaneously as 'beings' and 'becomings' who inhabit complex individual and social lives that are not limited to individualised embodiment:

> Wellbeing is not to be understood in terms of individual desire-satisfaction, even where the desires are both informed and of major significance in a person's life. If it is not a subjective matter in this sense, neither is it an objective matter of deriving it from features of our human nature. The [minoritarian] truth [with a small 't'] is more subtle. Wellbeing is still desire-dependent, but the desires in question are those not of an individual, but of a loose collection of people.... It is hard to be precise about who is inside this body [social body] and if inside, how far inside. I have been emphasising that nearly all of us are inside to some extent, and those who have a fuller acquaintance with different kinds of goods are further inside than others, but that there are no sharp lines at any point. This is where education comes in [and the role of non-binary definitions of inclusion/exclusion]. One of the purposes of education in a democratic society is to equip people for a flourishing life. As part of this aim they become better qualified to make judgments about human flourishing. They become better-informed contributors to the national and global conversation. (White, 2007, p 25)

Wellbeing is embedded in cultural and social experiences and:

> built around things *we* can do and experience.... When a society or a social group, rises above the level of subsistence and has the time, resources and this-world ethical outlook to make the best of our short human life, the activities it favours as elements in flourishing must be built around

such things as the exercise of our senses, physical activity, self-awareness. (White, 2007, p 27, original emphasis)

Wellbeing is a *concept* and can only be understood through its practice (and its effects). Complexity theory does not construct the world in ways that, following Martin Buber (1996), require an 'I–it' relationship – as the objective 'outside', which can be viewed from a standpoint. Instead, an idea of relational ethics sees the professional in an 'I–Thou' relationship, where 'the professional' and 'the object of professional activity' co-constitute each other, they are co-relational; but the 'object' also stands in co-relationships with the rest of the 'objects', which forms an ontology of education. Ontology here resembles a rhizome not a 'tree' (arborescent) structure (Deleuze and Guattari, 1980). This does not mean that the professional stands as an 'insider' (participant observer); instead, the dynamic 'object' as the partner of professional activity only comes into existence through the co-relation of the professional and the child through action:

> Let this be called 'participatory knowing'. To emphasize, the key aspect of participatory knowing, or consensuality, is that the 'knowing subject' becomes inscribed in context and thus epistemically intimate with 'it'. [Again, let us be mindful how the term 'it' tends to trigger objectification.] Here, 'object' is reconceived from being something that lies outside subject, 'out there', independent of perceiver, to becoming a phenomenon continuous with self, unfolding *creatively* through the self's perception. Now, the knower is part of what comes to be known, and the observer is part of the observed. (Bai and Banack, 2006, p 13, emphasis in original)

If I am 'part of what comes to be known', then:

> This ring that grounds the understanding of our relationship with the world and with ourselves does not describe our *desire for lucidity*, our refusal to be resigned *to doing without understanding*, since we know that *to try to understand, it is necessary to do* and that *to do assuming the responsibility for our acts, it is necessary to try to understand*. The intelligent action demands the recognition of the third included in the relation action and reflection, between experience and knowledge, between Pragmatics and Epistemics: Ethics, that teleological

crucible which is needed to be consciously stimulated so that the experience which ethic clarifies can be transformed into *new knowledge which transforms the knowledge that created it*. (Le Moigne, 2007, p 123, emphasis in orginal)

In the context of professional activity and the intersections of the conceptual plane that constitutes 'education', the professional act, as a relational ethics, has the potential to 'transform the knowledge that created it'. The development of a professional ethics, based on relationality, may take the form of a Deleuzean ethics that renounces life in opinion and representation in the hope of finding life in experience: 'Deleuzean ethics counterpose, affirmation to judgement: they restore encounter. Ethics concern relations rather than representations' (Goodchild, 1996, p 207).

An ethical encounter is mediated by *eudaimonia* (Nussbaum, 2001) – our personal (emotional) engagement with 'human flourishing'. The incorporation of a personal understanding of what constitutes 'human flourishing' – whether this be civic or personal love, friendship, concepts of nurture, social justice – guides our relationality to our 'objects' of encounter, through an emotional affirmation of engagement with that 'object', constituted as an 'I–Thou' (not as an 'OTHERED–it'). *Eudaimonia* cannot lead to a normative or deontological ethics, in that a *eudaimonistic* encounter is an emergent system of knowledge creation and transformation, not the measurement of predictable hypotheses (Bayliss and Thoma, 2008).

References

Abbott, D. (2012, forthcoming) 'Other Voices, Other Rooms: Talking to Young Men with Duchenne Muscular Dystrophy (DMD) about the Transition to Adulthood', *Children and Society*.

Adi, Y., Schrader Mcmillan, A., Kiloran, A. and Stewart-Brown, S. (2007) 'Report 3: Universal Approaches with Focus on Prevention of Violence and Bullying', in *Systematic Review of the Effectiveness of Interventions to Promote Mental Wellbeing in Primary Schools*, London: Health Sciences Research Institute (HSRI), Warwick Medical School, University of Warwick and Centre of Public Health Excellence NICE.

Ahonen, A., Alverby, E., Johansen, D.M., Rajala, R., Ryzhkova, I., Sohlman, I. and Villanen, H. (eds) (2008) *Crystals of School Children's Well-Being: Cross-Border Training Material for Promoting Psychosocial Well-Being through School Education*, Lapland: University of Lapland.

Ailwood, J. (2010) 'Playing with Some Tensions: Poststructuralism, Foucault and Early Childhood Education', in Brooker, L. and Edwards, S. (eds) *Engaging Play*, Maidenhead: Open University Press.

Alborz, A., Pearson, D., Farrell, P. and Howes, A. (2009) *The Impact of Adult Support Staff in Pupils and Mainstream Schools: a Systematic Review of Evidence*, London: Eppi-Centre, Institute of Education, University of London.

Alderson, P. (2002) 'Civil Rights in Schools', *National Children's Bureau Highlight No. 191*, London: National Children's Bureau.

Alderson, P., Sutcliffe, K. and Curtis, K. (2006) 'Children as Partners with Adults in Their Medical Care', *Archives of Diseases in Childhood*, 91: 300–3.

Alexander, J.C. and Pia Lara, M. (1996) 'Honneth's New Critical Theory of Recognition', *New Left Review*, 220: 126–36.

Alexander, R. (2010) *Children, Their World, Their Education. Final Report and Recommendations of the Cambridge Primary Review*, Abingdon: Routledge.

Alkire, S. (2005) *Capability and Functionings: Definition and Justification*, Human Development and Capability Association (www.hd-ca.org).

Allan, J. (2004) 'Deterritorializations: Putting Postmodernism to Work on Teacher Education and Inclusion', *Educational Philosophy and Theory*, 36: 417–32.

Allan, J. (2008) *Rethinking Inclusive Education: The Philosophers of Difference in Practice*, Dordrecht: Springer.

Allardt, E. (1976) 'Dimensions of Welfare in a Comparative Scandinavian Study', *Acta Sociologica*, 19: 227–40.

Alldred, P. and Burman, E. (2005) 'Analysing Children's Accounts Using Discourse Analysis', in S. Greene and D. Hogan *Researching Children's Experience: Approaches and Methods*, London/Thousand Oaks, CA:/ New Delhi: Sage, pp 175–98.

Alur, M. and Timmons, V. (2009) *Inclusive Education across Cultures: Crossing Boundaries, Sharing Ideas*, London: Sage.

Anand, A., Hunter, G. and Smith (2005) 'Capabilities and Well-Being: Evidence Based on the Sen–Nussbaum Approach to Welfare', *Social Indicators Research*, 74: 9–55.

Andreou, E., Didaskalou, E. and Vlachou, A. (2008) 'Outcomes of a Curriculum-Based Anti-Bullying Intervention Program on Students' Attitudes and Behavior', *Emotional and Behavioural Difficulties*, 13: 235–48.

Andrews, J. and Lupart, J. (2000) *The Inclusive Classroom: Educating Exceptional Children*, Scarborough, Ontario: Nelson Thomson Learning.

Archard, D. (2004) *Children, Rights and Childhood*, London: Routledge.

Aristotle (1847) *The Nicomachean Ethics*, London: The Walter Scott Publishing Co. Ltd.

Arneil, B. (2002) 'Becoming versus Being: "a Critical Analysis of the Child in Liberal Theory"', in Archard, D. and Macleod, C. (eds) *The Moral and Political Status of Children*, Oxford: Oxford University Press.

Arneson, R.J. (1999) 'Human Flourishing versus Desire Satisfaction', *Social Philosophy and Policy*, 16.

Avramidis, E., Bayliss, P. and Burden, R. (2000) 'A Survey into Mainstream Teachers' Attitudes towards the Inclusion of Children with Special Educational Needs in the Ordinary School in One Local Educational Authority', *Educational Psychology in Practice*, 20: 191–211.

Axford, N. (2008) *Exploring Concepts of Child Well-Being: Implications for Children's Services*, Bristol: Policy Press.

Axford, N., Green, V., Kalsbeek, A., Morpeth, L. and Palmer, C. (2009) 'Measuring Children's Needs: How Are We Doing?', *Child and Family Social Work*, 14: 243–54.

Baginsky, W. (2004) *Peer Mediation in the UK, a Guide for Schools*, London: NSPCC, Daphne Project.

Bai, H. and Banack, H. (2006) '"To See a World in a Grain of Sand": Complexity Ethics and Moral Education Complicity', *An International Journal of Complexity and Education*, 3: 1–20.

Ball, S.J. (2008) 'New Philanthropy, New Networks and New Governance in Education', *Political Studies*, 56: 747–65.

Ball, S. (2010) 'Social and Education Policy, Social Enterprise, Hybridity and New Discourse Communities', Social Policy Association Conference, University of Lincoln, UK.

Bamford Review of Mental Health and Learning Disability (Northern Ireland) (2007) *A Comprehensive Legislative Framework* (available online at www.dhsspsni.gov.uk/legal-issue-comprehensive-framework.pdf [accessed on 13.10.11]).

Bandura, A. (1997) *Self-Efficacy: the Exercise of Control.* New York, NY: W.H. Freeman.

Barnes, H. (2009) *Children's Views of an Acceptable Standard of Living for Children in South Africa*, Measures of Child Poverty Project Key Report 3, Pretoria: Department of Social Development, Republic of South Africa.

Bar-on, R. and Parker, D.A. (eds) (2000) *The Handbook of Emotional Intelligence*, San Francisco: Jossey-Bass.

Bayliss, P.D. (1995) 'Integration and Interpersonal Relations – Interactions between Disabled Children and Their Non-Disabled Peers', *British Journal of Special Education*, 22: 131–9.

Bayliss, P. (2009) 'Against Intrepetosis. Deleuze, Disability and Difference', *Journal of Literary and Cultural Disability Studies*, 3: 281–94.

Bayliss, P. and Dillon, P. (2010) 'Cosmologies and Lifestyles: a Cultural Ecological Framework and Its Implications for Education Systems', *Anthropological Journal of European Cultures*, 19: 7–21.

Bayliss, P. and Thoma, T. (2008) 'Towards a Relational Ethics in (Special) Education', in Kozlowska, A., Kahn, R., Kozuh, B., Kington, A. and Mazgon, J. (eds) *The Role of Theory and Research in Educational Practice*, Grand Forks, ND: the College of Education and Human Development, University of North Dakota.

BBC (British Broadcasting Corporation) (2007) 'UK Is Accused of Failing Children'. Available at: http://news.bbc.co.uk/1/hi/6359363. stm (accessed 14 December 2010).

BBC (2011) 'Analysis', documentary, broadcast 7 March.

Beauchamp, T. and Childress, J. (2001) *Principles of Biomedical Ethics*, Oxford: Oxford University Press.

Ben-Arieh, A. (2005) 'Where Are the Children? Children's Role in Measuring and Monitoring Their Well-Being', *Social Indicators Research*, 74: 573–96.

Bennett, N., Wood, L. and Rogers, S. (1997) *Teaching through Play*, Buckingham: Open University Press.

BERA (2003) *Early Years Research: Pedagogy, Curriculum and Adult Roles, Training and Professionalism* (available online at www.bera.ac.uk/files/reviews/beraearlyyearsreview31May03.pdf).

Bitel, M. and Roberts, L. (2003) *Leading by Example: the Evaluation of Young Mediators Network (Phase 2 – May 2001 to December 2002)*, London: Partners in Evaluation.

Blair, T. (1999) 'Beveridge Lecture', Toynbee Hall, 18 March. Reprinted as 'Beveridge revisited: A welfare state for the 21st century' in R. Walker (ed) *Ending Child Poverty: Popular Welfare for the 21st Century?*, Bristol: The Policy Press, pp 7-21.

Blair, T (2002) 'Queen's Speech', House of Commons, London.

Blair, T. (2006) 'Lecture on Social Exclusion', 5 September, Joseph Rowntree Foundation.

Boulding, E. (1989) *One Small Plot of Heaven: Reflections on Family Life by a Quaker Sociologist*, Wallingford: Pendle Hill Publications.

Boushel, M. (2000) 'Young Children's Rights and Needs', in Boushel, M., Fawcett, J. and Selwyn, J. (eds) *Focus on Early Childhood: Principles and Realities*, Oxford, Blackwell Science.

Boushel, M. (forthcoming) PhD in progress, working title: 'Making Sense of Children's Rights', University of Sussex.

Bowlby, J. (1969) *Attachment and Loss Vol. 1*, London: Hogarth.

Bowlby, J. (1988) *A Secure Base: Parent–Child Attachment and Healthy Human Development*, New York: Basic Books.

Bradford Academy (no date) 'Anti-Bullying Policy' (available online: www.bradfordacademy.co.uk/Home/media/Safeguarding/Anti-Bullying%20Policy.pdf).

Bradley, J. (1994) *Students with Disabilities and/or Learning Difficulties in FE*, Windsor: NFER.

Bradshaw, J. and Richardson, D. (2009) 'An Index of Child Well-Being in Europe', *Child Indicators Research*, 2: 319–51.

Bronfenbrenner, U. (1979) *The Ecology of Human Development*, Cambridge, MA: Harvard University Press.

Bronson, P. (2009) 'How Biased Science led to Emotional Intelligence Curriculum in all UK Schools', *Newsweek*. Available online at: www.newsweek.com/blogs/nurture-shock/2009/10/19/how-biased-science-led-to-emotional-intelligence-curriculum-in-all-uk-schools.html [accessed 21 October 2010].

Brooker, L. and Edwards, S. (2010) *Engaging Play*, Maidenhead: Open University Press.

Bruner, J. (1973) *The Relevance of Education*, New York: W.W. Norton.

Bruner, J. (1987) 'Life as Narrative', *Social Research*, 5: 11–32.

Buber, M. (1996) *I and Thou*, New York: Touchstone.

Bunt, K., Mcandrew, F. and Kuechel, A. (2005) *Jobcentre Plus Employer (Market View) Survey 2004*, London: Department for Work and Pensions.

Burghardt, G.M. (2005) *The Genesis of Animal Play*, Massachusetts, MA: MIT Press.

Burkard, T. and Clelford, T. (2010) *Cutting the Children's Plan: a £5 Billion Experiment Gone Astray*, London: Centre for Policy Studies.

Cajkler, W., Tennant, G., Cooper, P.W., Sage, R., Tansey, R., Taylor, C., Tucker, S.A. and Tiknaz, Y. (2006) 'A Systematic Literature Review on the Perceptions of Ways in Which Support Staff Work to Support Pupils' Social and Academic Engagement in Primary Classrooms (1988–2003)', Technical Report, Research Evidence in Education Library, London: EPPI-Centre, Social Science Research Unit, Institute of Education, University of London.

Cameron, C. (2004) 'Social Pedagogy and Care: Danish and German Practice in Young People's Residential Care', *Journal of Social Work*, 4: 133–51.

Cameron, C. (2005) *Building an Integrated Workforce for a Long-Term Vision of Universal Early Education and Care*, London: Thomas Coram Research Institute, Institute of Education, University of London.

Cameron, D. (2010) Speech to the Confederation of British Industry, London, 25 October.

Cameron, C. and Moss, P. (eds) (2011) *Social Pedagogy and Working with Children and Young People: Where Care and Education Meet*, London: Jessica Kingsley Publishers.

Camfield, L. and Tafere, Y. (2009) *'Children with a Good Life Have to Have School Bags': Diverse Understandings of Well-Being among Older Children in Three Ethiopian Communities*, Young Lives Working Paper Series, Oxford: University of Oxford.

Campbell, T.W. (1994) 'Psychotherapy and Malpractice Exposure', *American Journal of Forensic Psychology*, 12: 541 –62.

Canguilhem, G. (1989) *The Normal and the Pathological*, New York: Zone Books.

Cannella, G.S. (1997) *Deconstructing Early Childhood Education: Social Justice and Revolution*, New York: Peter Lang.

CASEL (Collaborative for Academic Social and Emotional Learning) (2009) 'CASEL 15 Year Report Past Present Future', in *Annual Reports*, Chicago, IL: Collaborative for Academic Social and Emotional Learning.

CASEL (2010) *Welcome to CASEL*, Chicago, IL: Collaborative for Academic, Social and Emotional Learning.

CE (Council of Europe) (1950) *European Convention on Human Rights*, Rome: Council of Europe.

CFE (Curriculum for Excellence) (2010) 'Health and Wellbeing, Experiences and Outcomes', in *Curriculum for Excellence* (available online: www.ltscotland.org.uk/curriculumforexcellence/healthandwellbeing/outcomes/mentalemotionalsocialphysical/mentalemotionalwellbeing/index.asp).

Challen, A., Noden, P., West, A. and Machin, S. (2009) *UK Resilience Programme Evaluation: Interim Report*, London: DFE.

Challen, A., Noden, P., West, A. and Machin, S. (2011) *UK Resilience Programme Evaluation: Final Report*, London: DFE.

Chamberlain, T., Golden, S. and Bergeron, C. (2011) *Children and Young People's Views of Education Policy*, London: National Foundation for Educational Research.

Channing-Bete (2010) *Paths (Promoting Alternative Thinking Strategies)* Deerfield MA: Channing-Bete.

Cheng, F. and Lam, D. (2010) 'How Is Street Life? An Examination of the Subjective Wellbeing of Street Children in China', *International Social Work*, 53: 353–65.

Child Poverty Action Group (2009) *Child Wellbeing and Child Poverty, Where the UK Stands in the European Table*, London: CPAG.

Cigman, R. (2008) 'Enhancing Children', *Journal of Philosophy of Education*, 42(3): 539–57.

Clark, A. (2005) 'Listening to and Involving Young Children: a Review of Research and Practice', *Early Child Development and Care*, 175: 489–506.

Clark, A. and Moss, P. (2001) *Listening to Young Children: the Mosaic Approach*, London: National Children's Bureau for the Joseph Rowntree Foundation.

Clark, A. and Moss, P. (2005) *Spaces to Play: More Listening to Children Using the Mosaic Approach*, London: National Children's Bureau.

Clark, K.B. and Clark, M.K. (1939) 'Segregation as a Factor in the Racial Identification of Negro Pre-School Children: a Preliminary Report', *Journal of Experimental Education*, 8: 161–3.

Clarke, M. and Wilkinson, R. (2011) 'The Collaborative Construction of Non-Serious Episodes of Interaction by Non-Speaking Children with Cerebral Palsy and Their Peers', *Researching the Lives of Disabled Children and Young People: ESRC Sponsored Seminar Series*, Bristol.

Clements, K. and Clements, V. (2000) *Conflict Prevention Newsletter*, 3(2): 1–2.

Cockburn, T. (2007) 'Partners in Power: a Radically Pluralistic Form of Participative Democracy for Children and Young People', *Children and Society*, 21: 446–57.

Cohen, D. (1993) *The Development of Play*, London: Routledge.

Cohen, R. (1995) *Students Resolving Conflict*, Glenview, IL: Good Year Books.

Cohen, S. (1972) *Folk Devils and Moral Panics: the Creation of the Mods and Rockers*, Oxford: Martin Robertson.

Cohen, S. and Hoberman, H. (1983) 'Positive Events and Social Supports as Buffers of Life Change Stress', *Journal of Applied Social Psychology*, 13: 99–125.

Coleman, J. (2009) 'Well-Being in Schools: Empirical Measure or Politician's Dream?', *Oxford Review of Education*, 35: 281–92.

Conrad, D. (2004) 'Exploring Risky Youth Experiences: Popular Theatre as a Participatory, Performative Research Method', *International Journal of Qualitative Methods*, 3: 1–24.

Cordova, D.I. and Lepper, M.R. (1996) 'Intrinsic Motivation and the Process of Learning: Beneficial Effects of Contextualization, Personalization and Choice', *Journal of Educational Psychology*, 88: 715–30.

CRAE (Children's Rights Alliance for England) (2008) *What Do They Know? Investigating the Human Rights Concerns of Children and Young People Living in England*, London: CRAE.

Craig, C. (2007) *The Potential Dangers of a Systematic, Explicit Approach to Teaching Social and Emotional Skills (SEAL)*, Glasgow: Centre for Confidence and Well-Being.

Craig, C. (2009) *Well-Being in Schools: the Curious Case of the Tail Wagging the Dog?*, Glasgow: Centre for Confidence and Well-Being.

Creating Confident Kids (2010) *Support from the Start*, East Lothian Council (available online: http://edubuzz.org/blogs/equallywell/2010/09/15/creating-confident-kids/).

Cremin, H. (2009) Cambridge University press release for conference presentation, *Working with Bullying in Schools: Exploring the Interventions*, (available online: www.admin.cam.ac.uk/news/press/dpp/2009072017).

CRESST (2011) 'Case Studies', *Conflict Resolution Education* (available online: www.cresst.org.uk/case-studies/).

Crisp, R. (2008) 'Well-Being', in *Stanford Encyclopedia of Philosophy*, (available online at www.plato.stanford.edu/).

Crivello, G., Camfield, L. and Woodhead, M. (2009) 'How Can Children Tell Us about Their Wellbeing? Exploring the Potential for Participatory Research Approaches Within Young Lives', *Social Indices Research*, 90: 51–72.

Crocker, J. and Park, L.E. (2004) 'The Costly Pursuit of Self-Esteem', *Psychological Bulletin*, 130(3): 322–414.

Cross, B. (2011) 'Becoming, Being and Having Been: Practitioner Perspectives on Temporal Stances and Participation across Children's Services', *Children and Society*, 25: 26–36.

Cruickshank, B. (1996) 'Revolutions Within: Self-Government and Self-Esteem', in Barry, A., Osborne, T. and Rose, N. (eds) *Foucault and Political Reason: Liberalism, Neo-Liberalism, and Rationalities of Government*, Chicago, IL: University of Chicago Press.

Csikszentmihalyi, M. (1988) 'The Flow Experience and Human Psychology', in Csikszentmihalyi, M. and Csikszentmihalyi, I.S. (eds) *Optimal Experience. Psychological Studies of Flow in Consciousness*, Cambridge: Cambridge University Press.

Csikszentmihalyi, M. (1990) *Flow. The Psychology of Optimal Experience*, New York: Harpercollins Publishers.

Cummins, R.A. (2005) 'Moving from the Quality of Life Concept to a Theory', *Journal of Intellectual Disability Research*, 49: 699–706.

Curriculum Review Group (2004) *Curriculum for Excellence*, Edinburgh: Astron, for the Scottish Executive.

Curriculum for Excellence (2010) 'Health and wellbeing across learning, responsibilities of all, principles and practice' (available online: www.ltscotland.org.uk/Images/hwb_across_learning_principles_practice_tcm4-540403.doc).

Curtis, S. and Boultwood, M. (1963) *A Short History of Educational Ideas*, London: University Tutorial Press.

Dahlberg, G. and Moss, P. (2005) *Ethics and Politics in Early Childhood Education*, Oxford: Routledge Falmer.

Dahlberg, G., Moss, P. and Pence, A. (1999) *Beyond Quality in Early Childhood Education and Care: Postmodern Perspectives*, Philadelphia, PA: Falmer.

Davies, B. and Harre, R. (1999) 'Positioning and Personhood', in Harre, R. and Van Langenhove, L. (ed) *Positioning Theory: Moral Contexts of Intentional Action*, Oxford: Blackwell.

DCSF (Department for Children, Schools and Families) (2005) *School and LA Resources from the SEBS Pilot 2005–2007 Secondary National Strategy*, London: Crown Copyright.

DCSF (2006) *The Origins of the Primary SEAL Programme*, London: Crown Copyright.

DCSF (2007a) 'Bullying: A Charter for Action' (available online: www.beyondbullying.com/uploads/84cac46900ea26030075093.pdf).

DCSF (2007b) *The Children's Plan, Building Brighter Futures*, London: The Stationery Office.

DCSF (2007c) *The Consolidated 3rd and 4th Periodic Report to the UN Committee on the Rights of the Child*, Nottingham: DCSF.

DCSF (2007d) *Guidance for Schools on Promoting Emotional Health and Wellbeing*, London: Crown Copyright.

DCSF (2007e) *Safe to Learn, Embedding Anti-Bullying Work in Schools*, London: Crown Copyright.

DCSF (2007f) *Social and Emotional Aspects of Learning for Secondary Schools*, Nottingham: DCSF Publications.

DCSF (2007g) 'Ed Balls announces cash boost for successful behaviour programme'. Available online at: www.dcsf.gov.uk/pns/DisplayPN. cgi?pn_id=2007_0123 [accessed 25 August 2010].

DCSF (2008a) *2020 Children and Young People's Workforce Strategy: 'Workforce: the Young Voice' Report Summary*, London: Crown Copyright.

DCSF (2008b) *Childhood Wellbeing, Qualitative Research Study*, London: Counterpoint Research.

DCSF (2008c) *The Play Strategy*, Nottingham: DCSF.

DCSF (2008d) *Primary Social and Emotional Aspects of Learning (SEAL) Evaluation of Small Group Work*, Manchester: University of Manchester.

DCSF (2009) *Promoting and Supporting Positive Behaviour in Primary Schools, Developing Social and Emotional Aspects of Learning (SEAL)*, London: Crown Copyright.

DCSF (2010) *Tellus 4, National Report*, London: DCSF.

Deci, E.L. and Ryan, R.M. (2008) 'Hedonia, Eudaimonia, and Well-Being: an Introduction', *Journal of Happiness Studies*, 9: 1–11.

Deleuze, G. (1989) *Cinema 2: the Time Image*, Minneapolis, MN: University of Minnesota Press.

Deleuze, G. and Guattari, F. (1980) *Thousand Plateaus*, Paris: Continuum.

Deleuze, G. and Guattari, F. (1983) *Anti-Oedipus*, Minneapolis, MN: University of Minnesota Press.

Deleuze, G. and Guattari, F. (1987) *A Thousand Plateaus*, Minnesota, MN: University of Minnesota Press.

Deleuze, G. and Guattari, F. (1994) *What Is Philosophy?*, London: Verso Books.

Deleuze, G. and Guattari, F. (2004) *A Thousand Plateaus – Capitalism and Schizophrenia*, London: Continuum International Publishing Group Ltd.

Deleuze, G. and Guattari, F. (2009) *What Is Philosophy?*, London: Verso.

Department for Culture Media and Sport (2006) *Time for Play: Encouraging Greater Play Opportunities for Children and Young People*, London: DCMS.

Derrida, J. (1976) *Of Grammatology*, Baltimore and London: the Johns Hopkins Press.

Devine, D. (2000) 'Constructions of Childhood in School: Power, Policy and Practice in Irish Education', *International Studies in Sociology of Education*, 10: 23–41.

Dewey, J. (1933) *How We Think*, Boston: D.C. Heath and Company.

DfE (Department for Education) (2010a) 'Statistical First Release: School Workforce in England', ONS, SFR 11/2010.

DfE (2010b) *The Importance of Teaching*, Schools White Paper, London Crown Copyright.

DfE (no date) National Strategies Website, www.education.gov.uk/schools/toolsandinitiatives/nationalstrategies [accessed 21 April 2011].

DfEE (Department for Education and Employment) (1999) *The National Healthy Schools Standard Guidance*, London: Crown Copyright.

DfEE (2005) *National Healthy Schools Standard Promoting Emotional Health and Wellbeing*, London: Crown Copyright.

DfES (Department for Education and Skills) (2001) *Inclusive Schooling for Children with Special Educational Needs: Local Education Authorities' Schools, Health and Social Services in England*, London: DfES.

DfES (2002) *Time for Standards: Reforming the School Workforce*, London: Crown Copyright.

DfES (2003) *The National Agreement on Remodelling the Workforce*, London: Crown Copyright.

DfES (2004a) *Every Child Matters: Change for Children*, London: Department for Education and Skills, Crown Copyright.

DfES (2004b) *Removing Barrier's to Achievement: the Government's Strategy for SEN*, London: Crown Copyright.

DfES (2005a) 'Excellence and Enjoyment: Social and Emotional Aspects of Learning Guidance', in *Primary National Strategy*, London: Crown Copyright.

DfES (2005b) *Primary National Strategy, Social and Emotional Aspects of Learning: Guidance*, London: Crown Copyright.

DfES (2005c) *Social and Emotional Aspects of Learning*, London: Department for Education and Skills.

DfES (2007a) *The Early Years Foundation Stage*, Nottingham: DfES Publications.

DfES (2007b) *Social and Emotional Aspects of Learning for Secondary Schools*, London: Crown Copyright.

DfES (2007c) *Social and Emotional Aspects of Learning for Secondary Schools, Further Reading Booklet*, London: Crown Copyright.

DfES (2007d) *Secondary National Strategy for School Improvement, Social and Emotional Aspects of Learning for Secondary Schools (SEAL)*, Guidance booklet, London: Crown Copyright.

DH (Department of Health) (2003) *The Victoria Climbié Inquiry: a Report of an Inquiry by Lord Laming*, London: the Stationery Office.

DH (2004) *National Service Framework for Children, Young People and Maternity Services*, London: the Stationary Office.

DH (2010) *Healthy Weight, Healthy Lives: the National Child Measurement Programme: Guidance for Schools 2010/11*, London: Crown Copyright.

DH and DfES (Department for Education and Skills) (2004) *Promoting Emotional Health and Wellbeing through the National Healthy School Standard*, London: Crown Copyright.

Diener, E. and Biswas-Diener, R. (2000) *New Directions in Subjective Well-Being Research* (available online: ediener@s.psych.uiuc.edu).

Dobrowolsky, A. (2002) 'Rhetoric versus Reality: the Figure of the Child and New Labour's Strategic "Social Investment State"', *Studies in Political Economy*, Autumn: 43–73.

Donzelot, J. (2009) 'Michel Foucault's Understanding of Liberal Politics', in Peters, M., Besley, A., Ollsen, M., Maurer, S. and Weber, S. (eds) *Governmentality Studies in Education*, Rotterdam: Sense.

Doyal, L. and Gough, I. (1991) *A Theory of Human Need*, London: Macmillan.

DHSSPS (Department of Health, Social Services and Public Safety) (2003) *Promoting Mental Health: Strategy and Action Plan 2003–2008, Investing for Health*, Belfast: DHSSPS.

DHSSPS (2006) *Protect Life: A Shared Vision – The Northern Ireland Suicide Prevention Strategy and Action Plan 2006–2011*, Belfast: DHSSPS.

Durlak, J., Weissberg, R., Dymnicki, A., Taylor, R. and Schellinger, K. (2011) 'The Impact of Enhancing Students' Social and Emotional Learning: a Meta-Analysis of School-Based Universal Interventions', *Child Development*, 82: 474–501.

Ecclestone, K. (2004) 'Learning or Therapy? The Demoralisation of Education', *British Journal of Educational Studies*, 52(2): 112–37.

Ecclestone, K. (2007) 'Resisting Images of the "Diminished-Self": the Implications of Emotional Well-Being and Emotional Engagement in Education Policy', *Journal of Education Policy*, 22: 455–70.

Ecclestone, K. and Hayes, D. (2008) *The Dangerous Rise of Therapeutic Education*, London: Routledge.

Ecclestone, K. and Hayes, D. (2009) 'Changing the Subject: the Educational Implications of Developing Well-Being', *Oxford Review of Education*, 35: 371–89.

Edinburgh Council (2008) 'Growing Confidence, Courses for Staff' (available online at: www.growingconfidence.org/).

Edwards, C., Gandini, L. and Forman, G. (1998) *The Hundred Languages of Children: the Reggio Emilia Approach*, New York: Ablex.

Eekelaar, J. (1994) 'The Interests of the Child and the Child's Wishes: the Role of Dynamic Self-Determinism', *International Journal of Law and the Family*, 8: 42–63.

Eichstellar, G. and Holthoff, S. (2011) 'Conceptual Foundations of Social Pedagogy: a Transnational Perspective from Germany', in Cameron, C. and Moss, P. (eds) *Social Pedagogy and Working with Children and Young People: Where Care and Education Meet*, London: Jessica Kingsley Publishers.

Eid, M. and Larsen, R.J. (eds) (2008) *The Science of Subjective Well-Being*, New York: the Guilford Press.

11 Million (2008) *Happy and Healthy: Summary of Children and Young People's Views on what makes them Happy and Healthy*, London: 11 Million (available from www.11million.org.uk).

Elliot, M. (2010) 'No Blame: Kidscape's Viewpoint', Press Release.

Ellis, S., Tod, J. and Graham-Matheson, L. (2008) *Special Educational Needs and Inclusion*, Birmingham: NASUWT.

Eraut, M. (1994) *Developing Professional Knowledge and Competence*, London: the Falmer Press.

Ereaut, G. and Whiting, R. (2008) *What Do We Mean by 'Wellbeing'? And Why Might It Matter?*, London: Linguistic Landscapes.

European Platform for Conflict Prevention and Transformation (2000) *Conflict Resolution in Schools: Report of the International Seminar*, Soesterberg, the Netherlands: European Centre for Conflict Prevention.

Evans, J. (2008) 'Teaching Emotional Resilience' (accessed online at www.politicsofwellbeing.com/2011/01/teaching-emotional-resilience.html), originally published in *The Sunday Times*, 18 February.

Evans, M. (2011) 'Teaching Happiness – a Brave New World?', *The Psychologist*, 24: 344–7.

Evetts, J. (2008) 'The Sociological Analysis of Professionalism: Occupational Change in the Modern World', *International Sociology*, 18: 395–415.

Eysenck, H. (2000) *Intelligence: A New Look*, New Brunswick, NJ: Transaction Publishers.

Facer, K. and Pykett, J. (2007) *Developing and Accrediting Personal Skills and Competencies*, Bristol: Futurelab.

Fattore, T., Mason, J. and Watson, E. (2007) 'Children's Conceptualisations of Their Wellbeing', *Social Indicators Research*, 80: 5–29.

Federle, K.H. (1994) 'Rights Flow Downhill', *International Journal of Children's Rights*, 2: 343–68.

Fielding, M. (2001) 'Beyond the Rhetoric of Student Voice: New Departures or New Constraints in the Transformation of 21st Centruy Schooling?'. *Forum*, 43: 100–9.

Fitzgerald, R., Graham, A., Smith, A.B. and Taylor, N. (2010) 'Children's Participation as a Struggle over Recognition', in Percy-Smith, B. and Thomas, N. (eds) *A Handbook of Children and Young People's Participation*, Abingdon: Routledge.

Flanagan, H. and Clark, J. (no date) *Restorative Approaches in Schools, a Guide for School Managers and Governors Restorative Solutions*, Chorley: Community Interest Company.

Fortin, J. (2005) *Children's Rights and the Developing Law*, Cambridge: Cambridge University Press.

Foucault, M. (1972) *The Archaeology of Knowledge*, London: Routledge.

Foucault, M. (1980a) *Power/Knowledge: Selected Interviews and Other Writings 1972–1977*, Toronto: Pantheon Books.

Foucault, M. (ed) (1980b) *Truth and Power*, New York: Prentice-Hall.

Foucault, M. (1983a) *The Birth of the Clinic: an Archaeology of Medical Perception*, New York: Pantheon.

Foucault, M. (1983b) 'On the Genealogy of Ethics', in Dreyfus, H. and Rabinow, P. (eds) *Michel Foucault: Beyond Structuralism and Hermeneutics* (2nd edn), Chicago: University of Chicago Press.

Foucault, M. (1991a) *Discipline and Punish: the Birth of the Prison*, London: Penguin Books.

Foucault, M. (1991b) 'On Governmentality', in Burchell, G., Gordon, C. and Miller, P. (eds) *The Foucault Effect: Studies in Governmentality*, Chicago: the University of Chicago Press.

Foucault, M. (1995) *Discipline and Punish: the Birth of the Prison*, New York: Vintage Books.

Freeman, M. (2007) 'Why It Remains Important to Take Children's Rights Seriously', *International Journal of Children's Rights*, 15: 5–23.

Funky Dragon (2008) 'Our Rights, Our Story: the Children and Young People's Assembly for Wales' (available online: www.funkydragon. org/attachments/article/98/Our%20Rights%20Our%20Story.pdf).

Furedi, F. (2003) *Therapy Culture: Creating Vulnerability in an Uncertain Age*, London: Routledge.

Gallagher, D. (2007) 'Challenging Orthodoxy in Special Education: on Long Standing Debates and Philosophical Divides', in Florai, L. (ed) *The Sage Handbook of Special Education*, London: Sage.

Gasper, D. (2004) *Human Well-Being: Concepts and Conceptualisations*, The Hague: Institute for Social Studies.

Gee, J.P. (1999) *Discourse Analysis: an Introduction to Theory and Method*, New York: Sage.

Gibson, E.J. and Pick, A.D. (2000) *An Ecological Approach to Perceptual Learning and Development*, Oxford: Oxford University Press.

Gibson, J.J. (1979) *The Ecological Approach to Visual Perception*, Boston, MA: Houghton Mifflin.

Gilligan, C. (1982) *In Another Voice*, Cambridge, MA: Harvard University Press.

Goleman, D. (1995) *Emotional Intelligence: Why It Can Matter More Than IQ*, London: Bloomsbury.

Goleman, D. (2006) 'Cluing in the Critics' (available online: www.danielgoleman.info/2006/12/18/cluing-in-the-critics/).

Goncu, A. and Gaskins, S. (eds) (2007) *Play and Development: Evolutionary, Sociocultural and Functional Perspectives*, Philadelphia, PA: Psychology Press (Formerly Lawrence Erlbaum Associates).

Good, J.M.M. (2007) 'The Affordances for Social Psychology of the Ecological Approach to Social Knowing', *Theory and Psychology*, 17: 265–95.

Goodchild, P. (1996) *An Introduction to the Politics of Desire*, London: Sage.

Goodley, D. (2007) 'Towards Socially Just Pedagogies: Deleuzeoguattarian Critical Disability Studies', *International Journal of Inclusive Education*, 11: 317–334.

Goodley, D. and Runswick-Cole, K. (2012, forthcoming) 'Celebrating Cyborgs: Photovoice and Disabled Children', *Children and Society*.

Gould, S.J. (1971) *The Mismeasure of Man*, Harmondsworth: Penguin.

Graham, A. and Fitzgerald, R. (2010) 'Supporting Children's Social and Emotional Well-Being: Does "Having a Say" Matter?', *Children and Society*, Online First: 1–11.

Groebel, J. and Hinde, R. (eds) (1989) *Aggression and War: Their Biological and Social Bases*, Cambridge: Cambridge University Press.

Gura, P. (ed) (1992) *Exploring Learning. Young Children and Block Play*, London: Paul Chapman Publishing.

Haas, P.M. (1992) 'Introduction: Epistemic Communities and International Policy Coordination', *International Organization*, 46: 1–35.

Hallam, S., Rhamie, J. and Shaw, J. (2006) *Evaluation of the Primary Behaviour and Attendance Pilot*, Nottingham: DfES Publications.

Hamalainen, J. (2003) 'The Concept of Social Pedagogy in the Field of Social Work', *Journal of Social Work*, 3: 69–80.

Hansard (2004) *House of Commons Hansard Debates 13 September 2004*, London: House of Commons.

Harber, C. (2002) 'Schooling as Violence: an Exploratory Overview', *Educational Review*, 1: 7–16.

Harris, B. (2008) 'Befriending the Two-Headed Monster: Personal, Social and Emotional Development in Schools in Challenging Times', *British Journal of Guidance and Counselling*, 36: 367–83.

Hegarty, S. (2001) 'Inclusive Education – a Case to Answer', *Journal of Moral Education*, 30(3): 243–9.

Heiman, T. (2000) 'Friendship Quality among Children in Three Educational Settings', *Journal of Intellectual and Developmental Disability*, 25: 1–12.

Held, V. (2005) *The Ethics of Care,* Oxford Scholarship Online Monograph, pp 8–12.

Herrnstein, R. and Murray, C. (1994) *The Bell Curve: Intelligence and Class Structure in American Life*, New York: Free Press.

Hill, M., Laybourn, A. and Borland, M. (1996) 'Engaging with Primary-Aged Children about Their Emotions and Well-Being: Methodological Considerations', *Children and Society*, 10: 129–44.

Hill, M., Davis, J., Prout, A. and Tisdall, K. (2004) 'Moving the Participation Agenda Forward', *Children and Society*, 18: 77–96.

Hilton, Z and Mills, C. (2006) *'I think it's about trust': The views of young people on information sharing*, London: NSPCC

Hird, S. (2003) *What Is Wellbeing? A Brief Review of Current Literature and Concepts*, Scotland: NHS.

HM Government (1998) *School Standards and Framework Act 1998*, London: Crown Copyright.

HM Government (2006) *Clarification of Inclusion Policy*, London: House of Commons Select Committee on Education and Skills Third Report.

Holdaway, S. and O'Neill, M. (2006) 'Institutional Racism after Macpherson: an Analysis of Police Views', *Policing and Society*, 16: 349–69.

Holt, J. (1975) *Escape from Childhood*, Harmondsworth: Penguin Books.

Honneth, A. (1995) *The Struggle for Recognition: the Moral Grammar of Social Conflicts*, Cambridge: Polity Press.

Houlston, C., Smith, P. and Jessel, J. (2009) 'Investigating the Extent and Use of Peer Support Initiatives in English Schools', *Educational Psychology*, 29: 325–44.

House, R. (2008) 'Play and Playfulness in Therapeutic and Educational Perspectives', *The European Journal of Psychotherapy and Counselling*, 10: 101–9.

Howard, J. (2002) 'Eliciting Young Children's Perceptions of Play, Work and Learning Using the Activity Apperception Story Procedure', *Early Child Development and Care*, 172: 489–502.

Howard, J. (2009) 'Making the Most of Play in the Early Years', in Broadhead, P., Howard, J. and Wood, E. (eds) *Play and Learning in the Early Years*, London: Sage Publishing Ltd.

Howard, J. (2010) 'Early Years Practitioners Perceptions of Play: an Exploration of Theoretical Understanding, Planning and Involvement, Confidence and Barriers to Practice', *Child and Educational Psychology* 27(4): 91–102.

Howard, J. and Mcinnes, K. (2010) 'Thinking through the Challenge of a Play-Based Curriculum: Increasing Playfulness Via Co-Construction', in Moyles, J. (ed) *Thinking about Play – Developing a Reflective Approach*, Maidenhead: Open University Press.

Howard, J., Jenvey, V. and Hill, C. (2006) 'Children's Categorisation of Play and Learning Based on Social Context', *Early Child Development and Care*, 176: 379–93.

Howe, R.B. and Covell, K. (2010) 'Miseducating Children about Their Rights', *Education, Citizenship and Social Justice*, 5: 91–102.

Hoye, S. (2010) 'The Prevention of Poverty through Education: a Review of Policy History and Current Movements', in *Public Policy and Advocacy, a Chicago Psychology Community Blog* (available online: http://chicagopsychology.org/advocacy/the-prevention-of-poverty-through-education-a-review-of-policy-history-and-current-movements/).

Hoyle, D. (2008) 'Problematizing "Every Child Matters"', *The Encyclopaedia of Informal Education* (available online: www.infed.org/socialwork/every_child_matters_a_critique.htm).

Huby, M. and Bradshaw, J. (2006) *A Review of the Environmental Dimension of Children and Young People's Wellbeing, a Report Prepared for the Sustainable Development Commission*, Sustainable Development Commission.

Humphrey, N. (2012, forthcoming) 'The Emperor Has No Clothes: Challenging the New Orthodoxy of the Social and Emotional Aspects of Learning (SEAL) Programme', in Adey, P. and Dillon, J. (eds) *Bad Education: Debunking Myths in Education*, Maidenhead: OUP/McGraw-Hill.

Humphrey, N., Lendrum, A. and Wigelsworth, M. (2010) *Social and Emotional Aspects of Learning (SEAL) Programme in Secondary Schools: National Evaluation*, Manchester: DFE.

Humphries, S. (1995) *Hooligans or Rebels? An Oral History of Working-Class Childhood and Youth 1889–1939*, Oxford: Blackwell.

IDEA (1990) 'Individuals with Disabilities Education Act', *Public Law*, 1: 101–476.

Ife, J. (2001) *Human Rights and Social Work: towards Rights-Based Practice*, Cambridge: Cambridge University Press.

International Play Association (2010) website, http://ipaworld.org.

Isenhart, M. and Spangle, M. (2000) *Collaborative Approaches to Resolving Conflict*, London: Sage.

James, A., Jenks, C. and Prout, A. (1998) *Theorising Childhood*, Oxford: Polity Press.

Jayne, L. (2010) 'Manchester Healthy Schools Evaluation Report', Manchester: Manchester Healthy Schools Partnership.

Jenks, C. (2001) *Childhood*, London: Routledge.

Jones, N. and Sumner, A. (2009) 'Does Mixed Methods Research Matter to Understanding Childhood Well-Being?', *Social Indices Research*, 90: 33–50.

Jordan, B. (2008) *Welfare and Well-Being: Social Value in Public Policy*, Bristol: the Policy Press.

Jowett, S. and Sylva, K. (1986) 'Does Kind of Pre-School Matter?', *Educational Research*, 28: 21–31.

Kamerman, S.B., Phipps, S. and Ben-Arieh, A. (eds) (2010) *From Child Welfare to Child Well-Being: an International Perspective on Knowledge in the Service of Policy Making*, London: Springer.

Kaptani, E. and Yuval-Davis, N. (2008) 'Participatory Theatre as a Research Methodology: Identity, Performance and Social Action among Refugees', *Sociological Research Online*, 13: 1–13.

Karrby, G. (1989) 'Children's Conceptions of Their Own Play', *International Journal of Early Childhood Education*, 21: 49–54.

Kay, C., Watson, D.L. and Tripp, J.H. (2006) 'To What Extent Are Pupil Drop-in Clinics Meeting Pupils' Self-Identified Health Concerns?', *Health Education Journal*, 65: 236–51.

Kilkelly, U., Kilpatrick, R. and Lundy, L. (2005) *Children's Rights in Northern Ireland*, Belfast: Northern Ireland Commissioner for Children and Young People.

Kingston Upon Hull City Council (2003) *Thinking about Buddy Schemes and Friendship Stops, a Brief Guide for Primary Schools Including Case Studies*, Hull: PHISA Team, Hull Education Centre.

Kjorholt, A.T., Moss, P. and Clark, A. (2005) 'Beyond Listening: Future Prospects', in Clark, A., Kjorholt, A.T. and Moss, P. (eds) *Beyond Listening: Children's Perspectives on Early Childhood Services* (2nd edn), Bristol: Policy Press.

Kleinig, J. (1982) *Philosophical Issues in Education*, London: Croom Helm.

Konu, A. and Rimpela, M. (2002) 'Well-Being in Schools: a Conceptual Model', *Health Promotion International*, 17: 79–87.

Konu, A., Lintonen, T.P. and Rimpela, M. (2002) 'Factors Associated with School Children's Subjective Well-Being', *Health Education Research*, 17: 155–65.

Kostenius, C. and Nystrom, L. (2008) 'Health Promotion with the Children in the Classroom', in Arto, A., Eva, E., Martin, J.O., Raimo, R., Inna, R., Eiri, S. and Heli, V. (eds) *Crystals of School Children's Well-Being: Cross-Border Training Material for Promoting Psychosocial Well-Being through School Education*, Lapland: University of Lapland.

Krasnor, L.R. and Pepler, D.J. (1980) 'The Study of Children's Play: Some Suggested Future Directions', in Rubin, K.H. (ed) *New Directions for Child Development. Children's Play*, San Francisco: Jossey-Bass Inc Publishers.

Kytta, M. (2002) 'Affordances of Children's Environments in the Context of Cities, Small Towns, Suburbs and Rural Villages in Finland and Belarus', *Journal of Environmental Psychology*, 22: 109–23.

Kytta, M. (2004) 'The Extent of Children's Independent Mobility and the Number of Actualized Affordances as Criteria for Child-Friendly Environments', *Journal of Environmental Psychology*, 24: 179–98.

Laevers, F., Vandenbussche, E., Kog, M. and Depondt, L. (1994) 'A Process-Oriented Child Monitoring System for Young Children', Belgium: Centre for Experiential Education.

Layard, R. (2005) *Happiness: Lessons from a New Science*, New York and London: Penguin.

Layard, R. (2007) 'Happiness and the teaching of values', *Centrepiece*, 12(1):18-23.

Layard, R. and Dunn, J. (2009) *A Good Childhood: Searching for Values in a Competitive Age*, Harmondsworth: Penguin.

Learning and Skills Council (2004) *National Employers Skills Survey 2003: Key Findings*, LSC (available online: https://ness.ukces.org.uk/Hidden%20Library/NESS03/national-employers-skills-survey-2003-key-findings.pdf).

Learning and Teaching Scotland (2010) *Curriculum for Excellence: Health and Wellbeing, Experiences and Outcomes* (available online: www.ltscotland.org.uk/myexperiencesandoutcomes/healthandwellbeing/index.asp).

Leavey, G., Galway, K., Rondon, J. and Logan, G. (2009) *A Flourishing Society, Aspirations for Emotional Health and Wellbeing in Northern Ireland*, Belfast: Northern Ireland Association for Mental Health.

Lee, N. (2001) *Childhood and Society: Growing up in an Age of Uncertainty*, Buckingham: OUP.

Lee, N. (2005) *Childhood and Human Value – Development, Separation and Separability*, Maidenhead: OUP.

Lemke, T. (2000) 'Foucault, Governmentality, and Critique', Rethinking Marxism Conference, University of Amherst (MA).

Le Moigne, J.L. (2007) 'The Intelligence of Complexity: Do the Ethical Aims of Research and Intervention in Education and Training Not Lead Us to a "New Discourse on the Study Method of Our Time"?', *Sisifo Educational Sciences Journal*, 4: 115–26.

Lester, S. and Russell, W. (2008) *Play for a Change*, London: Play England/National Children's Bureau.

Levinger, B. (1992) *Nutrition, Health and Learning: Current Issues and Trends*, School Nutrition and Health Network Monograph Series, Newton, MA: Education Development Centre.

Lewis, A. (2010) 'Silence in the Context of "Child Voice"', *Children and Society*, 24: 14–23.

Linklater, H. (2006) 'Listening to Learn: Children Playing and Talking about the Reception Year of Early Years Education in the UK', *Early Years*, 26: 63–78.

Lloyd-Jones, S., Bowen, R., Holtom, D., Griffin, T. and Sims, J. (2010) *A Qualitative Research Study to Explore Young People's Disengagement from Learning*, Cardiff: WAG, Crown Copyright.

LLUK (Lifelong Learning UK) (2007) *National Occupational Standards (NOS) for the Role of Learning Support Practitioner in the Lifelong Learning Sector*, London: Crown Copyright.

Lundy, L. (2007) '"Voice" Is Not Enough: Conceptualising Article 12 of the United Nations Convention on the Rights of the Child', *British Educational Research Journal*, 33: 927–42.

Lyon, C.M. (2007a) 'Children's Participation and the Promotion of Their Rights', *Journal of Social Welfare and Family Law*, 29: 99–115.

Lyon, C.M. (2007b) 'Interrogating the Concentration on the UNCRC Instead of the ECHR in the Development of Children's Rights in England?', *Children and Society*, 21: 147–53.

Mack, R.W. and Snyder, R.C. (1957) 'The Analysis of Social Conflict: Toward an Overview and Synthesis', *Journal of Conflict Resolution*, 1(2): 212–48.

MacNaughton, G. (2005) *Doing Foucault in Early Childhood Studies: Applying Post-Structural Ideas*, London: Routledge.

Maguire, R. and Marshall, K. (1999) *Values, Education and the Rights of the Child: Stage 2 Report for the Gordon Cook Foundation*, Glasgow: University of Glasgow.

Malloy, T. and Gazzola, M. (2006) *The Aspect of Culture in the Social Inclusion of Ethnic Minorities*, Flensburg, Germany: European Centre for Minority Issues (ECMI).

Manning, K. and Sharp, A. (1977) *Structuring Play in the Early Years at School*, East Grinstead: Schools Council Publications.

Manning-Morton, J. (2006) 'The Personal Is Professional: Professionalism and the Birth to Threes Practitioner', *Contemporary Issues in Early Childhood*, 7: 42–52.

Mansell, W. (2009) 'How children become customers', *The Guardian*, Tuesday, 9 June.

Maslow, A.H. (1943) 'A Theory of Human Motivation', *Psychological Review*, 50: 370–396.

Matthews, G., Roberts, R. and Zeidner, M. (2004) 'Seven Myths about Emotional Intelligence', *Psychological Inquiry*, 15(3): 179–96.

May, T. (1997) *Reconsidering Difference – Derrida, Levinas, Nancy and Deleuze*, University Park, PA: Pennsylvania State University Press.

Mayall, B. (2002) *Towards a Sociology for Childhood: Thinking from Children's Lives*, Buckingham: Open University Press.

Mayer, J.D., Dipaolo, M.T. and Salovey, P. (1990) 'Perceiving Affective Content in Ambiguous Visual Stimuli: a Component of Emotional Intelligence', *Journal of Personality Assessment*, 3–4: 772–81.

Mayo, C. (2000) 'The Uses of Foucault', *Educational Theory*, 50: 103–16.

McInnes, K. (2010) 'The Role of Playful Practice for Learning in the Early Years', unpublished PhD dissertation, Glamorgan: University of Glamorgan.

McInnes, K., Howard, J., Miles, G.E. and Crowley, K. (2009) 'Behavioural Differences Exhibited by Children When Practising a Task under Formal and Playful Conditions', *Educational and Child Psychology*, 26: 31–9.

McInnes, K., Howard, J., Miles, G. and Crowley, K. (2010) 'Differences in Adult–Child Interactions during Playful and Formal Practice Conditions: an Initial Investigation', *The Psychology of Education Review*, 34: 14–20.

McLaughlin, H. (2009) 'What's in a Name: "Client", "Patient", "Customer", "Consumer", "Expert by Experience", "Service User"– What's Next?', *British Journal of Social Work*, 39: 1101–17.

Meyer, L.H. (2001) 'The Impact of Inclusion on Children's Lives: Multiple Outcomes, and Friendship in Particular', *International Journal of Disability, Development and Education*, 48: 9–31.

Michalos, A. (2007) 'Education, Happiness and Wellbeing', Paper written for international conference, 'Is happiness measurable and what do those measures mean for public policy?', Rome, 2-3 April 2007, University of Rome.

Miller, A. (2008) 'A Critique of Positive Psychology or "the New Science of Happiness"', *Journal of Philosophy of Education*, 42: 591–608.

Mills, E. (2009) 'Schools of Thought', *Leader, the Education Leader Magazine* (available online: www.leadermagazine.co.uk/article. php?id=1321).

Mithaug, D. (1998) 'The Alternative to Ideological Inclusion', in Vitello, S. and Mithaug, D. (eds) *Inclusive Schooling – National and International Perspectives*, London: Lawrence Erlbaum.

Moon, J.A. (2000) *Learning Journals: a Handbook for Academics, Students and Professional Development*, London: Kogan Page Ltd.

Morrow, V. and Mayall, B. (2009) 'What Is Wrong with Children's Well-Being in the UK? Questions of Meaning and Measurement', *Journal of Social Welfare and Family Law*, 31: 217–29.

Moss, P. and Petrie, P. (2002) *From Children's Services to Children's Spaces: Public Policy, Children and Childhood*, London: Routledge Falmer.

Moyles, J.R. (1989) *Just Playing?*, Buckingham: Open University Press.

Moyles, J.R. (ed) (1994) *The Excellence of Play*, Buckingham: Open University Press.

Nancy, J.L. (1991) *The Inoperative Community*, Minneapolis: University of Minnesota Press.

NCCA (National Council for Curriculum and Assessment) (2009) *Aistear: the Early Childhood Curriculum Framework,* Dublin: NCCA.

NCPR (National Council for Public Responsibility) (2011) *Brown vs Board of Education*, Kansas, KS: Kansas Supreme Court. Available at: http://www.nationalcenter.org/brown.html

Neumann, E.A. (1971) *The Elements of Play*, New York: Mss Information Corporation.

Nevill, C. (2009) 'Feelings Count: Measuring Children's Subjective Well-Being for Charities and Funders', *Measuring Children's Well-Being*, London: New Philanthropy Capital.

Newbury, J. and Hoskins, M. (2010) 'Relational Inquiry: Generating New Knowledge with Adolescent Girls Who Use Crystal Meth', *Qualitative Inquiry*, 16: 642–50.

NICE (National Institute for Health and Clinical Excellence) (2009) *Public Health Draft Guidance on Promoting the Social and Emotional Wellbeing of Young People in Secondary Education*, London: NICE.

Noddings, N. (1984) *Caring, a Feminine Approach to Ethics and Moral Education*, Berkeley: University of California Press.

Noddings, N. (2002) *Educating Moral People*, New York: Teachers College Press.

Northern Ireland Assembly (2006) *Our Children and Young People, Our Pledge, a 10 Year Strategy for Children and Young People in Northern Ireland 2006 to 2016*, Belfast: Office of the First Minister and Deputy First Minister.

Northern Ireland Assembly (2009) 'Concurrent Meeting of the Committee for Education and Committee for Health, Social Services and Public Safety, Official Report (Hansard) "A Flourishing Society"', 21 October.

Northern Ireland Assembly (2010) *Written Answers, Friday 12 February 2010*, Office of the First Minister and Deputy First Minister (available online: www.niassembly.gov.uk/qanda/2007mandate/writtenans/2009/100212.htm).

Northern Ireland Department of Education (2005) *Pupil Emotional Health and Wellbeing Programme*, Belfast: Department of Education.

Norwich, B. and Kelly, N. (2004) 'Pupils' Views on Inclusion: Moderate Learning Difficulties and Bullying in Mainstream and Special Schools', *British Educational Research Journal*, 30: 43–65.

Nussbaum, M. (1992) 'Human Functioning and Social Justice: in Defence of Aristotelean Essentialism', *Political Theory*, 20: 202–47.

Nussbaum, M. (2000) *Women and Human Development: the Capabilities Approach*, Cambridge: Cambridge University Press.

Nussbaum, M. (2001) *Upheavals of Thought*, Cambridge: Cambridge University Press.

Nussbaum, M. and Sen, A. (1993) *The Quality of Life*, Oxford: Clarendon Press.

Nutbrown, C. (ed) (1996) *Respectful Educators – Capable Learners: Children's Rights and Early Education*, London: Paul Chapman.

Nutti, Y.J. (2008) 'Outdoor Days as a Pedagogical Tool', in Ahonen, A., Alverby, E., Johansen, D.M., Rajala, R., Ryzhkova, I., Sohlman, I. and Villanen, H. (eds) *Crystals of School Children's Well-Being: Cross-Border Training Material for Promoting Psychosocial Well-Being through School Education*, Lapland: University of Lapland.

O'Brien, R. (2003) 'From a Doctor's to a Judge's Gaze: Epistemic Communities and the History of Disability Rights Policy in the Workplace', *Polity*, 35: 325–46.

OECD (Organisation for Economic Co-operation and Development) (2004) *Learning for Tomorrow's World: First Results from Pisa 2003*, Paris: OECD.

OECD (2009) *Doing Better for Children*, Paris: OECD.

Office for National Statistics (2007) *Rise in Non Family Households* (available online: www.statistics.gov.uk/cci/nugget.asp?id=1866).

OFSTED (Office for Standards in Education) (2004) *Promoting and Evaluating Pupils' Spiritual, Moral, Social and Cultural Development*, London: OFSTED.

OFSTED (2005) *Promoting Emotional Health and Well-Being in Schools*, London: OFSTED.

OFSTED (2006) *Inclusion: Does It Matter Where Pupils Are Taught? Provision and Outcomes in Different Settings for Pupils with Learning Difficulties and Disabilities*, London: OFSTED.

OFSTED (2008) *Indicators of a School's Contribution to Well-Being*, London: OFSTED.

OFSTED (2010a) *Children on Rights and Responsibilities: a Report of Children's Views by the Children's Rights Director for England*, Manchester: OFSTED.

OFSTED (2010b) *Fairness and Unfairness: a Report of Children's Views by the Children's Rights Director for England*, Manchester: OFSTED.

OFSTED (2011) *The Evaluation Schedule for Schools: Guidance and Grade Descriptors for Inspecting Schools in England under section 5 of the Education Act 2005, from September 2009*, Crown Copyright (available online: http://dera.ioe.ac.uk/1103/1/The%20evaluation%20schedule%20 for%20schools_Apr%202010.pdf).

O'Hare, T., Sherrer, M.V., Smith Connery, H., Thornton, J., Labutti, A. and Emrick, K. (2003) 'Further Validation of the Psycho-Social Well-Being Scale (PSWS) with Community Clients', *Community Mental Health Journal*, 39: 115–29.

Olson, K. (ed) (2008) *Adding Insult to Injury: Nancy Fraser Debates Her Critics*, London: Verso.

Olweus, D. (2002) *Bullying at School*, Oxford: Blackwell.

O'Neill, O. (1998) 'Children's Rights and Children's Lives', *Ethics*, 98: 445–63.

Osgood, J. (2006) 'Deconstructing Professionalism in Early Childhood Education: Resisting the Regulatory Gaze', *Contemporary Issues in Early Childhood*, 7: 5–14.

Otto, H.-W. and Ziegler, H. (2010) *Education, Welfare and the Capabilities Approach: a European Perspective*, Warsaw: Barbara Budrich Publishers.

Oundle Primary School (2009) 'Play Buddies', Oundle: Oundle Primary School.

Palmer, S. (2007) *Toxic Childhood: How the Modern World Is Damaging Our Children and What We Can Do about It*, London: Orion.

PARC (1971) *Pennsylvania Association for Retarded Children (PARC) v Commonwealth of Pennsylvania*, 334 F Supp 1257.

Parfit, D. (1984) *Reasons and Persons*, Oxford: Clarendon Press.

Parham, L.D. (1996) 'Perspectives on Play', in Zemke, R. and Clark, F. (eds) *Occupational Science. The Evolving Discipline*, Philadelphia, PA: F.A. Davis Company.

Pascal, C. (1990) *Under Fives in the Infant Classroom*, Stoke-on-Trent: Trentham Books.

Patton, P. (2000) *Deleuze and the Political*, London: Routledge.

Payler, J. (2007) 'Opening and Closing Interactive Spaces: Shaping Four-Year-Old Children's Participation in Two English Settings', *Early Years*, 27: 237–54.

Payne, D. (2009) 'Building Self-Esteem through Peer Mentoring', *Focus Cymru*, 5: 7.

Pellegrini, A.D. (1991) *Applied Child Study*, New Jersey, NJ: Lawrence Erlbaum Associates Inc.

Pellegrini, A.D. and Bohn, C.M. (2005) 'The Role of Recess in Children's Cognitive Performance and School Adjustment', *Educational Researcher*, 34(1): 13–19.

Pellegrino, E.D. (1995) 'Towards a Virtue-Based Normative Ethics for the Health Professions', *Kennedy Institute of Ethics Journal*, 5: 253–77.

Percy, M. (2003) 'Feeling Loved, Having Friends to Count on, and Taking Care of Myself: Minority Children Living in Poverty Describe What Is "Special" to Them', *Journal of Children and Poverty*, 9: 55–70.

Percy-Smith, B. and Thomas, N. (eds) (2010) *A Handbook of Children and Young People's Participation: Perspectives from Theory and Practice*, Abingdon: Routledge.

Peters, G. (2009) *The Philosophy of Improvisation*, Chicago: University of Chicago Press.

Petrie, P., Boddy, J., Cameron, C., Heptinstall, E., Mcquail, S., Simon, A. and Wigfall, V. (2009) *Pedagogy: A Holistic, Personal Approach to Work with Children and Young People, across Services*, London: Thomas Coram Research Unit.

Phelan, A. (1996) '"Strange Pilgrims": Disillusionment and Nostalgia in Teacher Education Reform', *Interchange*, 27: 331–48.

Piaget, J. (1951) *Play, Dreams and Imitation in Childhood*, London: William Heinmann Ltd.

Piers, M.W. and Landau, G.M. (1980) *The Gift of Play: And Why Young Children Cannot Thrive Without It*, New York: Walker Publishing Co Ltd.

Pollard, E.L. and Lee, P.D. (2003) 'Child Well-Being: a Systematic Review of the Literature', *Social Indicators Research*, 61: 59.

Pollitt, E. (1990) *Malnutrition and Infection in the Classroom*, Paris: UNESCO.

Punch, S. (2002) 'Research with Children: the Same or Different from Research with Adults?', *Childhood – a Global Journal of Child Research*, 9: 321–41.

Pupil Voice Wales (no date) 'Rhoseni (sic) HS Peer Mentors', Pupil Voice Wales.

QCA (Qualifications and Curriculum Authority) (2005) *A Curriculum for the Future, Subjects Consider the Challenge*, London: Qualifications and Curriculum Authority.

Quennerstedt, A. (2010) 'Children, but Not Really Humans? Critical Reflections on the Hampering Effect of the "3 P's"', *The International Journal of Children's Rights*, 18: 619–35.

Qureshi, Y. (2007) 'Lessons on How to be Happy', *Manchester Evening News*, 8 May.

Qvortrup, J. (1991) *Childhood as a Special Phenomenon: An Introduction to a Series of National Reports*, Vienna: European Centre.

Raby, R. (2008) 'Frustrated, Resigned, Outspoken: Students' Engagement with School Rules and Some Implications for Participatory Citizenship', *The International Journal of Childrens Rights*, 16: 77–98.

Ravens-Sieberer, U., Kokonyei, G. and Thomas, C.E. (2004) 'School and Health', in Currie, C., Roberts, C., Morgan, A., Smith, R., Settertolbulte, W., Samdal, O. and Barnekow-Rasmussen, V. (eds) *Young People's Health in Context: Health Behaviour in School-Aged Children (HBSC) Study: International Report from the 2001/2002 Survey*, Denmark: WHO.

Rees, G., Bradshaw, J., Goswami, H. and Keung, A. (2010) *Understanding Children's Well-Being: a National Survey of Young People's Well-Being*, London: The Children's Society.

Report of the Discipline Task Group (2001) 'Better Behaviour, Better Learning', Scottish Government.

Reynaert, D., Bouverne-De-Bie, M. and Vandevelde, S. (2009) 'A Review of Children's Rights Literature since the Adoption of the United Nations Convention on the Rights of the Child', *Childhood*, 16: 518–34.

Rinaldi, C. (2006) *In Dialogue with Reggio Emilia*, Oxon: Routledge.

Ringrose, J. and Renold, E. (2010) 'Normative Cruelties and Gender Deviants: the Performative Effects of Bully Discourses for Girls and Boys in School', *British Educational Research Journal*, 36: 573–96.

Robinson, C. and Taylor, C. (2007) 'Theorizing Student Voice: Values and Perspectives', *Improving Schools*, 10(1): 5–17.

Robson, S. (1993) '"Best of All I Like Choosing Time": Talking with Children about Play and Work', *Early Child Development and Care*, 92: 37–51.

Roets, G. and Goodley, D. (2008) 'Disability, Citizenship and Uncivilized Society: the Smooth and Nomadic Qualities of Self-Advocacy', *Disability Studies Quarterly*, 28: 1–21.

Roffey, S. (2008) 'Emotional Literacy and the Ecology of School Wellbeing', *Educational and Child Psychology*, 25(2): 29–39.

Rose, N. (1996) *Inventing Our Selves*, Cambridge: Cambridge University Press.

Roulstone, A. and Prideaux, S. (2008) 'More Policies, Greater Inclusion? Exploring the Contradictions of New Labour Inclusive Education Policy', *International Studies in Sociology of Education*, 18: 15–29.

Rousseau, J.J. (1979) *Émile or on Education*, New York: Basic Books.

Rowe, F., Stewart, D. and Patterson, C. (2007) 'Promoting School Connectedness through Whole School Approaches', *Health Education*, 107: 524–42.

Rubin, K.H., Fein, G.G. and Vandenberg, B. (1983) 'Play', in Mussen, P.H. (ed) *Handbook of Child Psychology. 4th Edition. Vol. IV. Socialisation, Personaltiy and Social Development*, New York, NY: John Wiley and Sons.

Ruch, G. (2005) 'Relationship-Based Practice and Reflective Practice: Holistic Approaches to Contemporary Child Care Social Work', *Child and Family Social Work*, 10: 111–23.

Ruch, G., Turney, D. and Ward, A. (2010) *Relationship-Based Social Work: Getting to the Heart of Practice*, London: Jessica Kingsley Publishers.

Runswick-Cole, K. (2008) 'Between a Rock and a Hard Place: Parents' Attitudes to the Inclusion of Children with Special Educational Needs in Mainstream and Special Schools', *British Journal of Special Education*, 35: 173–80.

Rutter, M. (2008) 'Developing Concepts in Developmental Psychopathology', in Hudziak, J.J. (ed) *Developmental Psychopathology and Wellness: Genetic and Environmental Influences*, Washington, DC: American Psychiatric Publishing.

Ryan, R.M. and Deci, E.L. (2001) 'On Happiness and Human Potentials: a Review of Research on Hedonic and Eudaimonic Well-Being', *Annual Review of Psychology*, 52: 141–66.

Ryan, R.M., Huta, V. and Deci, E.L. (2008) 'Living Well: a Self-Determination Theory Perspective on Eudaimonia', *Journal of Happiness Studies*, 9: 139–70.

Ryan, S. (2005) 'Freedom to Choose: Examining Children's Experiences in Choice Time', in Yelland, N. (ed) *Critical Issues in Early Childhood Education*, Maidenhead: Open University Press.

Samara, M. and Smith, P. (2008) 'How Schools Tackle Bullying, and the Use of Whole School Policies: Changes over the Last Decade', *Educational Psychology*, 28: 663–76.

Saris, W.E., Van Wijk, T. and Scherpenzeel, A. (1998) 'Validity and Reliability of Subjective Social Indicators: the Effect of Different Measures of Association', *Social Indicators Research*, 45: 173–99.

Saussure, F.D. (1959) *Course in General Linguistics*, New York: Philosophical Library.

Scanlon, T. (1993) 'Value, Desire and Quality of Life', in Nussbaum, M. and Sen, A. (eds) *The Quality of Life*, Oxford: Clarendon Press.

Schalock, R.L. (1997) *Quality of Life Volume II: Applications to Persons with Disabilities*, Toronto, Washington, DC: American Association on Mental Retardation.

Scheper-Hughes, N. and Lock, M. (1987) 'The Mindful Body: a Prolegomenon to Future Work in Medical Anthropology', *Medical Anthropology Quarterly*, 1: 6–41.

Schjetne, E.C. (2008) 'Culture, Identity and Psychosocial Well-Being in the Barents Region', in Ahonen, A., Alverby, E., Johansen, D.M., Rajala, R., Ryzhkova, I., Sohlman, I. and Villanen, H. (eds) *Crystals of School Children's Well-Being: Cross-Border Training Material for Promoting Psychosocial Well-Being through School Education*, Lapland: University of Lapland.

Schön, D.A. (1983) *The Reflective Practitioner: How Professionals Think in Action*, USA: Basic Books.

Schwartzman, H.B. (1982) 'Play as Mode', *The Behavioural and Brain Sciences*, 5: 168.

Scourfield, P. (2007) 'Social Care and the Modern Citizen: Client, Consumer, Service User, Manager and Entrepreneur', *British Journal of Social Work*, 37: 107–22.

SE (Scottish Executive) (2004) *Happy, Safe and Achieving Their Potential: A Standard of Support for Children and Young People in Scottish Schools*, The National Review of Guidance,, Edinburgh: Scottish Executive.

SE (2006) *Building the Curriculum 1, the Contribution of Curriculum Areas*, London: Crown Copyright.

Sebba, J. and Robinson, C., with Boushel, M., Carnie, F., Farlie, J., Hunt, F. and Kirby, P. (2010) *Evaluation of Unicef's UK Rights Respecting Schools Award: Final Report*, September, Brighton and Sussex: University of Brighton and University of Sussex.

Seligman, M. (1990) *Learned Optimism*, New York: Knopf.

Seligman, M. and Csikszentmihalyi, M. (2000) 'Positive Psychology: an Introduction', *American Psychologist*, 55: 5–14.

Seligman, M.E.P., Ernst, R.M., Gillham, J., Reivich, K. and Linkins, M. (2009) 'Positive Education: Positive Psychology and Classroom Interventions', *Oxford Review of Education*, 35: 293–311.

Sellman, E. (2003) 'The Processes and Outcomes of Implementing Peer Mediation Services in Schools: A Cultural Historical Activity Theory Approach', unpublished PhD thesis, Birmingham: University of Birmingham School of Education.

Sen, A.K. (1985) 'Well-Being, Agency and Freedom', *Journal of Philosophy*, 82: 169–221.

Sen, A.K. (1993) 'Capability and Well-Being', in Nussbaum, C. and Sen, A.K. (eds) *Quality of Life*, Oxford: Clarendon Press.

Sevenhuijsen, S. (1998) *Citizenship and the Ethics of Care: Feminist Considerations on Justice, Morality and Politics*, London: Routledge.

Shaughnessy, J. and Jennifer, D. (2007) *Mapping the Statistics: Moving to a Shared Understanding of the Nature of Bullying and Violence in Schools across Birmingham Local Authority*, London: Roehampton University.

Shermer, M. (1997) *Why People Believe Weird Things: Pseudoscience, Superstition, and Other Confusions of Our Time*, New York: Freeman.

Simmons, B. (2009) 'The PMLD Ambiguity: Articulating the Life-Worlds of Children with Profound and Multiple Learning Difficulties', unpublished PhD thesis, Exeter: University of Exeter School of Education and Lifelong Learning.

Siraj-Blatchford, I., Sylva, K., Muttock, S., Gilden, R. and Bell, D. (2002) *Researching Effective Pedagogy in the Early Years*, London: Queen's Printer.

Smart, D. and Vassallo, S. (2008) 'Pathways to Social and Emotional Wellbeing: Lessons from a 24-Year Longitudinal Study', *Research Conference 2008: Touching the Future: Building Skills for Life and Work*, Melbourne: Australian Council for Educational Research.

Smith, M.K. (2004) 'Nel Noddings, the Ethics of Care and Education', *The Encyclopaedia of Informal Education* (available online: www.infed.org/thinkers/noddings.htm).

Smith, P. (2010a) 'Bullying: Recent Developments', *Highlight*, 261 (available online: www.anti-bullyingalliance.org.uk/pdf/bullying_NCB_LIS_highlight261.pdf).

Smith, P.K. (2010b) *Children and Play*, Chichester: Wiley-Blackwell.

Smith, P.K. and Whitney, S. (1987) 'Play and Associative Fluency: Experimenter Effects May Be Responsible for Previous Positive Findings', *Developmental Psychology*, 23: 49–53.

Sohlman, E. (2008) 'Promoting Psychosocial Well-Being through School Education: Concepts and Principles', in Ahonen, A., Alverby, E., Johansen, D.M., Rajala, R., Ryzhkova, I., Sohlman, I. and Villanen, H. (eds) *Crystals of School Children's Well-Being: Cross-Border Training Material for Promoting Psychosocial Well-Being through School Education*, Lapland: University of Lapland.

Spratt, J., Shucksmith, J., Philip, K. and Watson, C. (2006) 'Interprofessional Support of Mental Well-Being in Schools: a Bourdieuan Perspective', *Journal of Interprofessional Care*, 20: 391–402.

Spyrou, S. (2011) 'The Limits of Children's Voices: from Authenticity to Critical, Reflexive Representation', *Childhood – a Global Journal of Child Research*, 18: 151–65.

Stephen, D. and Squires, P. (2005) 'Rethinking ASBOs', *Critical Social Policy*, 25: 517–28.

Storey, P. and Smith, M. (2008) *Methods and Approaches to Improving the Emotional Health and Well Being of Children: A Briefing Paper Concerning Interventions to Prevent Internalising Disorders*, London: Thomas Coram Research Unit, Institute of Education, University of London.

Strauch, B. (2004) *The Primal Teen: What the New Discoveries about the Teenage Brain Tell Us about Our Kids*, New York: Anchor Books.

Student Health Education Unit (2010) 'SHEU News', newsletter, May.

Suissa, J. (2008) 'Lessons from a New Science? On Teaching Happiness in Schools', *Journal of Philosophy of Education*, 42: 575–89.

Sumner, L.W. (1996) *Welfare, Happiness, and Ethics*, Oxford: Oxford University Press.

Sutton-Smith, B. (1997) *The Ambiguity of Play*, Cambridge, MA: Harvard University Press.

Swann, J.W.B. and Pittman, T.S. (1977) 'Initiating Play Activity of Young Children: the Moderating Influence of Verbal Cues on Intrinsic Motivation', *Child Development*, 48: 1128–32.

Taylor, R., Sylvestre, J. and Botschener, J. (1998) 'Social Support Is Something You Do, Not Something You Provide: Implications for Linking Formal and Informal Support', *Journal of Leisurability*, 25(4): 114.

TDA (Training and Development Agency for Schools) (2007) *National Occupational Standards for Supporting Teaching and Learning in Schools*, Manchester: TDA.

Teaching Expertise (2009) *School Emotional Environment for Learning Survey*, Optimus Professional Publishing (available online: www.teachingexpertise.com/articles/school-emotional-environment-for-learning-survey-2519).

The Children's Society (2006) *The Good Childhood: a National Inquiry Launch Report*, London: the Children's Society.

The Independent (2000) 'Welsh Children's Homes in Abuse Shame', 15 February.

The National Institute of Adult Continuing Education (2001) *Young Adults Learning Partnership* (available online: http://archive.niace.org.uk/Research/YALP/default.htm).

Thomas, G. and Loxley, A. (2007) Deconstructing Special Education and Constructing Inclusion, Maidenhead: OUP.

Thomas, L., Howard, J. and Miles, G. (2006) 'The Effectiveness of Playful Practice for Learning in the Early Years', *The Psychology of Education Review*, 30: 52–8.

Thompson, F. and Smith, P. (2011) *The Use and Effectiveness of Anti-Bullying Strategies in Schools*, London: DCSF/Goldsmiths, University of London.

Together 4 All (no date) *Together 4 All Programme for Schools*, Craigavon: Together 4 All.

Tomlinson, S. (2001) *Education in a Post Welfare Society*, Buckingham: OUP.

Tronto, J. (1993) *Moral Boundaries: a Political Argument for the Ethics of Care*, London: Routledge.

Turney, D. (2010) 'Sustaining Relationships: Working with Strong Feelings – Love and Positive Feelings', in Ruch, G., Turney, D. and Ward, A. (ed) *Relationship-Based Social Work: Getting to the Heart of Practice*, London: Jessica Kingsley Publishers.

Tyler, K. (1998) 'A Comparison of the No Blame Approach to Bullying and the Ecosystemic Approach to Changing Problem Behaviour in Schools', *Pastoral Care in Education*, March: 26–33.

Tyrrell, J. (2002) *Peer Mediation: A Process for Primary Schools*, London: Souvenir Press.

UKCC (UK Children's Commissioners) (2008) *UK Children's Commissioners' Report to UN Committee on the Rights of the Child*, London/Belfast/Edinburgh/Cardiff: UN Committee on the Rights of the Child.

UN (United Nations) (1990) *United Nations Convention on the Rights of the Child*: Geneva, Office of the United Nations High Commissioner for Human Rights.

UN (2006) *Convention on the Rights of Persons with Disabilities*, Geneva: UN.

UN (2008) *Committee on the Rights of the Child: Consideration of Reports Submitted by State Parties under Article 44 of the Convention*; CRC/C//GBR/CO/4, Geneva: UN Convention on the Rights of the Child

UNESCO (United Nations Educational, Scientific and Cultural Organisation) (1994) *The Salamanca Statement and Framework for Action on Special Needs Education*, Salamanca: Spain.

UNICEF (United Nations Children's Fund) (2007) 'Child Poverty in Perspective: an Overview of Child Well-Being in Rich Countries', *Innocenti Report Card* 7, Florence: UNICEF Innocenti Research Centre.

UNICEF (2010) *Rights Respecting Schools Project*, UNICEF, UK.

Uprichard, E. (2008) 'Children as Beings and Becomings: Children, Childhood and Temporality', *Children and Society*, 22: 303–13.

Valentine, G. (2004) *Public Space and the Culture of Childhood*, Aldershot: Ashgate.

Vandenbroeck, M., Coussee, F., Bradt, L. and Roose, R. (2011) 'Diversity in Early Childhood Education: a Matter of Social Pedagogical Embarrassment', in Cameron, C. and Moss, P. (eds) *Social Pedagogy and Working with Children and Young People: Where Care and Education Meet*, London: Jessica Kingsley Publishers.

Veenhoven, R. (2000) 'The Four Qualities of Life: Ordering Concepts and Measures of the Good Life', *Journal of Happiness Studies*, 1: 1–39.

Vislie, L. (2006) 'Special Education under the Modernity. From Restricted Liberty, through Organized Modernity, to Extended Liberty and a Plurality of Practices', *European Journal of Special Needs Education*, 21: 395–414.

Vitello, S. and Mithaug, D. (1998) *Inclusive Schooling – National and International Perspectives*, London: Lawrence Erlbaum.

Vlachou, A. (1997) *Struggles for Inclusive Education*, Buckingham: OUP.

Wade, B. and Moore, M. (1993) *The Experience of Special Education*, Milton Keynes: Open University.

WAG (Welsh Assembly Government) (2001) *The Learning Country, a Paving Document, a Comprehensive Education and Lifelong Learning Programme to 2010 in Wales*, Cardiff: WAG, Crown Copyright.

WAG (2002) *Well Being in Wales*, Cardiff: Office of the Chief Medical Officer.

WAG (2008a) *Children and Young People's Well-Being Monitor for Wales*, Cardiff: WAG, Crown Copyright.

WAG (2008b) *School Effectiveness Framework: Building Effective Learning Communities Together*, Cardiff: WAG, Crown Copyright.

WAG (2008c) *Foundation Phase: Framework for Children's Learning for 3–7-Year-Olds in Wales*, Cardiff: Welsh Assembly Government.

WAG (2010a) 'Indicators for the Welsh Network of Healthy School Schemes National Quality Award'. Available at: http://wales.gov.uk/docs/phhs/publications/100730schoolawardindicen.pdf

WAG (2010b) *Thinking Positively, Emotional Health and Well-Being in Schools and Early Years Settings*, Cardiff: WAG, Crown Copyright.

Warnick, B. (2009) 'Dilemmas of Autonomy and Happiness: Harry Brighouse on Subjective Wellbeing and Education', *Theory and Research in Education*, 7: 89–111.

Warnock, M. (1978) *Report of the Committee of Enquiry into the Education of Handicapped Children and Young People*, London: HMSO.

Waterhouse, L. (2006) 'Multiple Intelligences, the Mozart Effect, and Emotional Intelligence: a Critical Review', *Educational Psychologist*, 41: 207–25.

Watson, D.L. and Emery, C. (2010) 'From Rhetoric to Reality: the Problematic Nature and Assessment of Children and Young People's Social and Emotional Learning', *British Educational Research Journal*, 36: 767–86.

Watson, D.L. and Robbins, J.H. (2008) 'Closing the Chasm: Reconciling Contemporary Understandings of Learning with the Need to Formally Assess and Accredit Learners through the Assessment of Performance', *Research Papers in Education*, 23: 315–31.

Watson, D.L., Bayliss, P.D. and Pratchett, G. (2011) 'Pondlife That "Know Their Place": Exploring Teaching Assistants Professional Positions through Positioning Theory', *International Journal of Qualitative Studies in Education*. Advance online publication. doi: 10.1080/09518398.2011.598195.

Watson, N. (2012, forthcoming) 'How Can Disability Theory Help Our Understanding of the Lives of Disabled Children?', *Children and Society*.

Weare, K. and Gray, G. (2003) *What Works in Developing Children's Emotional and Social Competence and Wellbeing?*, London: DfES, Crown Printers.

Wells, J., Barlow, J. and Stewart-Brown, S. (2003) 'A Systematic Review of Universal Approaches to Mental Health Promotion in Schools', *Health Education*, 103: 197– 220.

Wells, P. (2004) 'New Labour and Evidence Based Policy Making' PERC Research Seminar, Sheffield: University of Sheffield Political Economy Research Centre.

Wenger, E. (1998) *Communities of Practice: Learning, Meaning and Identity*, Cambridge: Cambridge University Press.

Whitby, K. (2005) 'The Employment and Deployment of Teaching Assistants', *Topic*, 33: 42–7.

White, J. (2002) 'Education, the Market and the Nature of Personal Well-Being', *British Journal of Educational Studies*, 50: 42–456.

White, J. (2007) 'Wellbeing and Education: Issues of Culture and Authority', *Journal of Philosophy of Education*, 41: 17–28.

White, J. (2011) *Exploring Well-Being in Schools: a Guide to Making Children's Lives More Fulfilling*, Oxon: Routledge.

White, S. and Petitt, J. (2004) *Participatory Approaches and the Measurement of Human Well-Being*, Helsinki: World Institute for Development Economics Research (WUN).

Whitty, G. and Wisby, E. (2007) *Real Decision Making? School Councils in Action*, London: Institute of Education, University of London.

WHO (World Health Organisation) (1999) *Creating an Environment for Emotional and Social Well-Being: An Important Responsibility of a Health-Promoting and Child-Friendly School*, Atlanta, GA: Division of Adolescent and School Health, Atlanta.

WHO (2004) 'World Health Organisation International Classification of Disability and Health', *ICDH-2*, Geneva: WHO.

WHO (2010) *What Is a Health Promoting School?* (available online: www.who.int/school_youth_health/gshi/hps/en/index.html).

Wickenden, M. (2011) '"Talk to Me Like a Teenage Girl": How Do Disabled Teenagers with Little or No Speech See Their Friendships?', Researching the Lives of Disabled Children and Young People: ESRC Sponsored Seminar Series, Bristol.

Wills, T.A. (1991) *Social Support and Interpersonal Relationships*, London: Sage.

Wing, L. (1995) 'Play Is Not the Work of the Child: Young Children's Perceptions of Work and Play', *Early Childhood Research Quarterly*, 10: 223–47.

Wood, E. (2009) 'Developing a Pedagogy of Play', in Anning, A., Cullen, J. and Fleer, M. (eds) *Early Childhood Education: Society and Culture* (2nd edn), London: Sage.

Wood, E. (2010) 'Reconceptualising the Play–Pedagogy Relationship: from Control to Complexity', in Brooker, L. and Edwards, S. (eds) *Engaging Play*, Maidenhead: Open University Press.

Woodhead, M. (1997) 'Psychology and the Cultural Construction of Children's Needs', in James, A. and Prout, A. (eds) *Constructing and Reconstructing Childhood*, London: Falmer Press.

Woodill, G., Renwick, R., Brown, I. and Raphael, D. (eds) (1994) *Being, Belonging, Becoming: an Approach to the Quality of Life of Persons with Developmental Disabilities*, Cambridge, MA: Brookline.

Woolley, H., Armitage, M., Bishop, J., Curtis, M. and Ginsborg, J. (2006) 'Inclusion of Disabled Children in Primary School Playgrounds', York: Joseph Rowntree Foundation (available online: www.jrf.org.uk/sites/files/jrf/0016.pdf).

Wyn, J., Cahill, H., Holdsworth, R., Rowling, L. and Carson, S. (2000) 'Mindmatters, a Whole School Approach Promoting Mental Health and Wellbeing', *Australian and New Zealand Journal of Psychiatry*, 34: 594–601.

Yelloly, M. and Henkel, M. (1995) 'Introduction' in M. Yelloly and M. Henkel *Learning and Teaching in Social Work: Towards Reflective Practice*, London: Jessica Kingsley Publishers.

Youell, B. (2008) 'The Importance of Play and Playfulness', *The European Journal of Psychotherapy and Counselling*, 10: 121–9.

Young, L. and Barrett, H. (2001) 'Adapting Visual Methods: Action Research with Kampala Street Children', *Area*, 33: 141–52.

Youth Justice Board (2004) *National Evaluation of the Restorative Justice in Schools Programme*, London: Youth Justice Board.

Yssel, N., Engelbrecht, P., Oswald, M.M., Eloff, I. and Swart, E. (2007) 'Views of Inclusion: a Comparative Study of Parents' Perceptions in South Africa and the United States', *Remedial and Special Education*, 28: 356–65.

Index

Note: The letter f following a page number indicates a figure, and t a table.